The Spy Who Came in from the Co-op

The Spy Who Came in from the Co-op

Melita Norwood and the Ending of Cold War Espionage

David Burke

THE BOYDELL PRESS

First published 2008
The Boydell Press, Woodbridge

ISBN 978-1-84383-422-9

The Boydell Press is an imprint of Boydell & Brewer Ltd
PO Box 9, Woodbridge, Suffolk IP12 3DF, UK
and of Boydell & Brewer Inc.
668 Mt Hope Avenue, Rochester, NY 14620, USA
website: www.boydellandbrewer.com

A catalogue record for this title is available from the British Library

This publication is printed on acid-free paper

Designed and typeset in Adobe Myriad Pro and Adobe Warnock Pro by
David Roberts, Pershore, Worcestershire

Transferred to Digital Printing

Contents

Illustrations

All illustrations are from the Melita Norwood papers
in the possession of David Burke.

Betweeen pp. 116 and 117

1   'Find Three Policemen': Suffragette card inscribed 'Sasha to Gertrude. Xmas 1906'

2   Alexander Sirnis with Tolstoy's grandchildren, 'Lulu' (Ilya) and Sonia, Tuckton House, 23 September 1907

3   The Gardening Brigade, Tuckton House, 13 May 1907. Alexander Sirnis is standing on the right.

4   Tolstoy's manuscripts in the safe at Tuckton House

5   The office, Tuckton House, 1907. Alexander Sirnis sits in front of the typewriter in foreground; Count Chertkov is standing, second from the right. The safe containing Tolstoy's manuscripts is in the background.

6   Alexander Sirnis, 1909

7   Tuckton Football Club, 1907; an old photograph reproduced in the *Christchurch Times*, 3 September 1971. Alexander Sirnis stands in the back row, fourth from the right.

8   Gertrude, Alexander and Alfred, aged 7, Christmas 1909

9   Melita and Alexander Sirnis, Davos, 10 June 1915

10   Theodore Rothstein, *c.* 1920

11   Jacob Miller in Moscow, 1930s

12   Take Three Spies – Melita, Gertrude and Gerty Stedman Sirnis, with Alfred Brandt, late 1920s

13   Charlie Job, Communist Party candidate, Bexley, 1950 (photograph by Hilary Norwood)

14   Hilary Norwood, *c.* 1953

15   Joint VOF–BSRP philately exhibition, Moscow, 25–30 June 1976. Hilary Norwood sits in the centre.

16   'To Letty – Sonya Salutes You.' The card that 'Sonya' sent to Melita Norwood with a copy of her memoirs.

Foreword

Dr David Burke is probably the only historian ever to have had a career-changing experience in Milton Keynes bus station. On Saturday 11 September 1999 he was on his way from Leeds to have lunch with Melita 'Letty' Norwood in Bexleyheath. To his astonishment, while changing buses at Milton Keynes, he saw Mrs Norwood's photograph on the front page of *The Times* with the memorable caption, 'The Spy Who Came In From The Co-op', which he has aptly chosen as the title of his biography. *The Times* that day began serialising *The Mitrokhin Archive: The KGB in Europe and the West*, which I had written in collaboration with the dissident KGB archivist, Vasili Mitrokhin, who had escaped to Britain with a hoard of KGB material, including notes on Mrs Norwood's file. But *The Times* was not the only newspaper interested in her extraordinary career as Britain's longest-serving Soviet spy. On looking round the newsstand at Milton Keynes, Dr Burke saw Mrs Norwood's photograph on the other front pages too, with the exception of *Sporting Life*. By the time he had got over his shock at the revelation of her involvement in espionage, he had missed his bus.

Mrs Norwood, meanwhile, was preoccupied but surprisingly unintimidated by the massed ranks of reporters outside her end-of-terrace house. 'Oh dear', she told *The Times* reporter, the only one allowed inside her house. 'This is so different from my quiet little life. I thought I'd got away with it. But I'm not that surprised it's finally come out.' 'Letty' Norwood had been offered accommodation elsewhere before the media storm broke, but decided to stay and face the reporters. The image of the great-granny spy walking down her garden path between well-tended rose trees to make a televised confession, despite the fact that it was distinctly (if unsurprisingly) economical with the truth, briefly caught the imagination of millions of viewers and newspaper readers. 'I'm 87', she began, 'and unfortunately my memory is not what it was. I did what I did not to make money, but to help prevent the defeat of a new system which had, at great cost, given ordinary people food and fares which they could afford, given them education and a health service.'

'Letty' Norwood was instantly inundated with lucrative media offers for

her life story. She turned all of them down. As during her long career as a
Soviet spy, she was uninterested in making money. Instead, Mrs Norwood
told much of her story to Dr Burke, impressed by his research on revolutionary émigrés from the Tsarist Empire, of whom her father had been one,
as well as by his broader understanding of both the Soviet Union and the
British Left. This outstanding biography demonstrates the wisdom of her
choice. Though, as with all pioneering spy biographies, this one contains
some controversial moments, Dr Burke's brilliant archival research has
successfully uncovered the many layers of Norwood's inconspicuous but
extraordinary career.

The Spy Who Came In From The Co-op also identifies some important
areas for future research, among them the revelation that in the mid-
1930s Soviet intelligence had identified Lawn Road Flats, Hampstead, at
the epicentre of London's chattering classes, as the most promising base
for its British operations, with residents who included the recruiter of the
celebrated Cambridge Five. That will be the subject of Dr Burke's next
book.

CHRISTOPHER ANDREW

Professor of Modern and Contemporary History, University of Cambridge

Convenor of the Cambridge Intelligence Seminar

Acknowledgements

I am indebted to a number of people who have made this book possible. First and foremost I would like to thank Professor Christopher Andrew of Corpus Christi College, University of Cambridge. Without his expert knowledge and encouragement this book would probably have never seen the light of day. I would also like to thank contributors and participants at the Cambridge University Intelligence Seminar, particularly Dr Peter Martland, whose observations on the various drafts were always illuminating.

This book has a long history, and the number of people who have commented on parts of it are too numerous to mention. However, I would like to thank Fred Lindop for his advice and encouragement, Dr Lewis Johnman of the University of Westminster, Professor Julian Cooper, Mike Cooper, Professor Bob Davies, Martin Dewhirst, Phil Tomaselli and David Rose. I would also like to thank Christopher Feeney and David Roberts for their patience and skill in preparing the text for publication.

DAVID BURKE

Abbreviations

Agitprop	Agitation and Propaganda Department	MNB	Moscow National Bank
ARCOS	All Russian Co-operative Society	NATO	North Atlantic Treaty Organisation
AWCS	Association of Women Clerks and Secretaries	NKGB	Narodnyi Kommissariat Gosudarstvennoi Bezopastnosti (Soviet security and intelligence service 1941–6; incorporated within NKVD, 1941–3)
BN-FMRA	British Non-Ferrous Metals Research Association		
BSP	British Socialist Party		
BSRP	British Society of Russian Philately	NKVD	Narodnyi Kommisariat Vnutrennikh Del (People's Commissariat for Internal Affairs)
CIA	Central Intelligence Agency		
CND	Campaign for Nuclear Disarmament		
CPGB	Communist Party of Great Britain	OGPU	Obyesinennoye Gosudarstvennoye Politicheskoye Upravleniye (Soviet Security and Intelligence Service 1923–34)
CPSU	Communist Party of the Soviet Union		
FBI	Federal Bureau of Intelligence		
FCD	First Chief (Foreign Intelligence) Directorate, KGB	OMS	Otdel' Mezhdunarodnykh Svyazey (Comintern International Liaison Department)
FCO	Foreign & Commonwealth Office		
FO	Foreign Office	RCMP	Royal Canadian Mounted Police
FSU	Friends of the Soviet Union	ROSTA	Rossiiskoe Telegrafnoe Agenstvo (Russian Telegraph Agency)
GRU	Glavnoye Razvedyvatelnoye Upravleniye (Soviet Military Intelligence)		
		RPC	Revolutionary Policy Committee (ILP)
HO	Home Office	S & T	Scientific & Technical Intelligence
HOW	Home Office Warrant		
IAEA	International Atomic Energy Agency	SFRF	Society of Friends of Russian Freedom
ICI	Imperial Chemical Industries	SIB	Special Intelligence Bureau (Eastern Mediterranean)
ILP	Independent Labour Party		
ISC	Intelligence and Security Committee	SIS	Secret Intelligence Service (MI6)
KGB	Komitet Gosurdarstvennoi Bezopastnoti (Soviet Security and Intelligence Service 1954–91)	SDF	Social-Democratic Federation
		SLP	Socialist Labour Party
		SVR	Sluzhba Vneshnei Razvedki (Post-Soviet Foreign Intelligence Service)
KPD	Kommunistische Partei Deutschlands (Communist Party of Germany)	TASS	Telegrafnoe Agentsvo Sovetskovo Soyuza (Telegraph Agency of the Soviet Union)
LAI	League against Imperialism		
LSE	London School of Economics	TNA	The National Archives
MAP	Ministry of Aircraft Production	VOF	All-Union Society of Philatelists
MI5	British Security Service (domestic)	WO	War Office
		WSF	Workers' Socialist Federation
MI6	British Intelligence (overseas)		

For William, Ted and Mollie

Prologue

I FIRST met Melita Norwood in 1997. I didn't know that she had been a spy, and like most people who knew or met her I found her a pleasant enough old lady with distinctly leftwing views. At eighty-five she was still an active member of the Campaign for Nuclear Disarmament and, for over twenty years, a fully paid-up member of the British Communist Party. Born before the Russian Revolution of 1917, she had spent over thirty-nine years in the service of the KGB and Lenin's Bolshevik Revolution. She had invited me to Sunday lunch to talk about her father, Alexander Sirnis, a Latvian disciple of the Russian novelist Leo N. Tolstoy. During the First World War Alexander had been responsible for the publication of the authorized English edition of Tolstoy's *Diaries* along with Dr C. T. Hagberg Wright of the London Library.

It was a frugal lunch, fish fingers and greens from her allotment washed down by tea served in Che Guevara mugs. My interest in her father went back to research undertaken at the Universities of Birmingham and Greenwich into the history of the Russian political émigré community in Britain during the twentieth century. Melita had kept several files on Alexander's activities and on other Russians living on the south coast of England in the early years of the twentieth century. It was interesting material. Although on a first reading these files appeared to have very little to do with espionage, apart from the occasional mention of Russians who I knew had been involved in the world of secrets and espionage, they acquired greater significance once she began to talk about her spying career. In fact, I found it amusing that she should have known such figures, and when questioned on them she would laugh and say things like, 'Oh, so and so. He was a bit of a devil.'

At the time I was teaching at Trinity & All Saints College, Leeds, and would travel by coach to London once a month to enjoy a Sunday lunch of fish fingers and greens (or the occasional kipper) and go through Melita Norwood's papers. They were enjoyable outings. Melita Norwood had a good sense of humour, and kept up with current affairs. Her favourite television personality was the presenter Jeremy Paxman, and she rarely missed an edition of *Newsnight.*

On 11 September 1999 I learnt that she had been a major spy. It happened at Milton Keynes coach station. I was on my way to visit her when the coach I was travelling on from Leeds to London's Victoria coach station pulled up as usual at Milton Keynes coach station to pick up and drop off passengers. It had been an ordinary journey, and we had five minutes before the coach continued on its way to Victoria. I got off and went into the shop and cafeteria by the bus shelter to buy a newspaper, and there I came face to face with Melita Norwood staring at me from the front page of *The Times.* She had been accused of passing on Britain's atomic secrets to Moscow. I was a little shocked, to say the least. When I got to London I immediately telephoned her. She sounded a little vague: 'Who is it?' 'It's me. Lunch, remember?' 'Oh, yes! You'd better come next week. I'm afraid I've been rather a naughty girl. Never mind. Come next week.'

When I finally arrived the following week Melita came to the door positively beaming, looking very relaxed and mischievous. She was wearing a long, tatty, old-fashioned brown woollen man's overcoat. A hat of sorts was perched precariously on her head, and she clutched a knife in one hand and sprouting broccoli in the other. She ushered me into the back room next to the kitchen. It was rather a bare room apart from a large kitchen table, an armchair, a television set and a Utility sideboard. French windows looked out on to what was still an attractive garden. Lying on the kitchen table were copies of the Communist Party's newspaper *The Morning Star.* At the age of eighty-nine, every Saturday she still delivered thirty-two copies of the paper to friends and supporters of the Party alike. I picked up the one she saved for me and read. The tin kettle on the stove began to whistle, increasing in shrillness as she reached down the two Che Guevara mugs she used for serving up Co-op tea. She shuffled back into the room, put the mugs down unsteadily and began. I asked her if I could record the interview but she said that she'd rather I didn't, but that I could take notes if I liked. It was a strange interview. It was obvious that she was still in a state of shock, and her eccentric, mischievous manner was her way of coping. I just listened. I hadn't prepared any questions, and so I just let her talk, jotting down notes as quickly as I could. All the names from Russian espionage that we had spoken about on previous occasions now entered the drama in a different capacity. It was fascinating: as she spoke she became more animated, younger even, the mischievous woman that she once was, her confidence regained. When I left she told me I was to come back in a couple of weeks.

On my return visit the conversation began with a story about her father. Although she was only six years old at the time of her father's death, her mother had kept his memory alive and had spoken constantly about his communist beliefs. Eighty years later, looking at old photographs of her father, she was clearly upset by her 'outing' as a spy. 'I thought I'd got away with it', she kept repeating to herself quietly over and over again, fearing that her exposure, not her spying, meant that she had let both her father and the Communist Party down. The interview, however, followed the same pattern as the last, and she became quite animated when recounting past exploits. This was not always the case.

On other occasions Melita would retract what she had said, not aggressively but firmly, and began to claim that she was 'not technical', had no idea what it was she had handed to her Russian controllers, or who they were. Once the initial shock of her 'outing' as a spy had subsided she was making some attempt to mislead me, at least on a number of minor points. On one occasion she couldn't remember who it was who had recruited her to the Russian secret service, when she had earlier been quite eager to talk about this. Nevertheless, she remained keen for me to write her biography, and passed me her personal papers, which remain in my possession. We had several meetings, all of them as intriguing as the first. She was reluctant for the book to appear while she was alive, but felt that her motives for spying needed to be treated in an unsensational manner. She enjoyed the sobriquet 'the spy who came in from the Co-op', and insisted in the months before her death that I assume responsibility for her Che Guevara mugs.

CHAPTER 1

The Secret Life of Melita Norwood

M ELITA Norwood was an idealist, a Marxist, who throughout her long life refused to believe in the degradation of Soviet democracy and the failure of the Soviet experiment.[1] For most of her lifetime British and European societies struggled for social cohesion, wracked by the class and ideological struggles of the twentieth century. These conflicts had their origins in the unregulated exploitation of labour markets in the nineteenth century and the labour disputes that followed. As early as 1848 the German philosopher Karl Marx and his collaborator Friedrich Engels had predicted the downfall of world capitalism in the *Communist Manifesto*, calling on the workers of the world to unite: 'You have nothing to lose but your chains'. Sixteen years later a group of working men met under the banner of the First International at St Martin's Hall, London, with the purpose of uniting a variety of British and foreign leftwing political groups and trade unions on the basis of the 'class struggle'. An eclectic body of trade unionists, anarchists, French socialists, Italian followers of Garibaldi and Mazzini, former Chartists and Owenites, the First International was riven with internal disputes, and as a result of unprecedented bitterness between the followers of Karl Marx and the disciples of the Russian anarchist Mikhail Bakunin collapsed in 1876. Nevertheless, the seeds of the international communist movement that would inspire the Bolsheviks 'to scale the heavens' of revolution in 1917 had been sown in London in 1848 and 1864. Ironically, for most of the nineteenth century very little was known about Karl Marx, or indeed the theory of 'class struggle', in Russia before a wave of strikes in St Petersburg in 1897. Before then the revolutionary movement in Russia was poorly organized, and was largely influenced by the nihilism of Bakunin's self-appointed apostle Sergei Nechayev – the model for Dostoevsky's nefarious Peter Verkhovensky in *The Possessed* and the inspiration behind the terrorism of the *Narodnaya Volya* (the People's Will). His nihilist manifesto, *The Revolutionary Catechism*, published in 1869, called for individual acts of terror against selected government officials and led to the formation of a populist terrorist group in 1876, the *Zemlya Volya* (Society of Land and Liberty). It was responsible for a number of high-profile attacks on government officials, culminating in the stabbing to death in 1878 of the head of the Russian secret police, General N. V. Mezentsev. Not all members of *Zemlya Volya*, however, favoured terrorism, and the following year the organisation split into two factions – the Black Partition, which favoured some form of political action, and the *Narodnaya Volya*, which remained wedded to Nechaevism. In 1881 a group of bomb throwers belonging to *Narodnaya Volya* assassinated the tsar, Alexander II, and in the wave of repression that followed the organisation was virtually destroyed, with many of its members seeking political asylum overseas. The British government of the time was not unsympathetic, and granted political asylum to a number of prominent Russian revolutionaries, among them the murderer of Mezentsev, Sergei Mikhailovich Kravchinskii, better known by the pseudonym Stepniak. Another welcome guest was 'The Anarchist Prince', Piotr Kroptkin, the adviser and philosopher to the whole anarchist movement, who had escaped from a Russian prison in 1876 and lived permanently in Britain between 1886 and 1917. Oscar Wilde described him in *De Profundis* as 'a man with a soul of that beautiful white Christ which seems coming out of Russia'.

The first wave of Russian political emigrants to these shores, however, were hostile to the West, and violently opposed to the spread of Western influences inside Russia. These influences were identified with the development of capitalism in Russia and the process of modernization, agitating revolutionaries and conservatives alike. Ever since Russia's humiliation in the Crimean War there had been a growing awareness among the forces for democracy that if Russia was to survive as a great power it would have to embark on a process of social and economic reform. By its very nature the kind of change envisaged was incompatible with the continuation of tsarist rule. In this respect Russia, as one historian has pointed out, was 'in the grip of a profound contradiction'.[2] Confronted with the strains of rapid industrialization and growing political disaffection across the empire the reaction of the Russian authorities was to step up its repression of dissidents and to intensify the oppression of minorities. From the mid-1880s onwards, religious dissidents, in particular the Jewish community, were persecuted by the Russian authorities and came under severe attack. Between 1882 and 1906, and again between 1911 and 1913, pogroms against the Jews forced many of them to leave Russia and seek refuge in the cities of Western Europe. In England they settled mainly in London's East End, Manchester and the Leylands area of Leeds. Those who left Russia for Britain can be divided into three groups: those who fled racial persecution and economic discrimination; those who fled from religious persecution; and those who fled political persecution. The latter brought with them various strands of socialism, anarchism and trade unionism, and played an important role in spreading the Marxist faith in Britain. They also included a number of individuals who, post-October 1917, would come to exercise a direct influence over Soviet society and the establishment of Soviet espionage networks in Britain. Among the descendants of such individuals was Melita Norwood, the daughter of a Latvian father and an English mother. Her parents first met at Tuckton House, a large Victorian mansion in the village of Tuckton just outside Bournemouth, and home to Count Vladimir Chertkov, Tolstoy's literary executor who had been in exile since 1899 for his part in defending the Doukhobors. Tuckton House was then a meeting place for the Russian political emigration in England, with most of Russia's émigré revolutionaries, at one time or another, making a point of visiting and paying their respects to Chertkov regardless of their politics or backgrounds. Among them were Prince Kropotkin and the Latvian Jacob Peters, linked with the Houndsditch Murders, a veteran from the Siege of Sidney Street, and a future high-ranking member of Lenin's security organization, the Committee for Combating Counter-Revolution and Sabotage (the Cheka), during the October Revolution and ensuing civil war. Many of them came to gaze reverently at the specially constructed safe that housed Tolstoy's manuscripts. At this time Tolstoy's works were heavily expurgated in Russia and Chertkov was printing unexpurgated editions at Tuckton House and smuggling them back into Russia. Gertrude Stedman, who lived in the nearby village of Pokesdown, was a frequent visitor to Tuckton House and married Alexander Sirnis in 1909. They had three children, Wilfrid, who died in infancy, Melita and Gerty.

Melita's childhood was very happy. Tuckton House she described as an enchanting place where all the trees were big. (Her mother, she told me, remembered them as small.) There were other children living in the community, among them Tolstoy's grandchildren, Lulu and Sonia. One member of that community whom she corresponded with until his death in 1973 was an Englishman, Stanley Carlyle Potter, who wrote an article on Tuckton House for a local newspaper, the *Christchurch Times* describing the various visitors to the house – 'Kropotkin, Verigin, Birukoff and others, also Heinemann and Beinstock (the English and French publishers interested in Tolstoy):[3] 'Not all members of the colony were Tolstoyans', he remarked. 'In the evenings there were keen discussions between socialists and philosophical anarchists and other schools of thought.'[4] A regular contributor to these discussions was the Marxist socialist Theodore Rothstein, Lenin's first secret agent in Britain. It was his son Andrew who recruited Melita to the Russian secret service, the NKVD, in 1934. At that time Melita was working as a secretary for the British Non-Ferrous Metals Research Association (BN-FMRA), a research organization with strong ties to Britain's armaments firms. She was regarded as a highly competent secretary, and became the personal secretary of the Assistant Director, G. L. Bailey. In 1944 Bailey was appointed Director, and she became his personal assistant. During the Second World War, as secretary to the Director of BN-FMRA, she was granted access to classified information on the Anglo-American atomic bomb project.

In the post-war period, when Britain, cut off from her American ally's nuclear secrets, put in place her own nuclear reactor and atom bomb programme, Melita came to be regarded so highly by the Soviets that Stalin's Chief of Intelligence, Pavel Fitin, instructed his agents in London to congratulate her on the material she was providing. Melita Norwood was a Soviet spy of some magnitude, and between 1941 and 1949 a major source of information on Britain's nuclear reactor and atomic bomb programme. Her outing as a spy by *The Times* on Saturday, 11 September 1999, following the revelations of the Russian defector Vasili Mitrokhin, came as something of a shock to her. That night, the longest-serving female spy in British history sat down and prepared a statement explaining why she had spied for the Soviet Union for thirty-nine years. The following morning she stepped out into her neatly tended front garden and addressed the world's media that had been gathering outside her house since the early hours of the morning:

I'm 87, and unfortunately my memory is not what it was. I did what I did not to make money, but to help prevent the defeat of a new system which had, at great cost, given ordinary people food and fares which they could afford, given them education and a health service.

Prime Minister Chamberlain had expected Hitler to attack Russia first, and we were expected to put cardboard over our fireplaces. Bombs were not expected.

Fortunately, Churchill was more realistic and co-operated with the Russians.

When I left my job to have a baby, as promised to fellow staff I gave my leaving present to Mrs. Churchill's Aid Russia Fund.

Personally, I only worked in the general office. I am not technical.

I thought perhaps what I had access to might be useful in helping Russia to keep abreast of Britain, America and Germany.

In general, I do not agree with spying against one's country.

My late husband did not agree with what I did.[5]

A quite remarkable *apologia*, but more so for what it leaves out than for what it states. Memory in this case is a good poet rather than a bad historian. The listener might be forgiven for believing that Melita Norwood spied for the Soviet Union as part of her patriotic duty, to prevent Hitler dropping gas pellets down British chimneys and, as a good communist, to keep bus fares low for ordinary folk in Moscow. The Soviet Union was to her little more than the embodiment of the post-war Labour government's commitment to the Welfare State, and atomic espionage was analogous to facing up to New Labour or Conservative Party attacks on scroungers, illegal immigrants and welfarism. But there was more to Melita Norwood, and the Melita Norwood story, than misplaced ideology. From the moment she stepped into her front garden and began talking to the world's media alarm bells began ringing across Whitehall and in the offices of the Security Service, MI5. A series of extraordinary events began to unfold between her outing as a spy by *The Times* in September 1999 and the report of the Intelligence and Security Committee (ISC) on the *Mitrokhin Inquiry Report* in June 2000.

On Monday 13 September 1999 angry voices had been raised in the

House of Commons calling for Mrs Norwood's prosecution. The Shadow Home Secretary, Anne Widdicombe, led the charge. Comparisons were made between Mrs Norwood's spying activities and the atrocities committed by the Chilean dictator, General Pinochet, then being held in Britain pending a claim for extradition to Spain for crimes against humanity. If Mrs Norwood was too old to be prosecuted, then so too was the kindly old General. The Home Secretary, Jack Straw, was accused of double standards. Others asked why had she been allowed to get away with it for so long. Had the security services no inkling of her activities or even of her existence over the four decades that she spied for the Soviet Union? This unassuming granny from Bexleyheath had it seemed topped the spying careers of Blunt, Philby and the like by twenty-odd years. Straw was embarrassed, and in his speech to Parliament on 13 September announcing the setting up of an ISC inquiry into the publication of the Mitrokhin archive admitted that 'There is no reason to doubt ... that the KGB regarded Mrs Norwood as an important spy.'[6] Within a few days, however, Jack Straw had performed a volte-face, convened a meeting with friendly journalists and outlined why Mrs Norwood was not a major figure in the spying game. On 13 December 1999 an article by Philip Knightley appeared in the *New Statesman* under the headline 'Norwood: the spy who never was'. In this article we were apparently told 'the truth about the granny spy', as Knightley went on to throw doubt on some of the major accusations made against Mrs Norwood in the *Times* article. Knightley claimed to have seen a Home Office document that showed that Mrs Norwood had in fact left the BN-FMRA in 1943 to have a baby and had not returned until 1946. This was not true. There was no such HO document. What did exist was a letter written to the HO in October 1999 by the Director of BN-FMRA between 1958 and 1972, Alex Cibula, claiming that the BN-FMRA was engaged in research only into nuclear energy, not nuclear weapons, and that Mrs Norwood was not employed by the BN-FMRA in 1945. A copy of this letter was passed to Philip Knightley, who in his article elevated the letter to the status of a HO document. This led him to the following conclusion:

> According to a report in Home Office files, Norwood had left BN-FMRA in 1943 to have a baby and did not return until 1946. In short, by the final months of the war – the supposed peak of her

spying career – Norwood was at home busy with nappy, not nuclear, matters.[7]

Well, not according to Mrs Norwood. As she told reporters outside her home, she had left her job in 1943 to have a baby. What she did not tell them was that she had returned to work at the beginning of 1944, after the Assistant Director of BN-FMRA, G. L. Bailey, for whom she had been working in the general office, was promoted to the position of Director. In fact, Bailey made a point of visiting her at home on more than one occasion, pleading with her to return to work as she alone among the secretaries at BN-FMRA had a grasp of the technical language involved. As she put it, she was asked to return to work because 'I knew the ropes. I was useful to them'.[8] Of that there can be little doubt. In September 1945, according to extracts released from KGB files to Allen Weinstein and Alexander Vassiliev, authors of a book on the American atomic spies, there was an important spy based in England, passing on vital information to the Soviet Union under the codename TINA.[9] The biographical details released in these extracts, particularly the information that the spy was an employee of BN-FMRA, a secret member of the CPGB and had access in 1945 to important atomic intelligence is sufficiently convincing to suggest that this spy was Melita Norwood. In 1946 the US Army Security Agency (SIGINT) began decrypting some of the wartime messages exchanged between Moscow Centre, the body concerned with foreign intelligence and counter-intelligence at KGB headquarters in Moscow, and its American residencies. Although SIGINT did not possess the biographical information later released to Weinstein and Vassiliev that would have given clues to Mrs Norwood's identity they nevertheless became aware of TINA's existence. According to these decrypts, later codenamed VENONA, TINA was supplying vital information on atomic intelligence linked to the Manhattan Project, codenamed ENORMOZ. The VENONA decrypts showed clearly that Moscow Centre was very interested in the information TINA was providing, issuing direct instructions to her to obtain more of the same:

From Moscow to London, No. 13.   16 September 1945
Ref. No. 1413 [a]

We agree with your proposal about working with TINA.[i] At the next meeting tell her that her documentary material on ENORMOUS

[ENORMOZ] [ii] is of interest and represents a valuable contribution to the development of the work in this field ... instruct her not to discuss her work with her husband and not to say anything to him about the nature of the documentary material which is being obtained by her.

15 September   Viktor[iii]

  [i] TINA: unidentified cover-name.

  [ii] ENORMOUS: Atomic Energy Project.

  [iii] Viktor Lt. Gen. P. M. Fitin.[10]

Yet by the time the ISC published the *Mitrokhin Inquiry Report* in June 2000 Mrs Norwood was no longer TINA but a rather dotty old lady – 'the spy who never was'. Jack Straw, to his credit, quite rightly decided against a prosecution. 'With the benefit of history', he told the House of Commons in June 2000, 'we know that less damage was done by Mrs Norwood's spying than might otherwise have been the case.' Straw conceded that Norwood had handed over information about nuclear reactors, but he added that the Soviets 'merely copied American designs that they had obtained' when it came time for them to make plutonium for an atom bomb of their own. But this is not strictly true. Although the Soviet reactor used in making the necessary plutonium was similar to the American version, it contained important differences. Far from copying the American design, the Soviets rejected one of its key features, namely a radioactive core in which the fuel rods were laid horizontally, in favour of the design adopted by British scientists at the Chalk River plant built 130 miles west of Ottawa, where the fuel rods were suspended vertically, making it easier to refine bomb-grade plutonium. The history of the Chalk River plant shows that the BN-FMRA played a key role in overcoming technical difficulties encountered by scientists in Canada.

Following the passing by the US Congress of the McMahon Act in 1946 and the arrest of the atomic spy Allan Nunn May in Britain, exchanges of atomic information between Great Britain and the United States were supposedly severely restricted. This, however, did not seem to apply to the Chalk River plant. According to Margaret Gowing, the official historian of the British nuclear power and weapons industry, America not only gave generous scientific help to the builders of Chalk River, but also supplied its uranium fuel rods. One of Chalk River's designers was allowed to visit the Hanford plant in Washington State. It was at Chalk River where the first reactor outside the United States provided the experimental tool around which Britain's post-war nuclear work was to grow. This work had at the outset the aim of producing plutonium for weapons of mass destruction. This went against the spirit of the United Nations Atomic Energy Commission, which sought to prohibit the use of nuclear fuel in atomic explosions or for the development, production or assembly of any atomic weapon. The UN General Assembly, at its seventeenth meeting in London on 24 January 1946, had unanimously adopted a resolution to establish a Commission to deal with problems raised by the discovery of atomic energy and other related matters; in particular it was agreed that the Commission should make specific proposals:

(a) for extending between all nations the exchange of basic scientific information for peaceful ends;
(b) for control of atomic energy to the extent necessary to ensure its use only for peaceful purposes;
(c) for the elimination from national armaments of atomic weapons and of all other major weapons adaptable to mass destruction;
(d) for effective safeguards by way of inspection and other means to protect complying States against the hazards of violations and evasions.[11]

The construction of nuclear piles at Chalk River in 1945 and Harwell in 1947 had as its purpose the secret production of plutonium for Britain's military nuclear programme, outside the guidelines laid down by the United Nations. BN-FMRA's identification with Chalk River and Harwell, as evidenced in correspondence between G. L. Bailey and scientists at Chalk River, meant that Melita Norwood was able to access information critical to Britain's atomic weapons programme and of genuine importance for the Soviet Union.

The first Soviet reactor was designed by Nikolai Dollezhal and was built in the industrial city of Chelyabinsk in the Urals in 1946. Like Chalk River, Chelyabinsk was built with the fuel rods suspended vertically, which made it easier to refine bomb-grade plutonium. In fact, all three early reactors – Hanford, Chalk River and Chelyabinsk – had important design differences. But common to all was the problem of creep and corrosion, particularly in the aluminium alloy 'canning' in which the bare uranium rods were clad and in the water-cooling tubes. Creep – the phenomenon whereby a metal slowly deforms and bends after prolonged exposure to high temperatures – is greatly exacerbated by radioactivity. In all three countries, it threatened the reactor's ability to function. Before the passing of the McMahon Act in 1946 the US government issued in (August 1945) the *Smyth Report: A General Account of the Development of Methods Using Atomic Energy for Military Purposes* under the Auspices of the United States Government 1940–1945. The Russian translation was published early in 1946 in an edition of 30,000 copies and distributed to scientists and engineers involved in the Soviet project.[12] Along with the information from spies, it exercised an important influence on the technical choices made in the Soviet programme. Warned by the report that the 'canning' problem was difficult to resolve, the scientist leading the Soviet atomic bomb project, Igor Kurchatov, organized research at the beginning of 1946 in four different institutes on methods of sealing the fuel rods. By this time the Russians were seeking a solution to canning problems from the British-based spies Karl Fuchs and Melita Norwood, as opposed to the American-based spy networks centred on the Rosenbergs. Pavel Sudoplatov, who had overall responsibility for the atom bomb spies, recorded in his memoirs that by the end of 1946 the American spy networks had ceased to function, forcing him to rely on 'sources in Great Britain.'

So why did the Home Secretary, Philip Knightley and the *New Statesman*, the security service (MI5) and the Intelligence and Security Committee seek to play down Melita Norwood's role in the spying game? Certainly the issuing of full security clearance to her in 1945, just as she was gaining access to important atomic secrets, was an intelligence blunder of significant proportions, particularly since (as shown in Chapter 8) the Security Service had connected her with Soviet espionage as early as 1938. In fact, the whole Melita Norwood affair betrays a number of MI5 'blunders', suggesting that either MI5 had been more heavily penetrated by communists and fellow-travellers than has hitherto been allowed, or that there was a rogue element pursuing an agenda that was often at odds with UN policy on non-proliferation. On the other hand, MI5 may simply have just 'blown it'. The contention that Moscow had a number of moles in the intelligence services is not a new one, and perhaps reached its apogee in the 1980s following the publication of Chapman Pincher's *Too Secret Too Long* in 1984 and Peter Wright's *Spycatcher* in 1987, repeating claims that the head of MI5 between 1956 and 1965, Sir Roger Hollis, had been a Soviet penetration agent. The case against Hollis, simply stated, was that he had been recruited in China by Soviet military intelligence in 1934 while working for British American Tobacco by the German communist Ursula Kuczynski. He then infiltrated British intelligence in early 1938, and became head of the section dealing with communist subversion before becoming Director-General of MI5 in 1956. The details of the case do not concern us here, other than to take note that Ursula Kuczynski, better known as 'Red Sonya', was Melita Norwood's controller between 1941 and 1944, and that during these years she was also the controller of the atom bomb spy Klaus Fuchs. Part of the case against Hollis was that clear evidence against Fuchs kept landing on his desk, and that he chose, on several occasions, to ignore it.

On top of this, once the evidence against Fuchs became overwhelming, Ursula Kuczynski, along with her brother Jurgen, was allowed to slip through the net and flee to East Germany. The Kuczynski network in Britain then simply dispersed, and Melita Norwood disappeared from the radar, at least for a while. It is impossible to say whether Hollis can be connected directly with the Norwood case. But it is interesting to note that when Hollis had responsibility for countering communist subversion in Britain the Kuczynski and Sirnis families, as Chapter 7 demonstrates in more detail, had developed closer ties than merely those of agent and agent-controller. The close bond of friendship that existed between them continued until Melita Norwood's death in 2005, and owed its existence to the building of a block of flats in Lawn Road, Hampstead in 1934. Following Hitler's accession to power in January 1933 the Kuczynski family fled the Nazi witchhunt of German communists and joined the growing number of German-speaking political exiles from Austrian and German fascism in London. Melita Norwood's sister Gerty befriended the patriarch of this family, Robert (René) Kuczynski, and with the help of their mother found them a house to rent in Lawn Road. The following year the Labour MP Thelma Cazalet opened the Lawn Road flats almost directly opposite the Kuczynski home in Lawn Road. These flats soon filled up with refugees from Austria and Germany, and were colonized by a number of Soviet spies, among them Arnold Deutsch, the secret agent responsible for the recruitment of the Cambridge spies: Anthony Blunt, Guy Burgess, John Cairncross, Donald Maclean and Kim Philby.

In 1934 Lawn Road was being prepared by the Russian intelligence service to take over from Paris and Den Haag as the centre of Soviet espionage in Britain, and the coming and goings of Austrian, British and German communists in this corner of Hampstead were closely monitored by Special Branch and MI5. By the outbreak of the Second World War, despite British intelligence having been run down to levels that threatened national security, the Security Service probably possessed enough information on Mrs Norwood and the Lawn Road spies to disrupt their activities and stop them becoming a threat to national security before they began. But for some reason this did not happen. In the case of Mrs Norwood she was investigated on no fewer than ten occasions – in 1938, 1941, 1945, 1949, 1951, 1962, 1965, 1992, 1993 and 1999 – and each time walked away unscathed. No wonder then that the Home Secretary, the Intelligence and Security Committee and MI5 were eager to play down Melita Norwood's role in the spying game, and elicited the help of the *New Statesman* to do so. The thorny question remains, however, how did she manage to get away with it for so long?

CHAPTER 2

'Is This Well?'

O N Sunday 12 September 1999 Mrs Norwood, an 87-year-old widow and great-grandmother, an atomic spy whose luck had held out, explained to the world's media over her garden gate why she had spied for the Soviet Union from 1934 to 1973. Outed the day before in *The Times* as the longest-serving female Soviet agent in the West, and charged with passing to her Soviet controller Britain's atomic bomb secrets, she remained defiant. Over her right shoulder in the window of her living room could be glimpsed a poster demanding 'Stop Trident'. A lifelong member of CND she had made her contribution to nuclear weapons proliferation by shortening the Soviet atomic bomb project by several years.

Mrs Norwood was born Melita, or Letty as her father fondly called her, Sirnis on 25 March 1912 at 402 Christchurch Road, Pokesdown, in East Bournemouth. Her father Alexander Sirnis was a revolutionary socialist, a member of the London branch of the Social-Democracy of Lettland, a militant organization affiliated to Lenin's Russian Social-Democratic Labour Party (Bolsheviks). He was also a member of the British Socialist Party, a Marxist body affiliated to the Labour Party, calling for the revolutionary overthrow of British capitalism. Letty's mother, Gertrude, who came from a well-to-do family of doctors and solicitors, was a suffragette and a supporter of the Labour Party; her views were thus no less progressive than her husband's. Letty shared many of the characteristics of her grandmother, Elizabeth Gurney Stedman (1851–1943), who possessed a literary and philosophical mind, and when quite a young woman had written a little book entitled *No Humbug*. According to her friends and acquaintances there was a strong vein of self-reliance in her character, and she needed no assistance in dealing with difficult situations. 'She used to claim she was "afraid of nothing on earth", but she had a horror of big spiders! Her memory was good.'[1]

Melita Norwood had been brought up in a family environment that, while not austere, was certainly hard working. On her mother's side the family ancestry was solid Sussex yeoman stock. The Stedman family had been landowners in Itchingfield, near Horsham, West Sussex, for over 600 years. An entry in *Sussex Genealogies* on Stedman of Itchingfield notes that the surname Stedman occurs with reference to Itchingfield as early as the year 1324 'when Simon Stedeman owned a messauge and half a virgate of land in Horsham and Hechyngefelde'. [2] Melita Norwood's grandmother, Elizabeth Gurney Stedman, had been 'interred in the family grave there on the 17th instant, in peaceful surroundings within the shadow of a Norman church and amid ancient yews planted to supply the English bowmen in the days of the crusades'. [3] The last of the Stedman male line to be buried in Itchingfield was Letty's uncle, Thomas Gurney Stedman (1883–1975) on 14 May 1975.

Letty's grandfather, Dr James Stedman (1836–1915), married Elizabeth Gurney on 21 January 1878 at Christchurch, Hants. He was then forty-two years old, a widower with four children, while Elizabeth was twenty-seven. The couple bought a large piece of land in Christchurch Road, Pokesdown, and built two houses. They had three children: Gertrude (1878–1967), Theresa (1882–1986) and Thomas (1883–1975). They were an unconventional couple and enjoyed quite separate lives. In the parlance of the time, they decided 'to go it alone', and lived in separate houses in Pokesdown.

Elizabeth, along with her three children, later moved to a large house in Gloucester Place, Boscombe, while Dr James Stedman took his two sons from his first marriage, Herman and Arthur, to America. In 1883 he opened a practice in Atlanta, and sent his two adolescent daughters, Edith and Agnes, to a finishing school in Switzerland. He returned to England three years later with Herman and rented a practice in Towcester, leaving Arthur in America. His two daughters from his first marriage, Edith and Agnes, joined them in Towcester later the same year.

In 1899 Edith returned to Berne and married a German-speaking Swiss national. Letty's mother, Gertrude, was invited to stay with them in 1900, and remained in their household for five years, becoming a fluent German speaker. She became engaged to Carl Adolf Brandt, the only son of Alfred Brandt, the engineer who had built the Simplon tunnel connecting Italy and France, and Anna Maria Brandt, an authority on Greek culture and a close friend of the German philosopher Friedrich Nietzsche. The couple married in England in January 1905 and then went to Spain, where Carl had secured work in the silver and lead mines of Cuevas de Vera in the province of Almeria. The following year, when Gertrude was four months pregnant, her father joined them to oversee her pregnancy. Gertrude's sister, Theresa, remained with her mother in Boscombe, while her brother, Thomas, moved to Bournemouth and began work with Tattershalls, a firm of solicitors.

Gertrude and Carl's son Alfred was born at Cuevas de Vera on 28 August 1906. Three months later Carl caught a local fever and died on 19 November 1906. Gertrude and Carl returned to England, and began visiting Tuckton House, where she met and fell in love with a Latvian translator of Tolstoy's works, Peter Alexander Sirnis (Sasha), the first man she had met who spoke enthusiastically about Mrs Pankhurst's suffragettes. At Christmas Sasha sent her a suffragette puzzle with the inscription 'Sasha to Gertrude. Xmas 1906'. The puzzle was to find three policemen, supposedly hidden within the picture of a suffragette waving a banner demanding 'Votes for Women'. The couple married on 3 November 1909.

Meanwhile, Gertrude's brother, Thomas, had left Tattershalls and joined Thomas Cotching, a firm of solicitors in Horsham that undertook legal work for the radical ex-diplomat, philanderer and adventurer Wilfrid Scawen Blunt, a 'kinsman' and hero of the future Cambridge spy, Anthony Blunt. At the time Wilfrid Scawen Blunt was regarded 'as politically and morally unsound' by Anthony Blunt's father, the Revd A. Stanley Blunt of Holy Trinity Church, Bournemouth, and his name, according to Anthony Blunt's brother Wilfrid, was 'barely to be mentioned amongst us'. [4] A member of the landed gentry and owner of an Arab stallion stud farm at Crabbett Park, Horsham, Wilfrid Scawen Blunt had gained political notoriety as a 'rebel' in 1889, when he stood in Ireland as a Home Ruler and had gone to prison for inciting Irish tenants to resist eviction. In 1906, he became involved in the protest against Britain's occupation of Egypt and published a book under the title *Atrocities of Justice under British Rule in Egypt*. The following year he formed the British–Egypt Association in support of the Egyptian nationalist movement of Mustapha Kamel, and campaigned for the withdrawal of British troops. Thomas Stedman became a member of the British–Egypt Association and acted as the group's solicitor. Among its more notable members were James Keir Hardie, the founder of the Labour

Party; Hilaire Belloc, the French writer; Mustapha Kamel, the Egyptian nationalist leader; H. N. Brailsford, the radical socialist; Lord Rutherford, the atomic physicist; a member of Sinn Fein, who also worked for the British secret service; and a Russian political émigré, Feodor Aaronovich Rotshtein (Theodore Rothstein) who in time would become Lenin's first secret agent in Britain.

Feodor Aaronovich Rotshtein was born at Kovno, now Kaunus, in Lithuania on 26 February 1871 to non-Orthodox Jewish parents. In Russia he had belonged to a clandestine study group organized by the *Narodnaya Volya* (People's Will), which over a period of two decades had been responsible for a number of high-profile murders across Russia in the belief that individual acts of terror would inspire a general insurrection. During the 1870s they were responsible for the killing of a number of leading government figures, culminating in the assassination of the tsar, Alexander II, on 13 March 1881. Their philosophy was both anti-Western and anti-capitalist, and was not Marxist. They hoped to exploit pan-Slav sentiment to stop capitalism, which they regarded as alien to Slavonic customs and traditions, gaining any foothold in Russia. They refused to believe that capitalism had a future in Russia and idealized the Russian peasant commune – the *mir*. Individual acts of terror, however, did not provoke a general insurrection, and in 1883 a section of the *Narodnaya Volya* broke away to form the Emancipation of Labour under the leadership of the Marxist Georgi V. Plekhanov. A fierce polemical struggle between the two groups broke out, with the literature of both organizations circulating in underground study groups. Fyodor Aaronovich Rotshtein, who had joined a similar study group in Poltava, where he was studying medicine, read the works of the Russian anti-capitalists Chernishevskii and Dobroliubov before reading the few Marxist texts that were then circulating underground in Russia: the *Communist Manifesto*, parts of the first volume of *Capital*, and Friedrich Engels's *Development of Socialism from Utopia to Science*. Rotshtein came to the attention of the authorities and after an 'anonymous tip-off' that he 'had better get out', in 1891 he fled with his family to Britain, where he changed his name to Theodore Rothstein.[5]

The Rothstein family initially went to Germany, where an older brother, Phoebus, lived in Danzig, before travelling to the northern industrial city of Leeds. On arrival Theodore's father leased an apothecary's shop in Chapeltown, a predominantly Jewish district of the city. Theodore became active in Russian political émigré politics and joined the Society of Friends of Russian Freedom (SFRF), an ad hoc body made up of Russian constitutionalists and English radicals calling for the establishment of democratic institutions across the Russian empire. He published several articles in the SFRF's Russian-language journal *Letuchie Listki* before being appointed honorary secretary. He also worked as an assistant editor for their English-language paper *Free Russia*, edited by the influential Liberal-Radical MP J. Frederick Green. In this capacity he worked closely with Kerensky's future secretary, David Soskice, a comradeship that had embarrassing repercussions. It was David Soskice's son, Sir Frank Soskice, who, as Labour Home Secretary in 1965, took the final decision to foreclose MI5 investigations into Letty Norwood's spying activities. And it was the son of his father's old comrade Theodore Rothstein, Andrew Rothstein, who had first introduced Letty to the world of spying in 1934.

In 1893 Rothstein moved to London to begin working on a Marxist history of Rome. He worked on this project for two years, supported by his family, studying mostly in the British Museum. Although this work was never finished he published articles on Plato, Socrates, Alexander the Great, Julius Caesar, Demosthenes and Cicero in the Russian journal *Zhizn zamechatel'nikh lyudei* (Lives of Famous People). He also published an article on Roman poetry under the *nom de plume* E. Orlov in the journal *Zhizn'* (Life). His literary output was impressive. He was employed on the Liberal Party leader Sir Henry Campbell-Bannerman's short-lived radical newspaper *The Tribune* and made a name for himself reporting on the engineers lock-out of July 1897 to January 1898. In London he initially settled in the predominantly Jewish area of Whitechapel and began editing two Yiddish socialist newspapers. He also joined the Whitechapel branch of the Marxist Social-Democratic Federation (SDF), founded in 1884 from the remnants of the Chartist movement by Henry Hyndman, a top-hatted stockbroker and Sussex county cricketer. The SDF faced an uphill task, and Hyndman once complained to Karl Marx that, 'At times I … must confess it seems hopeless to attempt to found a Labour party here. The men are so indifferent, so given over to beer, tobacco, and general laissez-faire.'[6]

Hyndman's pessimism was not misplaced. Theodore Rothstein, then resident in Whitechapel, was under no illusions. The area was notorious for street crime, thieves' kitchens and disorderly public houses. Nevertheless, the Jewish community of Whitechapel successfully created a vibrant political culture alongside a religious one. A number of secular, anarchist and socialist clubs sprang up in London's East End, and the Whitechapel branch of the SDF became a meeting place for many Jews. Theodore Rothstein met his wife-to-be, Anna Kahan, through the Whitechapel branch of the SDF in 1897, marrying her that same year. In 1898 they moved to Hackney, where their son Andrew was born. That same year they began visiting the Russian community at Tuckton. In 1900 he was invited by Tolstoy's literary executor Count Vladimir Chertkov, then living in exile at Tuckton House, to work as a translator and as a proof-reader on French editions of Tolstoy's works. By this time Theodore had become a leading figure in the SDF and a prominent campaigner against the Boer War (1899–1902). Under his influence the mood in Tuckton House began to shift away from Tolstoyism towards Marxism. In 1902 he met Vladimir Illich-Ulyanov, better known as Lenin, for the first time outside the blue-domed reading room of the British Museum. Lenin had arrived in London earlier that year to share the printing presses and offices of the SDF's Twentieth Century Press situated in Clerkenwell Green in order to continue publishing the Russian-language newspaper *Iskra* (The Spark) following its suppression by the German authorities. Soon after his arrival in London he met with Rothstein and the two men became firm friends. They were of similar ages: Lenin was 32 and Rothstein was 31. Their backgrounds were similar. In their youth they had both been members of the *Narodnaya Volya*, and both men understood fully the conspiratorial world of exile politics.

In 1903 *Iskra* was transferred from London to Geneva and Lenin left for Switzerland. He returned later in the year to attend the Second Congress of the Russian Social-Democratic Labour Party in London. It was at this congress that the famous split in the RSDLP between the Bolsheviks and Mensheviks took place. In the very first number of *Iskra* Lenin had written a short article entitled 'Urgent Tasks of Our Movement' in which he argued that the revolutionary party should consist only of full-time professionals 'who shall devote to the revolution not only their spare evenings, but the whole of their lives'.[7] Theodore Rothstein was in full agreement. At the Second Congress, however, Lenin's arguments in support of the creation of a professional revolutionary body were rejected in favour of a broader-based political party. The two factions split, with Lenin winning a small majority on another issue after many of the delegates had left for the continent. His faction then claimed the title Bolsheviki (majority), dubbing his opponents the Mensheviki (minority) and the two titles stuck. The Bolsheviks, with Theodore Rothstein in full tow, now wholeheartedly turned to the methods of conspiracy.

In 1907 Theodore cemented his contacts with liberal-radical elements in British politics and began working as a sub-editor for the Liberal *Daily News*, and as the London correspondent on Wilfrid Scawen Blunt's *The Egyptian Standard*, a weekly newspaper published by the British–Egypt Association in Cairo, London and Paris. On 14 September 1909 he addressed the second Egyptian national congress held in Geneva on 'The Fortunes of the Constitutional Movement in Egypt'. He was forthright in his condemnation of British policy in Egypt, and pointed out to his audience, Egyptian, French and British alike, that the overwhelming support for the nationalist movement in Egypt had now overridden the purely constitutional desire for political reform championed by British liberal-radicals. He spelt it out to reluctant British radicals that British opposition to reform had convinced the majority of Egyptians that reform would never take place without the removal of the British. He began visiting Wilfrid Scawen Blunt's estate at Crabbett Park on a regular basis, and in 1910 he published a book on the Egyptian question under the title *Egypt's Ruin*. 'I think', Wilfrid Scawen Blunt wrote in his diary, 'the book will be worth it politically. It has given me a deal of trouble, besides writing the introduction.'[8] Soon afterwards Scawen Blunt sent a copy to Asquith, 'with a letter requesting him to read it', a foolish attempt to influence British foreign policy that cost Theodore Rothstein his application for British citizenship.[9] By the end of the year, however, Asquith's censure notwithstanding, Theodore Rothstein had managed to secure his position on Fleet Street and had begun to contribute articles to C. P. Scott's *Manchester Guardian*. He would prove to be a lively addition to Fleet Street. As the twentieth century got underway his denunciations of the British empire became more forthright.

Following the assassination of the Turkish administrator of Egypt, Boutross Pasha, and the execution of his assassin Wardani in 1910, a wave of anti-British rioting had swept across Egypt in the first half of the year, leading Rothstein to locate the Egyptian question within the context of the European system of alliances and the balance of power. If the British government responded to the Egyptian crisis by dispatching troops to the region then it would have to face the common censure of Germany, Austria and the other Great Powers. Britain had no mandate from Europe condoning her occupation of Egypt. She had been allowed to remain in Egypt solely at the discretion of the European Powers, and only as long as she did not infringe the substantial rights of those Powers by seeking to annex or appropriate any exclusive advantage. Nor could she make any alteration in the status quo without the consent of the Powers. To send troops to Egypt would raise not only a diplomatic row with Turkey, who, in the face of the occupation of her autonomous province by foreign troops, would have no other choice but to demand the withdrawal of those troops and the occupation of Egypt by her own. In making such demands, Turkey would be confident of the support of Germany and Austria, and Britain would be left with no alternative but to fight or to surrender. Faced with such an alternative Britain could not afford to risk military repression in Egypt. To dispatch troops at this point would inevitably clash with the equal rights of other European nations in Egypt and raise the question of her stay there. The occupation of Egypt was beginning to destabilize international relations, and to threaten the European balance of power. Theodore Rothstein, by now a frequent visitor to the Russian colony at Tuckton House, began to put forward Lenin's case for revolutionary socialism not only as a vehicle of advance in their native Russia, but also as an antidote to British imperialism and a recipe for activism in their adopted land. Socialism and Tolstoyism, he told them, were not incompatible; both were based on the doctrine of cooperation. The fundamental difference lay in how society was to get from where it was to where it should be. He found his audience receptive.

In 1844 a small group of radical working men had met in Rochdale, the so-called Rochdale Pioneers, a meeting that gave rise to the modern movement of consumers' cooperation that was later to become the Co-operative Wholesale Society (CWS), better known as the Co-op. In Manchester, in 1905 the CWS established a cooperative journal, the *Millgate Monthly*, to publicize their programme of cooperation. In February 1909 the CWS, intrigued by a colony of Russian Tolstoyans espousing the philosophy of cooperation on England's south coast, dispatched an eager young journalist to Tuckton House to report on the progress being made by the cooperative movement in both Britain and Russia. Arriving full of optimism, this young man left Tuckton House in no doubt that the firebrand politics of the Russian colony in Bournemouth had worrying implications for Britain's future national security:

> Men of all classes and shades of opinion, men escaped from the military service they deem it a crime against their conscience to perform, persecuted suffering individuals, socialists, democrats, and the most profound revolutionaries, temporarily from Russia or en route from other lands, find a home and a refuge at Tuckton House. … There are even Englishmen among the ranks, those who come desiring to lead a simple life, or ardent revolutionaries who go far in their aims. It is a little centre, a port of call in a strange land, the magnet attracting all, the pivot of the whole machinery. From it the work of reform for Russia pours steadily forth. But the influence may be found permeating our own country. Is this well?[10]

CHAPTER 3

'Neither the Saint nor the Revolutionary'[1]

Tuckton House had been founded in 1900 by Tolstoy's literary executor, Count Vladimir Chertkov, to house the English branch of the Free Age Press, a small publishing business devoted to the production of cheap English-language editions of Tolstoy in which no copyright would be claimed, while unexpurgated Russian editions of Tolstoy's works were to be produced and smuggled back into Russia. To help him in this venture Chertkov recruited a young Englishman, A. C. Fifield, from the editorial staff of a large publishing house in London, who had already made a name for himself in the publishing world by overseeing the production and distribution of penny editions of Charles Sheldon's religious novels:

> My acquaintance with Tchertkoff goes back to 1897, soon after his exile to England. I was engaged on the editorial staff of a large publishing house in London, and learning also something of the production and distribution of books. Tchertkoff was busy with seeking newspaper avenues for Tolstoy's new writings. We met at Tamworth Hall, Croydon, at Paul Boulanger's house in Forest Hill, at my own house in Beckenham, and at Castle's Vegetarian Restaurant, Shoe Lane, London; and we became immediate friends.[2]

At this time Tolstoy's novels were subject to heavy censorship in Russia following Tolstoy's intervention on behalf of the Dukhobors, a persecuted religious sect who shared many of Tolstoy's precepts. Like Tolstoy they advocated chastity, vegetarianism, abstinence from alcohol and tobacco, the pooling of all goods and property, cooperation and non-resistance to evil. In keeping with the latter they refused to bear arms in the Russian army and as a consequence were subjected to a number of atrocities at the hands of Cossack troops. In December 1896 Leo Tolstoy wrote a manifesto, *Pomigite!* (Give Help!) on their behalf, which was signed by a number of influential literary figures, including Count Chertkov. A copy of the manifesto was sent to Tsar Nicholas II, who responded by banishing Tolstoy to his estates at Yasnaya Polyana and exiling Chertkov to the Baltic Provinces. However, following intercession by his mother, Yelizaveta Ivanovna, née Countess Chernyshova-Kruglikova (1831–1922), a former member of the imperial court and already in exile in Bournemouth for her Baptist convictions, Count Chertkov was allowed to go into 'permanent exile' in England.[3] Chertkov knew England well. His mother had been a follower of the English evangelist Lord Radstock and was related by marriage to Count P. A. Shulatov (1827–1889), the Russian ambassador to London between 1874 and 1879. The diplomatic world would rub shoulders with Tuckton House again when the future British Consul to Ekaterinburg, Thomas Preston, paid an unexpected and instructive visit to Tuckton House before leaving for Russia to take up his first diplomatic post:

> Before I left England I was invited by a maiden aunt to spend a few days at Bournemouth. Oddly enough it was this trip to England's bathchair-ridden seaside resort which first of all brought me into contact with Russians, with whom I was to have so much to do in after life.
>
> On a summer's day in July, whilst cycling on the outskirts of the town, hot and thirsty, I asked a nearby policeman where I could get a drink of water.
>
> 'Go and try them Roussians up at the big 'ouse,' said the man in blue, pointing to a large mansion standing in its own grounds just off the sea-front.
>
> 'They may be mad; but they plays football and are kind'arted to us folk. Some says they are bloody anarchists and that we should keep an eye on 'em – we don't want no bombs in England,' he added.[4]

The year was 1903 and it was hardly surprising that the 'man in blue' keeping a watchful eye on England's south coast should nurture suspicions about 'them Roussians up at the big 'ouse'. For over a decade, ever since a series of anarchist outrages had shocked Europe in the early 1890s, English novelists, playwrights and the popular press had portrayed Russian political exiles living in Britain as a sinister threat to national security.[5] In 1893 the Conservative MP Arthur J. Balfour, speaking in the House of Commons called upon continental governments to crack down upon anarchists prepared to use 'the resources of chemical discovery for the most brutal form of destruction of innocent men, women, and children'.[6] However, as Balfour's campaign against terrorism began to take effect, other influential governmental figures began to express their concerns. In a debate which echoes today's concerns about international terrorism, G. Lushington, the Permanent Under-Secretary at the Home Office, despatched a minute to Balfour advising him that 'if other states possess and exercise the power of expelling anarchists as from their own countries & England alone does not, all the anarchists are bound to come to England'.[7] Such fears periodically roused the House of Commons, and between 1894 and 1906 there were numerous protests in the House against countries who deported their anarchists to Britain. The press also expressed its outrage that Britain had become a dumping ground for the continent's political waste.

It was, therefore, with some trepidation that Thomas Preston approached 'a side door of a mansion on the outskirts of Bournemouth eyeing, suspiciously, a huge dog chained to a post near the door'. While his fears were soon allayed, his suspicions were not:

> The door opened to my timid knock and, much to my surprise, revealed a bearded, but smiling and not unkindly giant, attired in a red shirt, buttoned up to the neck and worn, Russian style, over baggy velvet trousers tucked into short top-boots.[8]

Before Preston had time to issue his modest request for a glass of water a heavy hand descended on his shoulder and he found himself 'half pushed, half led down a corridor into a kind of dining hall'. There, 'seated at a long table, were a score or more of young people of both sexes, the men attired in the same fashion as my host and the women in simple black frocks with white pinafores, such as were worn by girls at Tsarist gymnasium schools'. Pressed to join the diners he found himself 'seated at the table between a bearded Russian and an attractive young Russian girl who was introduced to him as Olga Nicolaevna'. He soon found himself bombarded with questions:

> Over a repast of borsch, kasha and sour cream, a vegetable dish and a kind of jelly, called kissel, I was the bewildered target of a perfect

barrage of questions. Did I speak Russian? Had I read Tolstoy? How long was England going to be ruled by an aristocratic oligarchy? Were not public schools and the privileged classes they produced a gross injustice to a nation supposed to be free? With the odds at about thirty to one I felt myself at a considerable disadvantage. Nevertheless I plucked up courage ... What was the Tolstoyan creed? I asked timidly.[9]

Olga Nicolaevna responded to the question warmly. 'Love should rule instead of law. We should agitate for non-co-operation with the State. If everybody refused to join the army, to pay taxes or to submit to the decisions of the law courts, the existing order would collapse.' Preston was shocked and yet at the same time smitten: 'It flashed through my mind that when the policeman had described these people as "bloody anarchists" he was not far wrong. Only Olga Nicolaevna was undoubtedly a "nice bloody anarchist".'[10]

During the summer of 1903 Gertrude Stedman's sister, Theresa Gurney Stedman, also visited Tuckton House. She could barely contain her excitement when she received an invitation from Count Chertkov to join him for tea at Tuckton House. Among the guests would be the anarchist Prince Piotr Kropotkin. This would be no ordinary invitation to an afternoon tea of cream cakes, strawberries and cucumber sandwiches, the staple summer fare of Edwardian country houses; but an invitation to black Russian tea imported from the Popov estates in the Caucasus, brewed and served from an enormous samovar. The samovar, long regarded as an invitation to conversation among Russians, was a novelty on England's south coast and Theresa eagerly anticipated her visit.[11] When Thomas Preston visited Tuckton House later that summer, having passed an enjoyable evening of musical entertainment and political discussion, it was quite late in the evening before he left. He had had a very pleasant evening for someone who had just knocked on a strange door in search of a glass of water. When he reached the gate he found the policeman who had pointed him to Tuckton House waiting for him:

'Seem to 'ave been 'aving a pretty long drink of water up at the Roussians. 'ope you 'aven't been gettin' up to no trouble,' he said, as I darted past him at the entrance of the drive to the Tchertkoff Mansion.[12]

The policeman was not far wrong. Before leaving Tuckton House Preston had taken advantage of a lull in the conversation – 'a sudden angel-passing silence' as he called it – 'to refer to the extraordinary coincidence of my finding my way into a Russian house, especially a centre of Russian culture in England, on the very eve of my departure for Batoum.' Spiritualists to a man, and 'with a superstition peculiarly Russian', they immediately placed 'all kinds of occult interpretations' on this unexpected meeting and pressed upon Preston 'a small confidential package for delivery to a friend of theirs in Batoum', a commission he undertook but regretted soon afterwards:

> On arrival at Batoum ... I was met by the Vice-Consul, in spite of whose energetic protests the Russian Customs officials insisted on searching my luggage. It struck me that they were looking for some definite object and, although I had no proof of it I could not help feeling that it might have been the packet I had so wisely flung into the sea at Constantinople.[13]

Preston was not alone in expressing his concern at the activities of the Tolstoyans living at Tuckton House, and their communication methods with Russia. The local postmistress who had responsibility for handling their mail was in a constant state of alarm lest the 'smuggled tracts might perhaps involve her in slight disfavour with the Russian court'.[14] Everything Tolstoy wrote was sent to Tuckton House. From there Count Chertkov liaised with publishers, both Russian and foreign, chose translators, supervised their work and decided upon publication dates. He insisted that Tolstoy's manuscripts should be housed in a specially constructed strongroom in the basement of Tuckton House, and in 1903 he took possession of the first three volumes of Tolstoy's *Diaries, Youth*, volume I, 1847–52, volume II, 1853–61 and *Later Years*, volume III, 1895–1903. He needed a translator for these works and sought advice from Tolstoy's secretary and biographer, Paul Biryukov, who recommended a twenty-two-year-old Latvian, Alexander Sirnis, who was then working on a ranch belonging to Russian exiles in San Jose on the outskirts of San Francisco.[15] Biryukov had been introduced to Alexander by a fellow signatory of *Pomigite!*, Bodniaski, who had made Alexander's acquaintance in exile in Lemsal following his banishment to Courland.

The contrast between San Jose and the leafy lanes of Hampshire at the beginning of the twentieth century could not have been more marked. One contemporary described Tuckton House, along with its Russian inhabitants, as standing between the old order and the new, a witness to the nineteenth century giving way to the pace of the twentieth:

England is a second home to Vladimir Tchertkoff, and the pleasant house, standing high above the banks of the sedgy Stour, seems wrapped in a quiet, reposeful atmosphere. Away in the distance gleams the blue of the changed ocean, the grey pile of Christchurch Priory rises proudly forth set betwixt meandering streams and emerald meadows; only the garish red-brick with which the beauty-destroying builder is rapidly covering the heathy, gorsey broken land adjacent to Southbourne strikes a dissonant note and mars an otherwise perfect prospect. Tuckton House stands between the old order and the new. Ancient Christchurch, with its storied fane and legendary lore – a home of past glories – and the jerry-built villa residencies of to-day, the brand new electric trams, and all the so-called goods of modern civilisation. And in the midst of these conflicting elements is the home of Vladimir Tchertkoff, pulsating with stern determination, vigorous life, and strenuous endeavour – a bit of Russia in the heart of English scenes and English customs.[16]

When Alexander arrived at Tuckton House he found himself in the company of a number of experienced publicists and revolutionaries drawn from across the Russian empire. It was without question a very professional enterprise, and would have made a strong impression on the twenty-three-year-old Sirnis. The printing works in Iford Lane boasted Russian type, Russian compositors, printing machines, machinists, imposing tables, stereotyping plant, wire-stitching machines, guillotines for cutting and all the other necessary plant of a small printing and paper-binding factory. The house itself had twenty bedrooms. At times as many as thirty people lived there, engaged in the community's various activities.[17]

Although Count Chertkov had a reputation for being a rather difficult man, he got on well with Alexander, and the two by all accounts established a good working relationship. Alexander had arrived at Tuckton with glowing references from Biryukov, who, as Tolstoy's official biographer, was in a position to greatly influence Count Chertkov's judgement. According to Alfred Brandt, Alexander's stepson, the count held a very high opinion of Alexander's linguistic abilities and would often defer to him on the finer points of Russian grammar:

> Mum once told me that whenever there was an argument at Tuckton, about the Russian meaning or construction, translation etc. Tchert-koff always took Sasha's [Alexander's] opinion as final. Although Russian was not his native language, he was a much better Russian scholar than the 'educated' Russians![18]

Count Chertkov was not without a sense of humour. Alfred Brandt remembers his mother saying of him that when he became a vegetarian, fried bacon was the last meat dish he gave up because the taste was so delicious. He also ate herrings once a year, 'to avoid becoming too narrow minded'.[19]

The Tuckton House community came to be well respected locally, and the observation of Preston's 'man in blue' that 'they may be mad; but they plays football and are kind'arted to us folk' was pretty accurate. The count remained a very popular figure with the 'locals', and set up the only English football club in history to be founded by an exiled Russian count – Tuckton Football Club, colours green and gold. Alexander by all accounts played a robust game on the left wing. The team enjoyed mixed fortunes. In the *Christchurch Times* of 6 January 1906 the team, then the bottom club, is reported to have beaten the top team, Pokesdown St James, by three goals to two. The following year, in a report of 21 December, after playing sixteen games the team was recorded as being second in Division II of the Bournemouth and District League and also second in Division III of the Bournemouth Saturday League.[20]

However, life at Tuckton didn't revolve entirely around Tuckton Football Club (they also had a cricket eleven), and was soon overtaken by events of a more dramatic nature unfolding in Russia. On Sunday 22 January 1905, a peaceful demonstration of workers led by an Orthodox priest, Father Gapon, marched on the Winter Palace in St Petersburg to present a petition to the tsar demanding an eight-hour day and a constitution. As the demonstrators approached the Winter Palace they 'were met with rifle fire; the troops even picked off little street boys who had climbed the trees in the Alexander garden to watch the show, in the same spirit as our urchins do to watch cricket at the Oval'.[21]

Once news of 'Bloody Sunday' spread from St Petersburg into the interior, strikes, mutinies and rural insurrections spread rapidly across Russia. On 27 June the crew of the battleship *Potemkin* mutinied, killing several officers, before sailing into the port of Odessa, where striking factory workers were already battling government troops. In October a general strike in Moscow quickly spread to St Petersburg and then to other major towns and cities. The nation had been brought to a standstill – no railways, no post, no telegraph, no newspapers, no public transport and no electricity. On 17 October, Nicholas II, under the pressure of events, agreed to the formation of a state Duma with limited powers, to be elected by universal suffrage. No piece of legislation, however, could pass into law without first gaining the Duma's approval. The new constitution proved divisive and while those liberals who feared the revolution spiralling out of control accepted it, the workers and peasants who rapidly set up their own instruments of government in the form of the Soviets did not. Disturbances increased in intensity, with strikes and mutinies taking place at Kronstadt and Sevastopol. In December street fighting in Moscow resulted in a heavy loss of life. In response the tsar sacked the moderate head of the government, Count Witte, replacing him with the unpopular and autocratic Stolypin. Six months later the Duma was dissolved, bringing the first phase of the Russian Revolution to a close. These events were watched closely in England.

In 1904 Britain settled its imperial differences with France by signing the Entente Cordiale, guaranteeing freedom of trade, free passage of the Suez Canal and the prohibition of fortifications opposite the Straits of Gibraltar. Following the Moroccan crisis of 1905 British and French diplomacy sought to exploit anti-German sentiment in Russia by forging an agreement with Russia aimed at containing German continental and imperial ambitions. One consequence of this policy was that the two parliamentary Great Powers, Britain and France, would not put pressure on the tsar in 1905, and withheld their support from those Russian liberals campaigning for constitutional reform. This was to prove an error of judgement of some importance. The failure of the liberal democracies to support reform in Russia between 1905 and 1907 led many reform-minded

Russians living in exile during these years to distrust and ultimately reject liberalism in favour of revolution. Sirnis, whose politics on arrival at Tuckton House had been an eclectic mixture of essentially pacifist, anarchist and Tolstoyan beliefs, now began to openly question the relevance of Tolstoyism to the social question and political reform in Russia. Between 13 May and 1 June 1907 the Fifth Congress of the Russian Social-Democratic Labour Party took place in London. It coincided with the dismissal of the short-lived Second Duma and the arrest of the Social-Democratic deputies in Russia. A demonstration to protest against these events was held in Trafalgar Square, where a section of the protestors broke away from the main demonstration and led a procession along Whitehall to protest outside the Foreign Office against any Anglo-Russian agreement. A number of skirmishes broke out between the demonstrators and the police, in which a number of Russian voices could be heard on both sides. Accusations followed in the socialist press that the British police had been working hand in glove with the Russian secret police, the Okhrana, to monitor and intimidate Russian dissidents living in Britain. This led to a significant shift in opinion within Britain's Russian political émigré community, and by the time the Liberal government and the tsar's government had signed a formal agreement in 1907, their politics had become noticeably more revolutionary.

On 29 December 1906, Alexander Sirnis, using the alias A. Brady, joined Lenin's section of the Russian Social-Democratic Labour Party, the Social-Democracy of Lettland, London branch.[22] Their meetings were held at the premises of the Communist Working Men's Club and Institute in Charlotte Street, London. Among the club's prominent members was Theodore Rothstein. Alexander also joined the East Bournemouth branch of the Social-Democratic Federation (SDF) and began editing a four-page leftwing newspaper, *The Southern Worker: A Labour and Socialist Journal* issued as a monthly, and published in Bournemouth by local socialists and trade unionists. Alexander's new politics made a profound impression on Count Chertkov. When the count received a copy of Tolstoy's *The Government, the Revolutionaries and the People* attacking the bloodthirsty methods of the revolutionaries, he read the tract 'with astonishment and wrote to Tolstoy imploring him to tone down his derogatory remarks about the Marxists'.[23]

Towards the end of 1907 the Third Duma convened under a restricted franchise, and the following year its liberal leader, Alexander Guchkov, offered an amnesty to the signatories of *Pomogite!*, making it possible for Count Chertkov to return to Russia in time to celebrate Tolstoy's eightieth birthday. Before his departure he arranged for an English cooperator, Frank Thompson, to take charge of Tuckton House, and passed financial responsibility for the 'Tolstoy Fund' and the publication of Tolstoy's works in English to Dr Hagberg Wright, the director of the London Library. Dr Wright, a Russophile, had received part of his education in Russia, and on Chertkov's advice he engaged Sirnis as his personal 'Russian secretary' and as an official translator of Tolstoy's diaries. The following year Thompson emigrated to Australia and Chertkov wrote to Alexander asking him to take over the duties of manager at Tuckton House. Alexander accepted, with the proviso that he continued living at Pokesdown. Gertrude, who was pregnant at the time, gave birth to their first child, Wilfrid, on 31 May 1910. Later that year Alexander was diagnosed with TB and the management was passed to Stanley Carlyle Potter. Chertkov's mother, Yelizaveta Ivanovna, who had remained in Bournemouth, 'wrote to him in excellent English "so that your dear wife can read it too" – typical aristocratic good manners, expressing her sorrow saying, "I must speak to my son to see what can be arranged." The upshot was that Chertkov arranged for Sasha [(Alexander)] to do translating work, which he would be able to do in Switzerland.' [24]

In 1911, therefore, in addition to working on Tolstoy's *Diaries* Alexander began work on a translation of Maxim Gorky's *Tales of Two Countries* for the London-based publisher Werner Laurie, and prepared to move his family to Davos. However, on 7 August 1911 their first child Wilfrid, just over a year old, died, and Gertrude, who was now two months pregnant, insisted that they postpone travelling to Switzerland until after the birth of their new child. In January 1913 Count Chertkov travelled to England to arrange for the shipment of Tolstoy's manuscripts back to Russia. By this time Alexander's health had worsened, and when Count Chertkov returned to Moscow he made hasty arrangements for Alexander to accompany him as far as Berlin to consult a lung specialist. He was again advised to go to Davos to seek a cure and Count Chertkov promised to help him financially. When they eventually left for Davos in October 1913 Gertrude was again pregnant and Switzerland promised a new start: 'That is how we came to go to Davos where Gerty was born. It certainly prolonged his [Sasha's] life several years.'[25] In Davos Alexander became friendly with the Swiss inventor Dr Wande, the creator of Ovo-Maltine, later marketed as Ovaltine and regarded as a prophylactic for TB. They skated together for hours on the frozen ice.[26] Letty, too, skated after a fashion: 'He took me (2–3 years old) on the frozen lake of Davos where I pushed a box about while the others skated.'[27] On 22 March 1914 Letty's sister Gerty was born:

> We lived in the top flat of Villa Surley, Wolfgang, Davos, where Gertrude ('Gerty') was born on the 22nd March 1914. We had a glorious view overlooking the Davoser See and the whole valley to the Tinzenhorn, miles away at the end.[28]

That summer Letty's uncle took a holiday from his work for the firm of Thomas Cotching and visited the Sirnis family in Switzerland. In July he sent a picture postcard of the panoramic view from his window over the lake to his friend Wilfrid Scawen Blunt:

> This view is from our windows, in a small villa by the lake. The air here is splendid – very dry.[29]

On 7 August, three days after Britain's declaration of war on Germany, he wrote to Blunt again in a very different, sombre tone, dark and foreboding:

> We had arranged to leave for England as soon as the Bank Holiday traffic was over but this infernal affair has of course stopped us and it seems very doubtful when we shall be able to get out of the country. The British Consuls are doing what they can to make arrangements for British visitors to return home either through France or via Genoa. On Wednesday we attended a meeting in Davos of the British residents to discuss matters – many are running short of cash. The Banks will not cash their customers' cheques for more than 50 francs at a time and then only once in 8 days. ... everything seems disorganised.[30]

In Britain the Bank Holiday Monday (3 August) crowds had already prepared for the worse. While the wealthy moved to secure their savings, the less wealthy withdrew their cash 'to make their annual spree go with a swing'.[31] Together they created a run on the banks that put the Bank of England under enormous pressure. 'The Bank Rate, which stood at 4 per cent on Thursday, 30 July, was doubled the following day, and pushed up to 10 per cent on Saturday, 1 August.'[32] That same day Germany declared war on Russia, and two days later was at war with France. On 4 August came news of Germany's invasion of Belgium, and of the ultimatum delivered by Asquith, the British Prime Minister, expiring at 11 p.m. (midnight in Berlin), calling upon Germany to withdraw from Belgium. As the fateful hour approached large crowds gathered in Trafalgar Square and Whitehall, waving Union Jacks and singing patriotic songs. When the British declaration of war against Germany was announced it was greeted with 'round after round of cheers'.[33] The war was widely expected to be over by Christmas, and in Britain it was 'business as usual'. Much the same sentiment prevailed in Germany, where a decision was taken not to invade Holland in order to 'trade freely with the rest of the world'.[34] The Germans expected to march through Belgium and take Paris. On 6 September they were halted on the Marne and driven back in defeat. Thomas Stedman, recently returned to England, would have found that enthusiasm for the war was already waning.

Ever since the formation of the Second International in July 1889 socialist workers had spoken out against militarism, and in 1907 a resolution had been passed at the Stuttgart Congress of the Second International calling on workers to do everything in their power to prevent a military conflict. If this strategy failed then they were to bring the conflict 'quickly to an end using the resulting economic and political crisis to rouse the people and thus hasten the downfall of capitalism'.[35] On 3 August 1914 the Second International had collapsed almost overnight when the SPD parliamentary group in the Reichstag voted in favour of the kaiser's war credits. The Austrian Socialist Party quickly followed suit as did the French and Belgian socialists. In Britain the overwhelming majority of trade unionists and the bulk of Labour MPs voiced support for the war, with the exception of a number of important individuals, among them Keir Hardie and Ramsay MacDonald. But, in general, all the European socialist parties adopted a vigorous patriotic line. There were two notable exceptions: the Serbian socialists and both factions of the Russian Social-Democratic Labour Party

– Mensheviks and Bolsheviks – who condemned the war as imperialist. As the war ground to a halt in September 1915 and it became clear that Europe was in for a long war of attrition a minority of European socialists began listening to these dissenting voices. A small group of international socialists opposed to the war met in the small village of Zimmerwald high up in the Swiss Alps, about ten kilometres from Berne. Thirty-eight delegates from eleven countries, including Germany and France (British delegates were refused passports), came together to denounce the war as the outcome of imperialist and capitalist rivalry. That same month Alexander and Gertrude Sirnis decided to leave the safe haven of neutral Switzerland and return to England to campaign for socialism and to work for peace:

> We returned to England September 1915 after many delays, owing to wartime difficulties. It took some 3 months for our French visas to come through, and during this time we stayed with Paul Birukoff and his family at ONEX, near Geneva. Birukoff, another Russian exile, was a great friend of Tolstoy and wrote his probably most authentic biography. It was a wonderful summer.
>
> The journey across France, by a roundabout route to avoid the war zone, took 2 or 3 days. Our boat across the Channel was accompanied by an aeroplane, because of the U. Boat menace. But what advantage the aeroplane would have been had we been attacked, I cannot imagine.[36]

CHAPTER 4

Lenin's First Secret Agent

W HEN Alexander Sirnis returned to England from Switzerland in September 1915 one of his first visitors was Theodore Rothstein. In August 1914 the leadership of the British Socialist Party (BSP)[1] had issued a Recruitment Manifesto and had urged pro-war members to appear on recruitment platforms alongside army recruiting sergeants calling on the workers to 'join up'. Rothstein had resigned from the BSP's Executive Committee in protest and had gathered around him a talented group of socialists opposed to the war, among them a close-knit group of Russian political émigrés including his sister-in-law, Zelda Kahan. On Alexander Sirnis's return to England in September 1915 he was approached by Theodore Rothstein and asked to join this opposition group.[2] However, unbeknown to Sirnis, Rothstein was also working for British intelligence, having been recruited to Military Operations 7 (MO7) sometime in 1915.

MO7 was an important branch of military intelligence and among its remit was the 'censorship of Press cables' and all 'articles of a military nature'. It was also responsible for transmitting the decisions of the General Staff to the directors of the Press Bureau and 'communiqués of prohibitory notices'.[3] In January 1916 a reorganization of the Imperial General Staff took place and MO7 became MI7. A sub-section, known as MI7(d), was later 'constituted to deal exclusively with the study of the foreign Press and the production of the *Daily Review of the Foreign Press* (DRFP), a digest of important information, military, naval, political or economic, collected by the readers of the foreign Press'.[4] The DRFP was under the 'general direction of the Director of Special Intelligence', and its brief was 'to read the foreign press and to produce *Daily Extracts* of military importance'.[5] The staff consisted 'at first of one junior officer and a small number of readers who were for the most part officials in other Government offices, or volunteers who wished for war work and were acquainted with languages and political and economic affairs. The papers were sent to these readers and the extracts which they marked and annotated, were translated and edited in the War Office, and then printed and circulated to the General Staff and to General Headquarters, France.'[6] According to Theodore Rothstein's son, Andrew, his father was seconded to this work when 'the authorities in some panic applied to the newspapers for any translators they could recommend, and C. P. Scott (editor of the *Manchester Guardian*) for whom TR had been doing just such translations in the form of articles on foreign affairs, asked him to take on this work.'[7] However, in a Foreign Office memo dated 29 October 1918 Rex Leeper, in charge of the Russian Department, talked of first making Rothstein's 'acquaintance in 1915 when he was reading Russian and German papers in the small office that had been set up by Mr. Muir and was at that time under the Home Office.'[8]

> When the reading of the foreign press was transferred to M.I.7 (d) at Watergate House, Mr. Rothstein became a member of the War Office Staff and has remained there ever since. Mr. Reynolds of M.I.7 (d) tells me privately that Mr. Rothstein has always co-operated very loyally and that it would be impossible to replace him owing to his extraordinarily wide knowledge of the Socialist movement in every European country. I know him very well personally and, in spite of violent disagreements on political questions, I have never been aware of any active steps taken by him against this country. He has often been accused to me of pro-Germanism, but he has always in conversation with me, expressed himself as the most bitter enemy of all that we are fighting against in Germany. His pro-Germanism only amounts to close association with and interest in the Socialist Movement in Germany before the war.[9]

In fact, at the time, Rothstein was a triple agent, working for Lenin's Bolsheviks, British intelligence and Turkish intelligence. He was also continuing his socialist and anti-war activities *sub rosa*, writing under two pseudonyms, John Bryan and W.A.M.M. His appointment to MI7(d) generated considerable alarm in the Special Intelligence Bureau (SIB) (Eastern Mediterranean), which had long suspected Rothstein of links with Turkish intelligence. On 11 June 1916 the Assistant Director of SIB wrote to MI5 informing them that Rothstein had been working for the Turkish secret service since 1908 through his association with Wilfrid Scawen Blunt's British–Egypt Association.[10] One of the London-based editors of the Association's newspaper, *The Egyptian Standard*, was described in this document as 'a Sinn Feiner, but long a good Loyalist' who had been working as an agent for the Special Intelligence Bureau (Eastern Mediterranean). He had successfully infiltrated Wilfrid Scawen Blunt's circle and had reported back that 'TH. ROTHSTEIN was a very violent man and almost an Anarchist and that he was of German Jewish origin. … We send you a copy of a note regarding Theodore ROTHSTEIN for your information and such action as may appear necessary.'[11] Sir Edward Pears, the Constantinople correspondent of the *Daily News*, had also informed SIB that Rothstein was working for 'a pro-Turk faction at the "Daily News" (Foreign Department) where he was employed largely under the direction of Mr. I. SACHER … a Viennese Jew, a relative of the Sacher family, the "JOSEPH LYONS" of that city and regarded as pro-Turk and anti-Russian'. The report concluded that Rothstein in 1914 was probably working for the Turkish secret service in London:

> The writer receives hints at Constantinople in 1914 that a Russian Jewish journalist working for English newspapers was in receipt of Turkish secret service money. This might be ROTHSTEIN.[12]

When MI5 examined Rothstein's bank account they discovered that it contained a 'little less than £20' and chose to ignore the warnings coming from SIB, pointing out that both the War Office and the Foreign Office spoke highly of his abilities. As he was not regarded as a threat to national security he was kept on at MI7, where he was paid £5.0.0 per week for reports culled from the foreign press on the European labour movement.[13]

Rothstein was undoubtedly one of the best-informed sub-editors on Fleet Street working on European socialist organizations. His capacity for work was quite remarkable. He worked evenings, from 7.30 p.m. to midnight, with the exception of Saturdays, at the offices of the *Daily News* in Bouverie Street, where he reviewed foreign newspapers and translated articles selected for insertion in the following day's newspaper. He also continued to write for the British socialist press under the pseudonyms John Bryan and W. A. M. M., and contributed occasional articles to the German leftwing publication *Neue Zeit*.[14]

On 20 June, following the introduction of conscription on 2 March 1916, Alexander Sirnis was invited to Bournemouth to see the Recruiting Officer. He was examined by the Medical Officer of Health on the 29th and exempted from military service on medical grounds on 3 July. Towards the end of the month he travelled up to London to meet the new General Secretary of the BSP, Albert Inkpin, and bought 'scooters for Letty and Gerty'. On 10 August 1916 he was back in Pokesdown, recording in his diary that 'Rothstein and Mrs. Rothstein called'. Before the Russian Revolution of March 1917 Lenin's articles had not been submitted to the British censor, and Rothstein had called on Alexander with MI7 material on Lenin and the Bolsheviks culled from the European socialist press. Four days after the visit he wrote in his diary 'Lenin's art. to Paul'. The situation, however, changed quite dramatically on Friday 16 March 1917, when Alexander was struck by the news in his morning newspaper: 'Russian Revolution could not believe my eyes when I opened the Daily Chronicle.'[15]

Almost overnight Rothstein's intimate knowledge of Russian socialistic questions and leaders made him a prized intelligence asset. But on 25 May 1917, following publication of Lenin's *April Theses* calling for the overthrow of the Provisional Government and Russia's withdrawal from the 'imperialist war', MI5 approached Lieutenant-Colonel Wake of MI7 questioning the wisdom of Rothstein's continued employment by the intelligence services. Wake leapt to Rothstein's defence, stating that he was 'a very valuable man' and that he would be 'very averse' to parting with him but would 'do so without demur' if it was considered absolutely necessary. He spoke of his concern 'that if he (Rothstein) was dismissed from M.I.7 he would be immediately snapped up by Count Gleichen, ex-head of Section E (Austrian and Turkish) of the Intelligence Department at the FO and a leading figure in Lloyd George's Special Intelligence Bureau.' Count Gleichen, he observed, had already borrowed Rothstein's 'services on one occasion and envies M.I.7 the possession of them'.[16] By June, however, new voices were warning the intelligence services about Rothstein. The Liberal MP Sir Donald Maclean, father of the future Cambridge spy Donald Maclean, wrote to MI5 expressing his concern at Rothstein's connections with the socialist movement in London. The veteran socialist leader Henry Hyndman warned that Rothstein was 'hand in glove with LENIN'. Dr Seton

Watson, a Russian scholar in the Foreign Office, also raised his objections to Rothstein's continued employment, describing him 'as a completely unreliable person who should on no account have access to confidential documents'. [17]

The Foreign Office, however, continued to view the matter differently. Initially the overthrow of the tsar had been greeted across the political spectrum as the welcome completion of the democratic revolution of 1905 and it was not until Lenin's return to Russia in April 1917 and the publication of the *April Theses* that the mood began to change. Lenin's doctrine of 'revolutionary defeatism', exhorting socialists in both the belligerent and neutral countries to work for the revolutionary overthrow and defeat of their respective governments, was unthinkable, and it now began to appear openly in the British socialist press. Alexander Sirnis, who had resigned from the BSP in September 1917 to join the rival Socialist Labour Party (SLP), had published two articles by Lenin in the June and September issues of the SLP's newspaper *The Socialist*. [18] Following the October Revolution the SLP now asked Alexander to submit a short biography of Lenin for a special Russian supplement to *The Socialist* to be published in January. The revolution was not expected to survive:

> Can you get a photo of Lenin, and supply a short outline of his life and activity together with a reference to his theoretical writings? If he manages to hold out successfully, we may need to translate one of his works. [19]

At the beginning of 1918, when the Bolsheviks, still a minority within the Soviets, split the revolutionary socialist movement inside Russia between those calling for a separate peace with Germany and those calling for the prosecution of a revolutionary war, the SLP pushed Alexander once more for a translation of one of Lenin's pamphlets:

> We think you would be the better judge of what would be most topical from Lenin's writings to be presented to British readers. Something about 32 pages, as per any of our pamphlets, would be sufficient as a preliminary feeler regarding Lenin's popularity in this country. I was under the impression that he had written something on theoretical Marxism on either economics or history. [20]

Alexander sent them a translation of Lenin's *Collapse of the Second International*, which castigated the old International for its readiness to admit other than avowedly socialist bodies. When the war came, Lenin argued, the International had proved too broad-based to organise any effective protest against it. Any future International would need to be based on revolutionary principles and to exclude all but 'leftwing' parties. By now, however, the British government was monitoring the SLP's correspondence, and quickly moved to shut down the SLP's printing presses.

The National Labour Press in Glasgow, which was part-owned by the SLP, and the SLP's own Socialist Labour Press received a special letter from the Home Office telling them that 'if they did any matter in connection with blocks and Russian revolution their Press would be dismantled and closed down.'[21] Alexander was warned by the SLP to be extra cautious: 'You put your address on the order to the Photo Company and our "friends" got it. Had the blocks not been delivered up there is no doubt they would have been on your track.'[22] The SLP now began to experience difficulties obtaining paper, and it was feared that *The Socialist* would be closed down at any moment. Alexander, who was providing a safe haven at his home in Pokesdown for the editor of *The Socialist*, William Paul, at the time 'on the dodge' from the military authorities -offered to buy paper from a supplier in Southampton to keep the paper alive.[23] He also made arrangements for an alternative printing press to be set up should the authorities dismantle the existing one, using equipment from the old Tuckton House printing works at Christchurch:

> Your offer re machine will most likely turn out very timely and I would like further particulars of it. It is most likely that the Press will be closed if we get out many more issues like the last, for although it is legally all right, it is not wise for an unscrupulous government to tolerate such for long. If we can rely on using the one you name it would be a help. If you can get the bursted portion mended I will be glad to cover cost even if we cannot use it. I presume it is in Bournemouth? If not you need not send details through the post. If you can give me a more detailed description of plant I will be very glad.[24]

The Socialist's problems were made worse by the activities of their business manager, who on his own initiative had begun to edit Alexander's translations, causing considerable delay in preparing articles and pamphlets for publication.[25]

Lenin's writings had never been published in Britain before, apart from a few articles translated by the socialist press and occasional extracts reappearing in the *Manchester Guardian*. On 13 June extracts from Trotsky's *War and Revolution*, which the SLP had recently published, were confiscated along with copies of *The Revolution* and *The Young Rebel*, monthly magazines published by the Glasgow and Newcastle Socialist Schools and printed by the Socialist Labour Press. On 6 July a further raid more or less effectively closed down *The Socialist*:

> On Saturday July 6th without any previous warning, a body of Police, accompanied by an engineer, entered our printing establishment ... and dismantled the machinery, and removed the vital parts, together with stocks of paper and printing materials to the Police Office. On being asked by our representatives for their authority for such action they replied that it was done on the order of the Crown, no other reason being given.[26]

On 17 July 1918 Sirnis received a cheque for paper purchased in Southampton a week after the raid. The accompanying letter expressed fears that the government's action would hinder still further the publication of *The Collapse of the Second International*:

> This will play havoc with us, for I believe it will take several hundreds of pounds to replace what was stolen. Where the money is to come from goodness knows. I expect this will prevent the publication of the works in hand, for I think it will take us all our time to keep the Socialist going if we can find someone to print.[27]

With such difficulties preventing the publication of Lenin by the SLP the initiative passed to the BSP and to Rothstein, who was now working closely with Maxim Litvinov, the Soviet representative in London. According to Virginia Woolf's husband, Leonard, who had been working closely with Rothstein on the Labour Party's Advisory Committee on International Questions, Rothstein had managed to gain access to Lloyd George and was conducting off-the-record talks with him on Lenin's behalf. Rothstein, he claimed, had recently been arrested by the London police and held 'on a ship lying in the Pool just below London Bridge awaiting deportation.' Leonard Woolf, who openly sympathized with the Bolsheviks, claimed that Rothstein had succeeded 'in getting a letter to Lloyd George smuggled out, and orders were immediately given to the police to release the Russian "ambassador"'.[28] Soon after his release, on 11 January 1918, unofficial diplomatic relations between Russia and the United Kingdom were concluded when Rothstein and Litvinov signed an agreement with two junior Foreign Office officials, Bruce Lockhart and Rex Leeper, 'over the luncheon table at a Lyons' coffee shop in the Strand.'[29] Under the agreement Bruce Lockhart was to travel to Russia as head of a special mission to establish 'unofficial' relations with the Bolsheviks. He would be granted all necessary diplomatic privileges without being recognized by Lenin's government, while Litvinov would be granted similar diplomatic privileges in London, including the use of ciphers and the right to a diplomatic courier:

> It was an amazing meal. Outside, the January sky was like lead, and the room, poorly lit at the best of times, was grey and sombre. Leeper and I were just thirty. Litvinoff was eleven years our senior. Rothstein was a year or two older than Litvinoff. Both men were Jews. Both had suffered persecution and imprisonment for their political convictions. Yet Litvinov, whose real name was Wallach, was married to an Englishwoman. Rothstein had a son – a British subject – in the British Army.
>
> The success of that luncheon was made by Rothstein, who supplied to the conversation the necessary mixture of banter and seriousness which afterwards I was to find so useful in my negotiations with the Bolsheviks in Russia. Small, bearded with dark lively eyes, he was a kind of intellectual cricket, whose dialectical jumps were as bewildering to us as they were amusing to himself.[30]

After a nervous beginning the talks went smoothly as 'there and then, on the rough linen of a standard Lyons' table, Litvinoff wrote out Lockhart's letter of recommendation to Trotsky.' The meal ended on a comic note:

As we were ordering a sweet, Litvinoff noticed on the menu the magic words: "pouding diplomate." The idea appealed to him. The new diplomatist would eat the diplomatic pudding. The Lyons "Nippy" took his order and returned a minute later to say there was no more. Litvinoff shrugged his shoulders and smiled blandly. "Not recognised even by Lyons," he said.'[31]

Despite the 'success of that luncheon', it was the seeming reluctance of Lyons to approve any thawing of relations between Bolshevik Russia and the government of Lloyd George that proved prescient. A series of crises in Anglo-Soviet relations in 1918, beginning with the signing of a separate peace treaty between Germany and Russia at Brest-Litovsk on 3 March, and ending with the expulsion of Litvinov from Britain in October, saw relations between the two countries plummet to an all-time low. The situation was aggravated by a split within the Cabinet between those, led by Lloyd George and the Foreign Secretary, Lord Balfour, who argued in favour of recognizing the Bolshevik government in Russia, and those grouped around Winston Churchill and Lord Curzon who disagreed. The ratification of the Brest-Litovsk Treaty on 12 March put Winston Churchill's group in the ascendancy, seriously weakening Lloyd George as the Liberal Party leader. Although Litvinov's appointment as unofficial Bolshevik plenipotentiary had been a purely Foreign Office affair, and one bitterly opposed by the Home Office, the FO also shifted its position once the Bolsheviks began to sue for peace at Brest-Litovsk. The conclusion of a separate peace tilted the balance in favour of those who argued for allied military intervention in Russia. The outbreak of Civil War in May further eroded any chance of Lenin's government being recognized by the British government, and threatened to end abruptly all communications between the two countries. A schism began to appear in the official labour movement, with Arthur Henderson and a majority of the parliamentary Labour Party and the Parliamentary Committee of the TUC moving away from reluctant support for Litvinov and the October Revolution towards open condemnation. At the Labour Party conference at the end of June the deposed leader of the provisional government, Alexander Kerensky, addressed delegates in place of Litvinov and called on them to support the governments' case for military intervention in Russia. By then the first large-scale incursion of Western troops on Soviet Russian soil had already taken place in the far north. By 1 July 1918 4,000 British, French, American, Canadian, Italian and Serbian soldiers were occupying Murmansk. On 4 July Litvinov, refused a platform at the Labour Party conference, issued an appeal to the British labour movement through the socialist press, to stop the Allied war of intervention:

> The Soviet Government, if overthrown at the present juncture, can only be superseded by the most brutal and barbaric military dictatorship, resting on foreign bayonets, with the inevitable subsequent restoration of Tsarism. Is British labour going to be a party to these dark schemes? Is the British proletariat prepared to take upon itself the responsibility before history for the crushing of the great Russian Proletarian Revolution?[32]

If the policy of military intervention was to be halted then the propaganda war had to be stepped up. A collection of Lenin's articles, written in the summer of 1917, had been translated in Petrograd and passed to the BSP for publication. They were published in July 1918 under the title *Lessons of the Russian Revolution*, priced very cheaply at threepence. In Scotland frantic efforts were being made to repair the damage inflicted on the Socialist Labour Press by the authorities, and to push ahead with publication of Alexander's translation of Lenin's *The Collapse of the Second International*. Alexander was now working flat out: apart from his work for the SLP he was also writing the International Notes in the *Workers' Dreadnought*, the leftwing newspaper edited by Sylvia Pankhurst, the youngest daughter of the suffragette leader Emmeline Pankhurst. His health began to deteriorate and on 18 June he wrote in his diary, 'In the night coughed up some colour – more than usually. More in the morning and again about 4 p.m. & 7 p.m.' The following day he wrote 'In the morning the doctor came & found there was not much secretion. Had a bad headache towards the evening – about 7 p.m. & felt sleepy & slightly seasick but felt relieved after some clots of blood had come up.' On 29 July he wrote that he was unwell and had been forced to stay 'in bed all day. Wrote Intern. Notes for the "Work. Dreadn."' Despite this illness he again raised the importance of publication of Lenin's work with the SLP. The *Manchester Guardian* had recently published a heavily censored article on the Bolshevik Constitution with the caveat that 'lack of space prevented them from printing the whole Constitution'. *The Socialist* now asked Alexander whether he could translate the complete Constitution if a copy could be located:

> Now this document will rank as important or even more important than the Communist Manifesto. I have today sent an article to A and asked him to obtain full text from Litvinoff. If he should do so, could you translate quickly for the Press. Perhaps you yourself are in possession of the Constitution. ... It would be a master stroke as well as good propaganda if we could get it out quickly.[33]

At this time relations between the British government and Lenin's Bolsheviks had completely broken down. On 1 September 1918 Bruce Lockhart, following an assassination attempt on Lenin, was arrested in Moscow and charged with distributing financial aid to pro-Ally organizations and of plotting against the Bolsheviks. In response the British government arrested Litvinov in London and imprisoned him in Brixton gaol pending deportation. On 3 September Alexander went to Tuckton House to meet those Lettish socialists who had decided to return to Russia with Litvinov, including Jacob Peters, recording the final days before Litvinov's departure in his diary.

> Tues. 3 September 1918.
> Down at T. House. The Letts and Russians going to leave with Litvinoff for Russia.

> Tues. 10 September 1918.
> Peter's first wife a nice girl in St. Petersburg. Present wife English – leaves little girl alone at home to go theatres, etc.

> Wednes. 25 September 1918.
> Got up early. Litv. & friends leaving. Train left at 7. Felt sad when the train moved out on the way to Aberdeen.

> Sun. 29 September 1918.

> Meeting at Communist Club to settle the affairs of the Lettish S.D. Branch – 4 members left now.

Alexander's health was by now deteriorating rapidly. The last entry in his diary in his handwriting is dated Saturday 5 October: 'Home to West-end. Walked home.' The diary was finally closed by Gertrude the day after Armistice Day:

Monday 11 November 1918.
[Gertrude's handwriting]
Armistice Day.

Tuesday 12 November 1918.
[Gertrude's handwriting]
Sasha died.

CHAPTER 5

Rothstein and the Formation of the Communist Party of Great Britain

WHEN Theodore Rothstein succeeded Litvinov as Lenin's unofficial diplomatic representative in London he immediately stepped up his clandestine activities on behalf of the Bolshevik government. One of his first acts was to approach Leonard Woolf and suggest that he publish in the *International Review* the full text of a number of Lenin's post-April 1917 speeches:

> The question was how the typescript of the translation of Lenin's speeches should be physically handed over by Rothstein, his agent, to me, the editor. Having had no experience of revolutionaries, secret agents, or spies, I naturally thought that it would be sent to me in the ordinary way through the post. Rothstein was horrified at such a crude and naïve idea. ...
>
> On Wednesday afternoon I was to walk down the Strand towards Fleet Street, timing it so that I should pass under the clock at the Law Courts precisely at 2.30. I must walk on the inside of the pavement and precisely at 2.30 I would meet Rothstein under the clock walking from Fleet Street to Trafalgar Square on the outside of the pavement. He would be carrying in his right hand an envelope containing Lenin's speeches, and, as we passed, without speaking or looking at each other, he would transfer the envelope from his right hand to mine.[1]

This early example of how to execute the 'brush pass' was a good illustration of the lengths 'the real underground revolutionary'[2] was prepared to go to overcome the government's efforts to control the reading matter of the British working class. Was it necessary? Certainly the government, the security services and Lord Beaverbrook, owner of the *Daily Express* and Director of the Ministry of Information, thought so. They had been so thoroughly alarmed by Bolshevik propaganda that they had recently invited the leading writer of spy fiction of the day, John Buchan, to write a novel about the threat socialism posed to the British Empire. In his first post-First World War novel, *Mr. Standfast*, the main danger to the British empire from foreign espionage may have remained German imperialist ambition, but 'the enemy within' in the shape of a rebellious working class manipulated by foreign revolutionaries was never far from the surface:

> 'Well, I'm a shop steward. We represent the rank and file against office-bearers that have lost the confidence o' the workin' man. But I'm no socialist, and I would have ye keep mind of that. I'm yin o' the old Border radicals, and I'm not like to change. I'm for individual liberty and equal rights and chances for all men. I'll no more bow down before a Dagon of a Goavernment official than before the Baal of a feckless Tweedside laird. I've to keep my views to mysel', for thae young lads are all drucken-daft with their wee books about Cawpital and Collectivism and a wheen long senseless words I wouldna fyle my tongue with. Them and their socialism! There's more gumption in a page of John Stuart Mill than in all that foreign trash. But, as I say, I've got to keep a quiet sough, for the world is gettin' socialism now like measles. It all comes of a defective eddication.'[3]

The message was clear – while Gladstonian liberal-radicalism was acceptable; revolution was not. A literary class-struggle was now underway and Leonard Woolf found himself thrust into the thick of it. Despite Rothstein's elaborate precautions he was observed by the head of Special Branch, Basil Thomson, handing over an envelope containing Lenin's speeches to Leonard Woolf at precisely 2.30 under the clock outside the Law Courts on the Strand. A few days later the police raided the printers of the *International Review*, seized the documents and the type that had already been set, and forbade publication of the material. Rothstein was not arrested, although he was kept under surveillance by the authorities.

At the time of Maxim Litvinov's arrest the editor of the *Manchester Guardian*, C. P. Scott, acting on behalf of Lloyd George, had approached Basil Thomson and asked him to speak 'quietly' with Rothstein. In a letter to the historian E. H. Carr, then a Foreign Office employee, Thomson was adamant that no 'further action' would be taken against Rothstein, and laid great emphasis on the point that he (Rothstein) 'will continue to be employed by the W.O.'.[4] The Foreign Office was in full agreement, and Rex Leeper, who had been present at the 1918 meeting between Litvinov, Rothstein and Lockhart at the Lyons restaurant in the Strand, was asked for his views. An authority on Eastern Europe, Leeper, who had known Rothstein since 1917, when the two men had sat together on the Labour Party's Advisory Committee on International Questions, was exactly the right person to ask.[5] He told his superiors that if Rothstein was 'sent back forcibly to Russia' he would prove a most 'dangerous opponent' of the British government:

> Owing to his very real ability, doctrinaire though he is, and his intimate knowledge of this country, extending over many years, he would be a dangerous opponent to us and of great assistance to the Soviet Government. On this ground I think his deportation inadvisable.[6]

Leeper, who was then working under Sir William Tyrell at the Foreign Office on the reconstruction of post-war Eastern Europe, believed that a softly, softly approach to Rothstein would prove the more effective. He suggested to Tyrell that he should approach Rothstein privately and warn him that any further activity on behalf of the Soviet government would result in his expulsion. His advice was accepted.[7]

Following the Polish invasion of the Soviet Union on 26 April 1920, and the occupation of Kiev in the Ukraine by Polish forces on 8 May, the campaign to end the West's war against the Bolsheviks was stepped up. On 27 May a Soviet trade delegation arrived in London, headed by Leonid Krassin, ostensibly for trade talks but also to seek an end to Britain's military intervention in Russia. Over the coming month Krassin held a number of talks with Lloyd George on the question of establishing trade links between the two countries in exchange for a negotiated peace and a guarantee that the Bolsheviks would cease hostile propaganda in the countries of the Entente. On 16 June he warned Lloyd George that Soviet foreign policy operated on two levels and was dominated by two opposing factions – one seeking trade and the normalization of relations, while the other, a minority, preferred world revolution to world peace.

In order to prevent any future attempts to deport Rothstein, soon after Krassin's arrival in London his name was added to those of the Russian trade delegation. At the time Rothstein was overseeing the complex and fractious negotiations then underway to form a united Communist Party in Britain from the numerous contending leftwing parties and socialist societies that openly supported the Bolshevik Revolution. The recently formed Russian Communist Party (Bolsheviks), in order to increase the pressure on European governments to stop the allied war of intervention and support for the Whites in the civil war then raging across Russia, now embarked on an aggressive policy of communist unity among the various leftwing groups in Europe under the direction of a newly created body, the Third International or Communist International (Comintern). The creation of the Comintern in March 1919 led to the formation of communist parties across Europe, splitting the Western labour movement along reformist and revolutionary lines. Those who were opposed to the creation of a revolutionary communist international now called for the resurrection of the 'collapsed' Second International, and a fierce conflict between the two International bodies ensued. In Britain both sides regarded control over the editorial policy of the labour movement's main newspaper, the *Daily Herald*, as essential to their cause. Yet despite the paper's growing importance it was in serious financial difficulties, and by the end of the year it was confronted with a near-embargo on supplies from British paper merchants and was on the verge of closure. In order to overcome these difficulties Francis Meynell, a director of the newspaper, approached Rothstein privately and requested his help in securing the *Daily Herald*'s future. Francis Meynell, the son of the writer Alice Meynell – a fierce anti-imperialist, and a member of the Women Writers' Suffrage League – belonged to a remarkably well-connected and talented family. The paper's satirical approach, along with its outright opposition to the war of intervention in Russia convinced Rothstein that the newspaper's survival would assist Bolshevik propaganda in Britain, and he introduced Meynell to members of the Soviet trade delegation at a luncheon party at Frascati's restaurant in London. Meynell raised the question of a subsidy for the *Daily Herald* and arrangements were put in place for him to visit Litvinov in Copenhagen on behalf of Litvinov's English-born wife Ivy (née Low), who had recently been refused permission to travel abroad. Meynell was told to arrange for his sister Viola, a close friend of Litvinov's wife, to collect a special gift from Ivy – a spotted necktie that would also contain a note from Rothstein – and to deliver it to Litvinov in Copenhagen:

> I said, 'Here, dear Maxim, is a present from Ivy', and gave him a care-fully parcelled new tie in which was sewn a note from Rothstein, who was substituting for Litvinoff in London. Maxim thanked me with an understanding glance and went into his bed-room. In a few minutes he returned, wearing the new tie. When we were seated, and chat-ting, the door open all the time, he said, 'You English, are great pipe smokers. Here is some Russian tobacco to try', and he tossed me a tobacco pouch. I knew that he knew that I never smoked a pipe, so I guessed that the pouch contained an answer to Rothstein. It did – a practical one; for when I got back to my hotel I opened the pouch and found two strings of pearls.[8]

Meynell made a number of such trips to Litvinov in Copenhagen, each time transporting jewels back to Rothstein for sale on London's black mar-ket. During one 'jewel-trip' he smuggled two strings or pearls buried in a jar of Danish butter. On another occasion he posted a large and expensive box of chocolate creams, each containing a pearl or diamond, to his friend, the philosopher and future broadcaster Cyril Joad. Once back in London Meynell was taken to Scotland Yard and searched but nothing was found. Two days later Meynell and his wife recovered their chocolates from Joad and 'spent a sickly hour sucking the chocolates and so retrieving the jewels'.[9] Despite these elaborate precautions, the Bolsheviks' diplomatic codes had been successfully broken by the government's Code and Cypher School, allowing Sir Basil Thomson to closely monitor Meynell's and Roth-stein's activities:

> Among the remittances received by Rothstein from Russia was a packet of diamonds. Some of these now adorn the persons of Mrs. Rothstein and her daughter, but the rest have been converted into money. ... Besides the Bolshevik code, of which the Authorities pos-sess a copy, Rothstein has a pass-word, which is confided to very few persons.[10]

Basil Thomson knew from agents placed inside the labour movement that Rothstein's codename was Mozart, and that Mozart was working closely with Meynell. He also knew, from the same source, that the Soviet trade delegation was financing the *Daily Herald*:

> The Russian Delegation ... appear to have felt it safer to communi-
> cate Soviet Government news to the 'Herald' than to deliver money
> from hand to hand. For this purpose they appointed an intermediary,
> one Mozart, who was to receive the money from the delegation and
> to deliver it to Francis Meynell. It has now been pretty conclusively
> proved that this Mozart is no other than Theodore Rothstein, and
> the name Mozart is an anagram of the Yiddish Dmsart = Red-stone
> = German = Rothstein.[11]

It was now only a matter of time before the authorities closed down the Rothstein network. When Leonid Krassin's assistant, Nicholas Klishko, was summoned to Scotland Yard on 28 May 1920 to attend an interview with Basil Thomson it was made clear that Rothstein's career as a secret agent in London was all but over:

> Ques. We know a good deal more than you think we do. There is no
> object in telling you all I do know. But it is rather a dangerous game
> from your point of view. You all agreed that you came over only on
> this question of trade. Our complaint is that you are not playing the
> game by us.

> Ans. You consider that I, personally, have not played the game on
> this matter.

> Ques. Yes. You understand ... I think you will be well advised to cut
> off relations with Mr. Rothstein until we settle about him. He has
> for a long time been interfering in politics here. We do not think it
> important enough to take any action, but there comes a time when it
> may be expedient to act. After all, he is a Russian.

> Ans. I quite see that.[12]

Klishko, who was apparently visibly unsettled by this encounter, imme-diately made contact with Meynell and asked him to look after a number of platinum bars for the Russian trade delegation:

> 'There is danger,' he [Klishko] told me, 'that we shall be expelled.

We have here a large quantity of platinum. We do not want to take it with us. Will you guard it for us till our return?' I agreed, and struggled down the stairs with a barely portable suitcase in each hand. In the street I hailed a taxi. The first suitcase went safely in. When I lifted the second its handle came off and several wrapped bars of platinum fell on the pavement. A policeman helped me lift them on to the taxi's floor. 'Heavy, ain't they?' he said.[13]

Rothstein was not so fortunate. Basil Thompson's agents followed him to a converted Pullman car at Tophill, Lake Windermere, where he was known to be co-ordinating the secret negotiations for the formation of a Communist Party in Great Britain.[14] There were three main socialist bodies vying for control of the nascent British communist movement: the British Socialist Party (BSP), the Socialist Labour Party (SLP) and Sylvia Pankhurst's Workers' Socialist Federation (WSF). It was the activities of Sylvia Pankhurst, the youngest daughter of the suffragette leader Emmeline Pankhurst, which would eventually lead to Rothstein's downfall and expulsion.

Rothstein was still a well-known political figure in the BSP, and he was able to lead the BSP into the Communist Party without too many problems. In October 1919, following a ballot of members on the question of affiliation to the Third International, ninety-eight branches voted in favour, with four votes against. The SLP and the WSF, however, would not join a Communist Party dominated by the BSP because of the BSP's insistence that the Communist Party should seek affiliation to the Labour Party, and participate in parliamentary politics. To overcome this opposition Rothstein approached both parties claiming to be Lenin's 'official' representative in Britain, and, quoting from Lenin's *Left-wing Communism: An Infantile Disorder*, insisted that they adopt Lenin's position on affiliation to the Labour Party. He had a measure of success with the SLP, and began to channel some of the money earmarked for Meynell's *Daily Herald* to an 'unofficial' group inside the SLP hoping to force through a change of policy. However, he had no success whatever with Sylvia Pankhurst, who claimed that she, not Rothstein, was the authentic voice of Leninism in Britain:

It is believed that when Litvinoff left for Russia he appointed Theodore Rothstein to represent him, but Rothstein had a competitor in

Sylvia Pankhurst, whose restless activity appears to have impressed the continental Bolsheviks to such effect that she was invited to attend the International Congress in Moscow at the beginning of 1919, an invitation that she would gladly have accepted if she could.[15]

Lenin was called upon to adjudicate and effectively ruled in favour of the formation of two communist parties in Britain, a communist group affiliated to the Labour Party working inside parliament, and a revolutionary body outside.[16] Lenin's ruling, however, made little impression on Sylvia Pankhurst, who by now had been tipped off about Rothstein's British intelligence connections. A Cabinet report on 'Revolutionaries and the Need for Legislation' dated 2 February 1920 remarked that 'Sylvia Pankhurst distrusts Rothstein', while 'Rothstein has a contempt for Sylvia Pankhurst's intelligence and discretion. But the real division is between those who favour using the Communist Party in Parliamentary elections and those who, like Sylvia Pankhurst, will have nothing to do with Parliament at all. Lenin has been kept accurately informed of these differences, and in a letter to an English supporter, which was quoted in one of my recent reports, he says that he would favour a Communist Party in Parliament (for the conversion of the other Parties) and a Communist Party outside working in collaboration with it.'[17]

The 'unofficial' SLP sided with Lenin; Sylvia remained defiant. In July she journeyed to Moscow in order to remonstrate with Lenin and to complain to him about Rothstein's behaviour. She was forthright and made her point with some force. As a consequence, Rothstein decided to travel to Moscow to report on the progress being made towards Communist Unity in Britain. Basil Thomson could barely hide his pleasure:

> Rothstein's recall to Moscow is connected with Miss Pankhurst's presence in that city. She claims that Rothstein has appropriated for his personal use money given him for propaganda and that he has mismanaged propaganda in this country.[18]

He would not miss this opportunity, and as soon as Rothstein left the country in August he persuaded the Home Office to act: 'Orders have been issued that Rothstein shall be refused leave to land if he should return to this country.'[19] Lenin, fearful that such 'a dirty trick' was about to be played, dashed off a letter on 15 July telling Rothstein that he was to remain where he was.[20] The letter missed him, and as soon as he was out of the country the government declared him *persona non grata* and refused him the right of re-entry. By this action the long-drawn-out saga over whether he should be dismissed from MI7 and deported was finally brought to an end.

The following month Sylvia Pankhurst's WSF, the 'unofficial' SLP, the BSP, the ILP (Left-Wing) and the South Wales Socialist Society all came together to form the Communist Party of Great Britain (CPGB). One of their first acts was to apply for affiliation to the Labour Party, which was turned down. The CPGB then developed more or less along the lines advocated by Lenin in his letter to an English comrade (Sylvia Pankhust) published in the September 1920 edition of the *Kommunisticheskii Internatsional* recommending the formation of two communist organizations – the one 'open' and the other 'secret'. In effect, outside the main political party and unbeknown to the rank-and-file, an underground organization was created for purposes of espionage.

CHAPTER 6

Recruitment

AFTER Alexander Sirnis's death his widow, Gertrude, received a final sum of £25 from Dr Hagberg Wright on behalf of the London Library. In order to make ends meet, Gertrude Sirnis, with a son of sixteen and two daughters of six and four, took in lodgers, did some typing for local firms, gave piano lessons and taught Spanish in the evenings. She also worked for her French brother-in-law, Jules Valois, who owned a market garden at Hedgend, in return for vegetables. Although not a communist Jules Valois throughout the 1920s subscribed to *L'Humanité*, the newspaper of the French Communist Party.[1]

In 1923 the three children, along with their mother, moved to Thorn-hill Cottage, Bitterne, in the borough of Southampton, sharing a house and garden with their aunt, Theresa Valois, her husband, Jules, and their two children. The house was large enough to accommodate both families comfortably. In many respects their lifestyle appeared idyllic and recreated that of Tuckton House. The coach-house had a stable where Gertrude kept goats, an orchard with chickens and a vegetable garden. They made their money by selling fresh herbs and vegetables to liners docked at Southampton, delivering their produce by horse and cart. The junior and secondary schools were not far away and Melita and Gerty attended Westend Infants School, where they were allowed to arrive later than the other pupils to avoid the scripture lesson. Their mother insisted on this because Sasha had wanted his children to grow up without a bias towards religion.[2] In 1923 Melita won a scholarship to Itchen School, a mixed secondary school, where in 1928 she became school captain and the originator of a school joke which continues to this day: 'Why is the River Itchen? Because it has a current in its bed.'

Gertrude Sirnis joined the Labour Party in Southampton and remained in touch with William Paul and other friends of her late husband who had joined the Communist Party of Great Britain (CPGB) in 1920. She remained in close contact with the new manager of Tuckton House, Stanley Carlyle Potter, author of a book on the Russian Revolution, who lived with a young Russian woman called Holah.[3] In 1921 Gertrude worked with the Society of Friends (Quakers) on famine relief during the devastating Russian famine of that year, and made contact with Willi Munzenburg's International Workers' Aid. Through this work she met the head of the Moscow National Bank in London, N. V. Gavrilov, who in 1926 was known to be helping Britain's striking miners during the General Strike. Gertrude was also connected with the case, prompting MI5 to link a Personal File (Russia) on her with a Subject File on Gavrilov and the activities of the Moscow National Bank:

Name	P.F. Number and Name	S.F. Number – Serial
Gavrilov N. V.	PFR 1154. SIRNIS	(32A)(36A)(37A)[4]

On 18 June 1926 MI5 intercepted a telegram between the Telegraph Agency of the Soviet Union (TASS) in Moscow and TASS in London establishing a further link between agent Sirnis and Gavrilov:

> Activity of the Moscow National Bank Ltd., London. Report made by the Chairman of the Board [N. V. Gavrilov] PFR 1154 Sirnis on the activity for the bank for 1925.[5]

The TASS correspondent in London at this time was Andrew Rothstein, Theodore Rothstein's eldest son, known to Gertrude and described by the security services as a 'Communist of the purest water'.[6] He was also a well-connected Oxford graduate. During the war years he had given up his studies at Balliol College, Oxford, to serve in the British Army and had risen to the rank of lance-corporal. He had returned to Oxford in 1919 where he became the 'leader of the Communist set at Oxford and an extremely active propagator of intellectual Bolshevism'.[7] By all accounts he was an able student and had only just missed getting a first in June 1920. His strident communist views had landed him in trouble with the college authorities, and he was refused permission to continue in residence. In 1920 after applying to go to Russia for the long vacation he was sent down.[8] At the end of the year he visited Moscow with two of his Oxford undergraduate friends, and achieved some notoriety at a Moscow dinner party when he claimed to be 'primarily responsible for the preparation of the list of persons to be shot in

England when the Red revolution dawned. When asked by another diner how he selected persons for inclusion on this list, he refused to give any understandable answer.'[9] On his return to London he was attached to the Soviet trade delegation and took over his father's activities. He managed the trade delegation's Information Bureau (the forerunner of TASS), and served as the main link between the Soviet Government and the CPGB. In 1924 he was appointed London correspondent of a new press agency, the Russian Telegraph Agency (ROSTA), and was admitted to the inner circle of the Russian-British section of the Communist 'underground' movement, the organization responsible for co-ordinating clandestine intelligence operations in the UK.[10] In 1925, using the alias C. M. Roebuck, he was appointed to the CPGB's Central Executive Committee and served as the 'connecting link between Soviet institutions in the UK and the CPGB'.[11] MI5 at first had difficulty identifying C. M. Roebuck as Andrew Rothstein and dubbed him 'the mystery man of the Party'. It was not until the end of 1925 that enough information had been gathered 'from various inside quarters' and they were able to make the connection between C. M. Roebuck and Andrew Rothstein. A 'comparison of the hand-writings of the two men clinched the matter':

> 'Roebuck' or Rothstein is reported to be the man who most actively controls the Communist Party in this country and 'Roebuck' to be the man who deals with the money forwarded by Theodore Rothstein from Moscow for the use of the Communist Party. Knowledge of 'Roebuck's' identity is restricted to an extremely small circle. It is furthermore asserted that if he were removed the Communist Party would receive a shattering blow.[12]

Earlier in the year (July 1925) Moscow Centre had issued instructions for Andrew Rothstein to resign his management of ROSTA and to take over as London correspondent of the telegraph agency TASS. Moscow Centre's instructions were quite detailed: he was to retain his seat on the CPGB's Central Executive Committee using the pseudonym Roebuck; but 'to keep more in the background' so as to reduce 'the risks of his secret communist activities compromising official Russian concerns in Britain'.[13] In June 1926, when MI5 intercepted the telegram between TASS and Gavrilov linking Sirnis with the activities of the Moscow National Bank in London,

Andrew Rothstein was arguably one of Russia's most important agents in Britain. The situation changed rapidly, however, following the collapse of the General Strike, and the purge of communists from the official labour movement.

Despite the Communist Party's low membership figures – at the end of 1926 it had no more than 7,900 members – there were approximately 1,500 communists known to be active in the Labour Party itself. Until 1926 there had been nothing to stop individuals from becoming members of both the Labour Party and the CPGB, while trade unions could elect communists as delegates to Labour organizations and meetings. At the end of 1926 as many as 1,544 communists still belonged to the Labour Party as individuals, and another 242 were trade union delegates to Labour organizations.[14] The leaders of the Labour Party, in accordance with a decision first adopted at the 1924 Labour Party Annual Conference, began to purge the communists from its ranks in 1926. Local Labour parties who refused to expel their communists were simply disbanded and 'official' parties set up in their place. This purge of communists was made easier in 1927 by changes taking place inside the CPGB in response to directives coming from the Communist International. In 1927 the Ninth Conference of the CPGB, despite the witchhunt directed against communists in the Labour Party, passed a resolution calling for a struggle to bring down the Conservative government and its 'replacement by a Labour government pursuing a working class policy under the control of the labour movement'. No sooner had this conference finished than a telegram arrived from the President of the Comintern, Nikolai Bukharin, informing the British party that the attitude of the communist parties to their respective social-democratic parties was under review. The following year the Sixth World Congress of the Communist International adopted Stalin's policy of 'Class against Class', whereby all the social democratic parties were condemned as social-fascist; the CPGB was ordered to stop supporting the Labour Party at elections and to drop its policy of affiliation to the Labour Party.[15] Andrew Rothstein and other members of the National Executive Committee were dismayed and argued that the British Labour Party was not yet a social-democratic party in the accepted meaning of the term. They quoted from Lenin's *Left-wing Communism: An Infantile Disorder* to argue that affiliation to the Labour Party gave the Communist Party a direct link to the masses. The Communist International was not amused. In 1929, following the May General Election and the return of a minority Labour government, Andrew Rothstein was summoned to Berlin by the Executive Committee of the Communist International to explain his support for a policy of 'class collaboration' and continued communist accommodation with the Labour Party. He had fallen from grace. At the Eleventh National Congress of the CPGB, along with other leading members of the party, he was dismissed from the National Executive Committee on account of alleged 'right' deviation. The Central Committee of the CPGB even went so far as to conclude that Andrew Rothstein was a 'danger' to the British party, and 'placed him at the disposal of the Russian Communist party'. In January 1930 he left England to work with his father, who was then Director of the Press Department of the Commissariat for Foreign Affairs in Moscow. [16] Roebuck also vanished from view.

That same year Melita Sirnis was accepted by Southampton University College to study Latin and logic. She was a poor student and her only achievement was to learn how to ride a motorcycle. She never completed her studies and after a year on a motorcycle left the university and went to Paris, causing her mother some anxiety. In the spring of 1931 Gertrude and Gerty decided to rent a flat in Heidelberg and arranged to collect Melita from Paris and travel to Germany. According to Letty her mother wanted them all to have a clear knowledge of that country because of the First World War, and to adopt an internationalist outlook. A friend of the Sirnis family found them a flat in Heidelberg, and they visited friends in nearby Mannheim. In Germany they were visited by Ralph Morley, a Labour MP from Southampton. They became involved in the social life around them, and struck up a friendship with Thomas Mann's son, Klaus. They also began attending lectures in anatomy at the University of Heidelberg, where the head of anatomy, Professor Munther, managed the ladies' hockey team. Both Gerty and Melita played for this team, and developed a friendship with the professor (who boasted an impressive duelling scar). Professor Munther was a leftwing member of the Social-Democratic Party, and took part in street demonstrations against the Nazis. The Sirnis family went with him. Melita often spoke of the impression made on her by the Brownshirts massed on the banks of the River Neckar: 'One evening the Brownshirts were due to have a meeting near the river. So after dark people went out, and we did too. There was a leftwing counter demonstration you see and we joined it.'[17] This experience, along with the suicide of an unemployed workman near their flat in Heidelberg, convinced Melita that the Left alone had the solution to Germany's problems. After Hitler's rise to power in January 1933 and the harassment of lecturers who continued to teach Jewish students, Professor Munther, his wife and nine-year-old son Klaus were forced to leave Germany for England. 'We weren't physically threatened', Klaus said, 'but it would have come to that, Dad helped Jewish students.'[18] According to Melita: 'Professor Munther wasn't going to teach on racial origins and genetics. He was anti-fascist and decided to leave Germany. Mother took them in. She had an influential circle of friends and with the help of the Quakers she found them suitable accommodation in London.'[19]

When the Sirnis family returned to England in September 1931 they initially rented a flat in Earls Court before moving to a larger house at 173 Hendon Way in Golders Green. Following their experiences in Germany both sisters joined political parties – Melita joined the Independent Labour Party (ILP) and Gerty the Communist Party. Gerty went on to study law at the London School of Economics (LSE) and became a member of the student–staff communist group that had been in existence there since 1931. Melita, who had opted to take a secretarial course in Paddington, moved into a basement flat in the same house where her future husband Hilary Norwood (then Nussbaum) was living with his family. The Nussbaum family was part of that Russian–Jewish diaspora that had fled the Pale of Russia at the beginning of the twentieth century and had known the Sirnis family for almost twenty-five years. Hilary's father, Bronislaw, boasted that he had made his way to London in 1907 to join the anarchist club, 'according to his own statement with the sole object of beating one of the members who was an expert chess player, which accomplished, he resigned'.[20] Between 1909 and 1913 he was a fully paid-up member of the National Union of Clerks, and joined the British Socialist Party in January 1912. He was also elected a member of the Communistischer Arbeiter-Bildungs-Verein (Communist Working Men's Club and Institute) in Charlotte Street on 3 August 1910, where he made the acquaintance of Theodore Rothstein, Maxim Litvinov, Jacob Peters and Alexander Sirnis.

In 1932 Hilary was studying chemistry at the Northern Polytechnic Institute in London and teaching Russian part-time. Melita was working in the offices of an engineering firm in Praed Street, Paddington which supplied equipment to bakeries. She worked there for several months, leaving in 1932 to take up employment as a clerical worker at the British Non-Ferrous Metals Research Association (BN-FMRA) in Euston; that same year her politics took a decisive shift to the left when the ILP disaffiliated from the Labour Party. Ever since the election of the Labour government in 1929 and Ramsay MacDonald's failure to halt Britain's slide into depression the parliamentary Labour Party and the ILP had been at one another's throats. Disputes over unemployment and the means test between Labour and ILP MPs during the 1929–31 parliament had led many disaffected Labour Party supporters to seek out more radical solutions to the nation's problems. When in August 1931 MacDonald joined forces with the parliamentary opposition to form a National Government, an act regarded by both left and right of the Labour movement as one of betrayal, the ILP refused to work alongside MacDonald's National Labour group in parliament. The ILP, however, was itself split between the supporters of the ILP Chairman Fenner Brockway and those belonging to the ILP Revolutionary Policy Committee (RPC) led by a close friend of Hilary Nussbaum, the young Jewish lawyer Jack Gaster.[21] The National Government's decision to come off the gold standard in 1931 convinced Gaster that capitalism was collapsing, and he argued that Brockway's reformism must give way to a revolutionary programme. Gaster was now drawing closer and closer to the CPGB, and called on the ILP to cooperate with the Communist Party and the Communist International's policy of 'Class against Class'. At the ILP's 1933 conference the RPC's arguments won through and a motion was passed calling on the ILP to enter into negotiations with the Comintern. Melita, who had been attending ILP meetings regularly, accepted that the RPC's position was the right one. Every Friday evening and Saturday morning she could be seen selling the ILP's paper the *Labour Leader* and the Communist Party's *Daily Worker* outside Golders Green tube station with Hilary. Hilary now introduced her to Jack Gaster and to his communist friend Andrew Rothstein, back in England since 1931 and once more London correspondent of TASS. In 1933 Rothstein identified Melita as a potential intelligence asset, and began the vetting process that was to lead to her recruitment by the *Narodnyi Kommissariat Vnutrennikh Del,* People's Commissariat for Internal Affairs (NKVD), in 1934.

At this time Andrew Rothstein was setting up Scientific & Technical Intelligence (S & T) networks in Britain, and the BN-FMRA was a prime target. Founded in Birmingham on 21 January 1920 with the specific aim of co-ordinating British research into 'non-ferrous metals' for the armaments industry, the BN-FMRA had strong links with Britain's military establishment. Among its affiliated members were the Admiralty, the Aeronautical Research Committee, the War Office, the Research Department at the Woolwich Arsenal and the Royal Aircraft Establishment at Farnborough. In 1930 it expanded its operations and transferred its offices from Birmingham to premises in Reynart Buildings, off Euston Street, London, where it occupied the basement and three floors. The atomic scientist Lord Rutherford was invited to address the opening of the new headquarters, and gave an excellent summary of the Association's progress since its inception in 1920:

> In these days, metals are required to withstand conditions of work which were probably unthought of twenty years ago, and it is important to obtain metals for example that will maintain a certain tensile strength at a high temperature and yet be free from corrosion and free from the danger of 'creep'. The choice of the best substance for that purpose can only be made after an intensive study of the alloys of various metals and their behaviour under experimental test. I understand that your Association has been greatly interested in this problem, and I am glad to hear of the marked success that has attended these experiments for obtaining a type of metal that will stand a high temperature, with small 'creep', and at the same time have high tensile strength.[22]

To mark the occasion the Association appointed a new Director of Research & Development, G. L. Bailey, the main focus of whose work would be the development of a comprehensive theory of corrosion. The *Annual Report* of the Association for 1932 remarked:

> It looks as if, for the first time, we are beginning to understand the causes of corrosion, and with this definite knowledge it may prove

possible, by the addition of suitable material, to reduce or prevent corrosion to a very large extent.[23]

When Andrew Rothstein was introduced to Melita Sirnis for the first time in 1933 her potential worth as a spy was as great as that of those spies already being cultivated in Britain's universities. In June 1934 MI5 was alerted to Andrew Rothstein's interest in the Cavendish Laboratories at the University of Cambridge when they intercepted a telegram from Moscow instructing Rothstein to collect a message of about 250 words from the Cambridge-based Russian physicist Professor Piotr Kapitza on his 'new plant for the dilution of helium'. In July a further MI5 report on Kapitza commented that the Soviet Ambassador, Ivan Maisky, and members of the Soviet Embassy staff were 'making mysterious motor-car drives to Cambridge and other neighbouring towns'.[24] That same month Melita, along with her mother and sister Gerty, attended a meeting of the Friends of the Soviet Union (FSU) in Finchley. A week before this meeting Melita's mother had presented her with a breadboard with the initials FSU carved on one side. She told Melita that arrangements had been made for her to have a private talk with the president of the FSU, Andrew Rothstein, after the meeting.

The final stage of Letty's recruitment to the NKVD took place later that year, again after a meeting of the FSU in Finchley. Andrew Rothstein had been invited to Finchley to talk on the shortage of spare parts for tractors on Soviet collective farms and afterwards Melita approached him with an offer of spying:

> I must have thought then I wonder if any of the work the BN-FMRA was doing, not secret stuff, might be useful. But I didn't immediately think of pinching it. I made the approach; it happened Andrew Rothstein lived over that way in Finchley. I knew he was connected with the FSU. I was recruited in the sense that he took me on board. It wasn't that I had to see him whenever I got anything, it wasn't regular.[25]

That evening she was recruited to the NKVD, the forerunner of the KGB. Her future husband and mother had played a significant part in her recruitment. They had been instrumental in bringing her and Rothstein together, and had acted as go-betweens. At the time Gertrude Sirnis's address at 173 Hendon Way was regarded as a safe address for correspondence between Moscow Centre and CPGB headquarters in King Street. The NKVD's secret agents, including Melita, relied upon an 'illegal' network of wireless operators to maintain communication with Moscow. To ensure a regular supply of wireless operators they had set up a secret training school in Moscow, the Wilson Radio School, to train wireless operators recruited from the communist parties abroad. One such recruit was a young economics graduate, Jacob (Jack) Miller, who had joined the CPGB while at the University of Sheffield.[26] In 1934 the communist historian Robin Page Arnot,[27] a founder member of the CPGB and a member of its National Executive Committee with overall responsibility for the recruitment of volunteers in Britain to the Wilson Radio School, wrote to the General Secretary of the CPGB, Harry Pollitt, via Gertrude Sirnis, recommending Jack Miller for radio work. Gertrude Sirnis was an important point of contact:

> Jack Miller c/o Sirnis 173 Hendon Way, London NW2.
> Candidate for radio work.
> Sending Jack Miller to Moscow giving address for radio work.
> Safe address for information from Moscow to London.[28]

On 7 June 1934 Jack Miller's activities had also come to the attention of MI5 following his violent ejection from a meeting of the British Union of Fascists held at London's Olympia Hall. He had bought a ticket from a group of leftwing students at the University of Sheffield with the intention of heckling Mosley at Olympia. Once inside the hall, however, he had second thoughts:

> The hall was so large and the loudspeaker so powerful that it was useless. Worse were the uniformed Fascists everywhere, displaying their knuckle-dusters and other weapons, and their attacks on people who stood up and appeared to shout. I was too afraid, but forgot the fear (and the intention) when the Leader said infamous things about Jews who had come to England from Eastern Europe. I was probably the last heckler and received special treatment before being thrown into the street and taken to hospital. The case became news, and on

my return to the university the group informed me that I was now a member of the Communist Party.[29]

The savagery of the attack on Jack Miller, which resulted in his hospitalization and his photograph appearing on the following day's front pages, brought him to the attention of Special Branch, who kept a list of all those taken to hospital as a result of fascist beatings. The activities of the Wilson Radio School were also at this time being closely monitored by British intelligence, and intelligence reports on the school's activities were labelled 'Most Secret'. As a consequence, at the beginning of 1936 MI5 wrote to the deputy chief of MI6, Major Valentine Vivian, concerning Jacob Miller and the Wilson Radio School, employing language reminiscent of Robin Page Arnot's letter to Harry Pollitt sent via the Sirnis household:

29th January 1936
MOST SECRET & PERSONAL.

Dear Major Vivian,

With reference to your M.S.M. No. 4989/U.K. dated 24th January, I am very much inclined to think that the MILLER in question is Jacob MILLER, a copy of whose photograph and description I enclose. This man was secretary of the Sheffield Anti-War Movement, and while at the University he took an Honours Degree in Economics. As far back as 1935, MILLER was expressing a desire to go to Russia. He had been recommended by the Sheffield University for the Cutlers Company scholarship: it is essential for this scholarship to study some foreign language in a country approved by the Cutlers Company.

MILLER's parents, Harris and Sarah MILLER are both Russian subjects, and have been in this country since 1898 and 1902 respectively.

In your M.S.M. No. 3970/U.K., dated 18th October, 1935, there was the message 'MILLER is willing to radio position. Will we send him immediately?'[30]

Were MI6 and MI5 at this time monitoring Gertrude Sirnis, and if so were they now monitoring Melita Sirnis along with Andrew Rothstein?

On 31 October 1935 Melita Sirnis became a communist. She resigned from the ILP along with Hilary Nussbaum and the bulk of Jack Gaster's Revolutionary Policy Committee, and joined the CPGB. The following month, with Jack Gaster acting as his solicitor, Hilary formally changed his name from Nussbaum to Norwood. They wanted to anglicize Hilary's surname because they feared the spread of anti-Semitism in England, and to do so before their marriage in December 1935. The notice in the *London Gazette* announcing the change of surname on 22 November made no mention of Melita. 'I was never a Nussbaum', she told me. 'I was always a Norwood.' The change of name deed was signed on 19 November 1935 and cost ten shillings. Andrew Rothstein advised Melita to resign from the 'open' Communist Party and to join the Party's 'secret organization'. Before leaving for Moscow in May 1936 Jacob Miller received similar instructions, and joined a secret branch of the Communist Party meeting in the Home Counties under the guise of a vegetarian group.[31]

CHAPTER 7

The Lawn Road Flats

B ET WEEN 1935 and 1937 Melita Norwood did little to hide her leftwing views and she became a trade union organizer for the women's clerical trade union, the Association of Women Clerks and Secretaries (AWCS) at BN-FMRA. She had been recruited to the AWCS by her aunt, Margaret Stedman, the first wife of Melita's uncle Thomas, who had been Wilfrid Scawen Blunt's solicitor before the First World War.

The AWCS was a left-leaning trade union led by Anne Godwin, and Melita was well known for her militancy. At the 1934 and 1935 AWCS annual congresses she moved resolutions calling on the union to affiliate to the British anti-war movement and the women's branch of Wilhelm Münzenberg's World Committee against War and Fascism. On the first occasion she made her views on the leaking of classified information quite clear, calling on delegates to 'decide their loyalty to employers and their loyalty to humanity, and to be sure and make public war information that came their way in the course of their employment'. Her resolution was strongly opposed by Anne Godwin, who rejected it 'on the grounds that the Anti-War Movement was not a Peace Organisation' but a revolutionary organization that 'had as one of its objects the overthrow of Governments'. Nevertheless, anti-war sentiment ran high among the delegates, and after Melita had replied to Anne Godwin a vote was taken, resulting in a thirteen–thirteen split, which meant the resolution was not carried. The following year Letty Norwood tried again, presenting the resolution:

That the A.W.C.S., aware of the acute war danger and realising the necessity for the Trade Union Movement to organise against imperialist war, agrees to work in association with the Women's World Committee against War and Fascism, and arrange for a delegate from each branch and from the executive committee of the Association to help in the work of the British Committee.[1]

The resolution was carried by thirteen votes to one, a personal triumph for Melita Norwood but a cause for concern in certain circles. Despite Andrew Rothstein's exhortations that she was to refrain from open communist and trade union activity, Melita had clearly not done so. Following Hitler's rise to power in Germany, and the shift in communist strategy to counter the fascist threat, her openly anti-fascist activities began to worry those responsible for the agent networks in London. At the beginning of 1934 the Communist Party of the Soviet Union (CPSU) began to redefine the political aims of the Comintern in response to Hitler's accession to power. On the diplomatic stage Stalin sought 'collective security' through the League of Nations and an alliance with the democratic countries against Nazi Germany; while at the Seventh Congress of the Comintern in August 1935 the communist parties were instructed to move away from the divisive politics of 'Class against Class' and adopt a 'Popular Front' strategy – the alliance of all leftwing parties in opposition to Fascism. This strategy would be severely tested in Spain, where the political parties of the left and right had already forged two opposing pacts under the military term 'front' and were on the verge of civil war. In the elections of 16 February 1936 the 'Popular Front', a pact between the Socialists, Communists and Republican Liberals, confronted the National Front alliance of the Catholic Party, Agrarians, Monarchists and others sympathetic to the fascist regimes of Hitler and Mussolini. Between them stood the centre parties – the Radicals, Progressives, Basque Nationalists and others. Although the country was more or less evenly divided – if the centre and the right parties had added their votes together they would have secured a small numerical majority – the democratic forces of the Popular Front emerged from the elections triumphant. The National Front immediately rejected the election result and called for a Nationalist rising against the Republic, which began on the night of 16/17 July in Melilla, Spanish Morocco, spreading to the mainland over the next few days and plunging Spain into a bloody civil war that lasted until March 1939.[2]

During the conflict Melita Norwood, in common with many on both the communist and democratic left, as well as many progressive liberals, came out in open support of the Republic's struggle against Fascism. The leader of the Labour Party, Clement Attlee, in a resolution at a conference in London of the Labour and Co-operative movements on 20 July pledging 'all practicable support', voiced the sympathies of the Labour Party and the English working class for their Spanish comrades.[3] Far from remaining on the sidelines and following Rothstein's advice to break with the CPGB, Melita began distributing leaflets and selling socialist and communist literature in support of the Spanish Republican government at work. As newspaper reports of atrocities committed by both sides grabbed the headlines, many people who would normally regard themselves as apolitical or moderate in their political views voiced their concerns. Even Letty's boss, the Director of the BN-FMRA's Research Department, G. L. Bailey, bought literature from her, telling her at the same time 'to put those away now'.[4] One evening a week she joined her sister at her mother's house, stamping and addressing envelopes for the British Medical Aid Committee.[5] Rothstein was worried that Melita was in danger of losing her value as a secret agent before she could be fully employed. He was right to have worried; Gerty in 1933 was ensuring the family's commitment to spying as a result of her friendship with Professor Robert Kuczynski, a German-Jewish political émigré from Hitler's regime, and a leading member of the German Communist Party (KPD).

Gerty had met Robert Kuczynski at a meeting of the Communist Group of the London School of Economics (LSE) in May 1933 two weeks after his arrival in England. He was a charming character who had spent most of his life living in constant fear of arrest or worse. His outspoken views on a number of issues, and his previous position as chairman of the committee set up to oversee the expropriation of the property of the former kaiser's family and the land-owning nobility, had led the authorities to regard him with some suspicion during the years of the Weimar Republic. As a leading member of the German League of Human Rights he had been placed under surveillance by the German security forces in August 1927 when he campaigned against the death sentences imposed on the Italian anarchists Sacco and Vanzetti in the USA. Later that year he led a delegation to Moscow for the tenth anniversary celebrations of the Russian Revolution, leading MI5 to open a K file on the Kuczynski family (a 'Keep an Eye on Them' file), based on information from MI6 agents working inside Germany.[6] When Hitler came to power in 1933 he unleashed a wave of state-sponsored terror and repression against his political opponents. Communists were particularly savagely repressed. Individuals were brutally beaten, tortured, seriously wounded or killed, with total impunity. Communist meetings were banned and the activities of the KPD curtailed. Many of its leaders and supporters, Robert Kuczynski among them, came to believe that self-imposed exile was better than a life of constant fear.[7] An effective and well-organized underground network of agents existed under the umbrella of Willi Münzenberg's International Workers' Aid to smuggle leading communists out of Germany. Following the burning of the Reichstag on the evening of 27 February 1933 by Marinus van der Lubbe, a former member of a Communist Party youth organization in Holland, Hitler's terror campaign intensified and Robert Kuczynski, with the help of Münzenberg's organization, fled to Britain, arriving in London as a refugee in April 1933. There he took up a post lecturing in demography at the LSE.

Robert Kuczynski's status in Britain as a refugee in 1933 was insecure, and he confided in Gerty, telling her that he had been forced to leave his wife, Berta, and three of his daughters in Berlin, where they were now in acute danger. Although secret arrangements had been made for them to come to London he needed suitable accommodation to press their case for refugee status. Gerty's mother was then working for the British Committee for the Relief of the Victims of Fascism, a Quaker organization working closely with German and Austrian refugees in Britain, and agreed to help. She made arrangements for the Kuczynskis to move into 12 Lawn Road, Hampstead, already a focal point for German and Austrian political refugees from fascism and soon to become the centre of the NKVD's secret agent networks in London.[8]

In November 1935, less than a year after the Kuczynskis moved into 12 Lawn Road, two underground NKVD agents, an Irishman named Brian Goold-Verschoyle and Charlotte Moos, a Jewish communist refugee from Nazi Germany, moved into 9 Lawn Road, two doors along from the Kuczynskis.[9] Goold-Verschoyle, 'a public schoolboy type', 'highly-strung', 'a nervous individual' and 'the least suitable person' for the world of spies, had arrived in England from his native Donegal in 1929 to work for the English Electric Company in Stafford as an apprentice engineer.[10] He joined the CPGB in 1931, and was appointed Communist Party organizer in Stafford in 1933. He was then put under surveillance by Special Branch, who described him as 'a reticent young man who spent most of his spare time reading Russian and Communist literature'.[11] In July of that year he made the first of many trips to Soviet Russia to visit his brother, Hamilton Neil Stuart Goold-Verschoyle, who had been an active communist in Ireland during the civil war years (1922–3), and had left for Moscow in 1930 to work as a translator. There he had met and married a Russian woman, Olga Ivanovna, a NKVD agent. In Moscow Brian Goold-Verschoyle worked as an electrician in a Moscow factory and began courting a friend of Olga's, Irina Adler, also a NKVD agent. However, at the last moment, when Brian was confident that he would be granted the right of residence in the Soviet Union, Olga introduced him to two men wearing dark-green uniforms who impressed upon him the secret nature of their meeting. They told him that permission to reside in the Soviet Union could not be given just yet and that he was to return to England. Once there he must resign his 'open' membership of the CPGB, move to the Kings Cross area of London and obtain employment with the BBC. One year later, however, having heard nothing from the Russians, he gave up his BBC job and returned to Moscow. A few days after his arrival he was again visited by two people in dark-green uniforms, who reprimanded him for having come back to Moscow without permission and instructed him to leave for London at once.[12] At the end of May 1935 Brian ignored these instructions and returned to Moscow, where he was immediately confronted by two NKVD agents who told him never to come back to Russia without permission because he had made himself quite useless by these journeys to and from Moscow. The men were restless, pacing up and down the room chain-smoking. But all of a sudden the mood changed. They explained the difficulties they faced in arranging his affairs in London. They hadn't been able to make use of him in London because there was not, as yet, any 'organization' in place in England. But if he needed something it was not necessary to travel to Moscow; there was a contact address in Paris he should use. He was to forget about Moscow altogether for the present.

Once back in London he made arrangements with Charlotte Moos to move into 9 Lawn Road. In August 1935, a Special Branch detective who had been tailing them for some time noted that they were socializing with people who were suspected of underground communist activity, among them Edith Tudor-Hart: 'These persons have been seen recently in the flat occupied by Mrs Edith Tudor Hart at 158a Haverstock Hill, N.W.3. They are also believed to be friendly with a Dr. Bone who formerly resided at 9

Lawn Road and who associated with someone residing at 4 Lawn Road.'[13] 158a Haverstock Hill, on the junction of Haverstock Hill and Lawn Road, was the photographic studio of Edith Tudor-Hart, née Edith Suschitsky, a communist refugee from the fascistic Dollfuss regime in Austria. Both Edith Tudor-Hart and Dr Edith Bone were suspected of NKVD activity co-ordinated from a newly built block of flats in Lawn Road.

The Lawn Road flats, commissioned by a well-connected, progressive, entrepreneurial couple, Jack and Molly Pritchard, from the Canadian architect Wells Coates, were opened in 1934 by the Labour MP for Islington, Thelma Cazalet. Inspired by the work of the architect le Corbusier and the Bauhaus's Walter Gropius, Wells Coates and the Pritchards had embarked on an architectural experiment in 1929 with the aim of building a block of flats that would meet the needs of the modern age. Jack Pritchard was convinced that a rational and planned approach to everyday living would encourage a creative use of space, and spoke of a 'minimalist' brave new world. Wells Coates described the thinking behind their project in an interview published in the *Listener* on 24 May 1933: 'We cannot burden ourselves with permanent tangible possessions', he wrote, 'as well as with our real new possessions of freedom, travel, new experience – in short what we call "life."' His thinking was purely egalitarian:

> Because that idea of property – so much of this little garden is for you m'dear and this tweeny little wishy bit is for me, so there! – is dead, dead, dead. It's that idea which makes peoples, nations, set up borders, and put troops on them and forts too, and which makes wars between nations ...
>
> My scheme provides a place which every actor in this drama can call his own place, and further than that my idea of property does not go. This is the room where I sleep, this where I work, and this where I eat. That is the roof garden where everybody can turn out ... This is the garden where everybody goes. It's like a park.[14]

Wells Coates's vision appealed to those artists and communists, exiled from their native Germany and Austria, whose natural instincts were cosmopolitan. Among the earliest tenants of the flats were the Bauhaus refugees Walter Gropius, László Moholy-Nagy and Marcel Breuer; the Austrian Marxist and sexologist Arnold Deutsch, responsible for the recruitment of the Cambridge Five, along with his wife, Josefine, a Comintern-trained wireless operator; the London organiser of the KPD, Jurgen Kuczynski, who recruited the atom spy, Klaus Fuchs. There were others, including Jurgen's sisters, Brigitte and Barbara, and a number of English-born Soviet spies, among them Andrew Rothstein and the Colman-Reckitt's mustard heiress Eva Collett Reckitt, the owner of Collett's leftwing bookshop in Charing Cross Road. Hidden among them were the crime writer Agatha Christie, Nicholas Monserat, the author of *The Cruel Sea*, and Trevor Eaton Blewitt, who translated the works of Arthur Koestler and Stefan Zweig from German into English.

The Lawn Road flats building was four storeys high and had a number of distinct advantages for spies, not least the site layout, which was governed by two railway tunnels running close together under the site. The London County Council would not allow more than one storey to be built over the tunnels, which had left the architect Wells Coates very little room to manoeuvre. In the end the south corner of the flats marked one tunnel edge while the garage was built over the other tunnel. This meant that the building, which was long and thin, was angled to the road in such a way as to make surveillance difficult. There was also easy access to Belsize Park Tube station from the rear of the flats, which were situated in secluded woodland. Just as important, access to the flats would have exposed any casual visitor to unwanted curiosity. Staircases at the north and south ends of the building were the only means of access. The north staircase was internal, while the south staircase was external. These were the only link between the various levels of the deck-access galleries. Once a visitor had entered the flats it would be extremely difficult to keep track of their movements from Lawn Road itself, and any character on a resident's or visitor's tail would have been conspicuous.

In total there were thirty-two flats: twenty-four minimum-space dwellings and eight larger flats. The dwellings themselves were functional, with the larger flats split into two types, four studio flats at the north end of the building and four double flats at the south end. Each of the minimal flats had a total floor area of approximately 25 square metres, of which 6 square metres was bed- and dressing-room space. The rest of the floor area was divided into a small kitchenette and living space. During the Second World War Agatha Christie wrote her only spy novel, *N or M?*, in her apartment. Other famous residents included the sculptor Henry Moore, Agatha Christie's second husband, the archaeologist Max Mallowan, and his colleague at the Institute of Archaeology, the communist prehistorian Gordon Vere Childe. Living in the flats was a social experience. In 1937 the Half Hundred club was opened in the flats as a poor man's food and wine society, so-called because it had a membership of twenty-five, and each member was expected to bring one guest. The club's chef, Philip Harben, later achieved fame and celebrity status as the first television chef, appearing on BBC television as early as 1947 and often using his own rations to demonstrate the recipes. The club was overwhelmingly socialist. Among its members were the wine connoisseurs and historians of the labour movement G. D. H. Cole and Raymond Postgate, with their wives (Margaret Cole, Raymond Postgate's sister and a crime writer herself, and Daisy Postgate, daughter of the veteran Labour leader George Lansbury). All were on speaking terms with Andrew Rothstein as well as his father's old colleague from the pioneering days of Soviet espionage, Francis Meynell. Probably the most famous spy of all inside the Lawn Road flats before the Second World War, however, was Arnold Deutsch.

Arnold Deutsch was an Austrian Jew who had travelled to London from Vienna in May 1934 with instructions from Moscow Centre 'to cultivate young radical high-fliers from leading British universities before they entered the corridors of power'.[15] In 1936, along with his wife Josefine, a trained NKVD wireless operator, he moved into flat 7 at Lawn Road, a furnished studio flat on the ground floor at a monthly rent of £4.4.0, to be paid in weekly instalments. Deutsch's flat was only two doors away from that of another Soviet agent, Brigitte, the daughter of Robert Kuczynski, who lived in flat 4 with her English husband, A. G. Lewis, a member of the CPGB. Gertrude Sirnis, who knew the Pritchards through her work with the Quakers, had made the arrangements for Brigitte to move into the Lawn Road flats in 1934. By 1936, therefore, a Soviet spy network could be said to have successfully colonized Lawn Road and the Lawn Road flats as well as the neighbouring streets. This was a remarkable achievement, given the importance of the Kuczynskis and Deutsch to the Soviet intelligence networks operating in 1930s London.

Soviet foreign intelligence-gathering at this time was the responsibility of three organizations. First, the Comintern's *Otdel' Mezhdunarodnykh*

Svyazey (OMS) set up in 1921 to run a clandestine network of agents overseas. Second, the Foreign Department of the OGPU (the predecessor of the NKVD), put in place on the third anniversary of the All-Russian Extraordinary Commission for Combating Counter-Revolution and Sabotage, the Cheka, on 20 December 1920. And third, the Fourth Department of the General Staff, later the GRU, *Glavnoye Razvedyvatelnoe Upravlenie*, or military intelligence. At the beginning of the 1930s the heads of the GRU, the Foreign Department of the OGPU and the international liaison department of the OMS – General Jan Karlovich Berzin, Artur Khristyanovich Artuzov and Iosif Aronovich Pyatnitsky – agreed on a strategy of agent penetration as a means of gathering foreign intelligence. Foreign intelligence-gathering on the ground was to be the responsibility of the Third Section of the GRU's Fourth Department.

Third Section agents were top spies who always worked abroad and were divided into two main categories – 'legal' and 'illegal' residents. Their status and vulnerability to detection as 'legals' or 'illegals' could not have been more different. 'Legal' residents enjoyed diplomatic immunity and held official postings at Soviet embassies or legations, and their main function was to act as live letterboxes for 'illegal' residents. They also arranged for the cyphering of reports and oversaw the general running of the Intelligence Department. 'Illegal' residents did not have diplomatic status and were consequently more vulnerable to detection. They lived on the edge. There were three types of agents – head agents, who were in control of organization; resident agents, who held responsible permanent posts or worked as principal assistants to the senior agent or resident; and 'speculants'. These were mainly Austrian, Czechs, Hungarians or Rumanians, restless people from the newly created nations that had emerged from the collapse of the Austro-Hungarian empire at the end of the First World War, people who had become outlaws from their own countries on account of their communist activities. They had nothing to lose by employment in the Fourth Department and hoped to gain a good deal. Arnold Deutsch (codename Stefan Lang) was an Austrian Jew who belonged to this category. Among his successes in Britain was the recruitment of the Cambridge spies, Anthony Blunt, Guy Burgess, John Cairncross, Donald Maclean and Kim Philby. He was helped in this by another communist refugee from Vienna, Edith Tudor-Hart, who was well known to MI5 and Special

Branch in connection with Brian Goold-Verschoyle and Charlotte Moos. Her photography studio on the corner of Haverstock Hill and Lawn Road was known to MI5 as 'a rendezvous of persons interested in communist matters'.[16]

Edith Tudor-Hart, née Suschitzky, was born in Vienna on 28 October 1908 and had first been brought to the attention of MI5 in October 1930, when an undercover Special Branch officer spotted her in conversation with a number of leading CPGB figures at a demonstration in support of the Workers' Charter in Trafalgar Square. At the time she was living at 5c Westbourne Gardens, Bayswater, with Alexander Ethan Tudor-Hart, a communist medical student at St Thomas's Hospital. Notwithstanding the fact that she had lived and worked in Britain as a teacher since 1925 she was told to leave the country, and after repeated warnings left for Austria on 15 January 1931. There she became the official TASS photographer in Vienna. Two and a half years later Alexander Ethan Tudor-Hart married Edith Suschitzky in Vienna, allowing her to return to England.[17] Before they left for London in August 1934 Deutsch recruited them to Soviet intelligence. They were to use the joint codename of STRELA ('Arrow').[18]

The previous year Kim Philby had graduated from Trinity College, Cambridge with a respectable second-class degree in economics and a prize of £14.0.0, which he spent on the collected works of Karl Marx. His father gave him £50.0.0 for correcting the proofs of his latest book on the Arabian desert, *The Empty Quarter*, and he bought a motorcycle, announcing 'that he was riding off to Austria for a few months'.[19] At the time Vienna was in a state of near civil war. The first serious clashes between left and right had taken place seven years earlier on 1 July 1927, when the *Heimwehr*, a private army led by a dissolute aristocrat, Prince Starhemberg, opened fire on a socialist demonstration, killing a child. In response the people's militia, the *Schutzbund* or Republican Defence Corps, attacked individual members of the *Heimwehr* and violent clashes between the two groups became the norm. In early 1934, after four days of violent street battles in Vienna had left a thousand dead, the *Heimwehr* had brought up artillery and simply demolished the Karl Marx Hof and the Goethe Hof, two of the biggest blocks of workers' flats. The left literally went underground. Philby, whose communist lover Litzi Friedman had been forced into hiding, helped the underground movement smuggle countless Austrian social-democrats and communists out of the country. To save Litzi from certain arrest he married her on 24 February 1934 and took her with him to England. Three months later Edith Tudor-Hart introduced him to Arnold Deutsch on a park bench in London's Regents Park. Philby's recent experiences in Vienna ensured that this would be a meeting of like minds:

> So Philby was there when the Karl Marx Hof and the Goethe Hof were shelled. He helped a group of workers who had escaped from the flats to hide in a nearby sewer. … Everywhere the left was on the run and it did not take long for Philby to decide that he had seen the lesson: ordinary democratic socialism was apparently incapable of resisting Fascism.[20]

By this time Edith Tudor-Hart had become a frequent visitor to the Lawn Road flats, both to Arnold Deutsch and to Jack and Molly Pritchard. She had the perfect alibi: her husband's sister, Beatrice, described by Special Branch in 1934 'as a well-known extremist, and a known sympathizer with the Friends of the Soviet Union', ran a nursery school for the Pritchards in nearby Platts Lane.[21] Beatrice was also Jack Pritchard's lover. Around this time Arnold Deutsch switched apartments from number 7 to number 12 Lawn Road.

While he was in London Arnold Deutsch served under three 'illegal' residents: Ignati Reif, Alexsandr Orlov and the Hungarian, Teodor Maly. It was Maly who gave Deutsch the assignment to act as Philby's controller in London. In January 1936 Maly received instructions from Moscow Centre to leave Vienna for London, where he was to take control of a leading spy in the British Foreign Office, the cipher clerk John Henry King, who had been controlled hitherto from Holland by the Dutch artist Henri Christiaan (Hans) Pieck. Until the Lawn Road network had been set up in London in 1934 The Hague in Holland and the French capital Paris had acted as the point of entry for Soviet 'illegals' to Britain. Brian Goold-Verschoyle, working from his flat next to the Kuczynskis in Lawn Road, was to serve as the initial contact between Maly and King. However, at the end of January Goold-Verschoyle's application to train as a wireless operator in Moscow was approved by Moscow Centre and on 18 February he left for the Soviet Union. Charlotte accompanied him to the station, where, she later recalled, a strange incident took place: 'When we sat in the train talking an old man (white beard) came to the train window and asked B. whether he would post a picture of Edward VIII for him in Paris and handed the picture, rolled in a big roll, into the compartment. I felt this to be very strange, but B. laughed at me. This was about the time when Edward VIII became King.'[22] Goold-Verschoyle travelled via Paris to Moscow, where he met with Henri Christiaan Pieck, telling him that contact with Theodore Maly should be arranged through his Lawn Road address.

In Moscow Brian Goold-Verschoyle at first lived in a very elegant room in the Hotel Moskva until Charlotte arrived on an Intourist visa, unannounced, three months later. The Russians were incensed. He was turned out of the Hotel Moskva and put into an empty hall in the Hotel Metropole, where there was nothing but two beds, a table and a microphone. Brian fell ill and since his room didn't have any windows Charlotte moved him into her room in the Novaya Moskovskaya. He was still ill with fever, when a 'superior person, who spoke German' called and insisted that Charlotte leave the room. He 'then shouted with Brian so furiously that the hotel resounded'. When she was readmitted, she was told that she 'had no right to be there, that Brian had no right to have her come and change his room etc'. A few months later Brian was told that he was being posted to Germany, and Charlotte would have to stay in Russia on her own or leave. On 18 October 1937 she returned to 9 Lawn Road. Some days later she received a telephone call from Brian Goold-Verschoyle in Paris letting her know that he was on his way to Spain 'to fight against Fascism'.[23] That was to be the last time they spoke together. Suspected of Trotskyism, he was lured on board a Soviet ship and transported to Odessa before being shot in the back of the head on 12 April 1937 in a Moscow dungeon dubbed the 'shooting gallery'. In Spain he had been known by the nickname 'Friend'. An account of his kidnapping and transportation to Russia appeared in the Soviet defector Walter Krivitsky's book *I Was Stalin's Agent*.[24]

In 1936 Professor Robert Kuczynski's only son, Dr Jurgen Kuczynski, a leading member of the KPD since July 1930, fled Germany and joined his father in London. The previous year he had visited Moscow and had met with the KPD leader in exile, Walter Ulbricht (the first East German leader), who instructed him to leave Germany and to write to him when he had found a safe place of refuge. In January 1936 along with his wife, Marguerite, he moved to London initially staying with his father at

12 Lawn Road before moving to nearby Upper Park Road, from where he organized the KPD underground in Britain. He took a job with the British government as an economics statistician specializing in Germany. Among his contacts were a number of leftwing members of the British Labour Party including Ellen Wilkinson, the future Minister of Education, who was closely involved with Willi Münzenberg's organization, John Strachey and his wife, Celia, who was also a member of the CPGB. Among his close circle of influential friends were Aneurin Bevan, Cecil Day-Lewis and Lilian Bowes-Lyon, cousin of Elizabeth Bowes-Lyon (later Queen Elizabeth the Queen Mother).[25] Hampstead had finally taken over from Paris and The Hague.

CHAPTER 8

The Woolwich Arsenal Case

THE contrast between the leafy suburbs of Hampstead and industrial Woolwich on the southern side of the Thames could not be greater. What they shared in the 1930s, however, was a central role in the history of Soviet espionage in this country. In Hampstead the spies lived together in the Lawn Road flats and in the neighbouring streets; whereas in Woolwich they worked alongside one another in the less salubrious – albeit more palatial – engineering sheds of the Woolwich Arsenal, a munitions factory built in 1641 and sprawling over some 1300 acres. The Hampstead and Woolwich spies, however, could not have been more different. While the spies in Lawn Road were university-educated Austro-Hungarians, working in London for the Third Section of the Fourth Department, the Woolwich spies were English and working class. The ringleader of the Woolwich spies was a former member of the CPGB's Executive Committee, Percy Glading, who had been dismissed from his employment as an Examiner in the Naval Ordnance Department at the Woolwich Arsenal in 1928 for holding communist beliefs His sacking was quite abrupt:

> Naval Officer: 'Are you Percy Glading?' 'Yes.'
>
> Naval Officer: 'You are an active Communist. It is not the policy of the Admiralty to employ Communists and unless you disavow Communism within 48 hours you will be discharged.'[1]

Glading refused, and in a subsequent statement to the Arsenal authorities questioned the practice of testing Arsenal workers for 'political fitness':

> I was told that it is no longer the policy of the Admiralty to employ Communists. I was not aware that the Admiralty employed Communists, Labourists, Liberals and Tories, but Engineers and Craftsmen, and the test was fitness for the job. Now it appears we are to have a test of technical fitness and a test of political fitness.[2]

Glading's dismissal from the Arsenal – solely on the grounds of Communist Party membership – played no small part in his decision to spy for the NKVD. In October 1929, after a six-month period of employment at a private engineering firm in East London, he travelled to Moscow to study at the Lenin School using the pseudonym, James Brownlie.[3] He returned to London in April 1930 and there he was employed in the Colonial Department of the Communist Party until August 1930. Between May 1931 and March 1937 he worked as the Assistant Secretary for the League against Imperialism (L.A.I.).[4]

In July 1931, Glading met with a leading communist organiser, T. Thurlow,[5] who, unbeknown to Glading, had been befriended by an MI5 agent known only as 'B.1.' working inside the Communist Party. Thurlow had been selected for 'agitation work' among dock workers in the Woolwich area and before his departure for Woolwich, Glading told him, according to 'B.1.', 'to pay special attention to the work of trying to increase our contacts in the Arsenal, especially with skilled workers, but to be cautious as there is a certain amount of alarm among the fellows already there, owing to the risky way the job was done before. They have reported that in the past, there has been too much openness, and that has played into the hands of informers and others, and therefore for sometime our chaps have been lying "Doggo".'[6] Thurlbeck told 'B.1.' that the policy of lying 'doggo' was paying dividends: 'because if we give the impression that our influence in the Arsenal is dead, that will give us a better chance to build our contacts there quietly. Our fellows now inside have a fairly good idea of the views of others working there, but have to be careful. Also the lying quiet stunt will let us slip into the Arsenal other jobs. They [those now inside] are expecting to get about four more in shortly.'[7] The immediate reason behind the NKVD's concentration on the Woolwich Arsenal was the controversy taking place inside the Soviet Navy between advocates of the 'Big Ocean-Going Fleet' and those backing the doctrine of a 'Small War at Sea'. In short, were Soviet shipyards to build battleships or light craft and submarines? There can be little doubt that to Stalin big gun-armed ships were a symbol of naval superpower status, and as Jurgen Rohwer and Mikhail S. Monakov, historians of Stalin's ocean-going fleet, have pointed out: 'a battleship, a dreadnought, was a direct historical predecessor of the atomic bomb, a symbol of the highest grade of power; a most powerful and mobile instrument of power politics, that the world had ever known.'[8]

In the 1920s and 1930s the Soviet Navy had only four battleships, inherited from pre-revolutionary days, equipped with 12-inch (305 mm) guns. During the 1930s the Soviet Navy attempted to buy battleships from foreign suppliers – the hulls were to be built in Soviet shipyards, while the machinery, armour plate and heavy guns were to be imported. However, existing treaty agreements limiting the size of naval guns restricted the Soviet Navy's ability to build big gun-armed ships; it was obvious that without gun technology the construction of battleships was senseless. The USSR clearly needed this technology and attempted to acquire it by both open and covert means. Percy Glading's spy network in the Woolwich Arsenal was an important part of this set-up. Melita Norwood too played her part in this, working on the periphery of Glading's network and maintaining a safe house in Finchley for stolen documents. When the Glading network was broken up, and the principal actors in the affair sentenced to various terms of imprisonment, however, she managed to slip through the net. This was an event that would have dramatic consequences for American and British security once her employers, British Non-Ferrous Metals Research Association, began working on the Anglo-American atomic bomb project during the Second World War.

The drama began on the evening of 21 January 1938, when an officer from Special Branch observed Albert Williams, an employee at the Woolwich Arsenal, handing over a brown-paper package to Percy Glading in the station yard at Charing Cross railway station. They were both arrested, and on examination the brown-paper package was shown to contain blueprints with arrangements and details of a pressure bar apparatus for testing detonators. A search of Glading's house revealed negatives of a textbook on explosives used by the military in 1925 and five developed plates of a plan of a fuse used in anti-submarine bombs. There was only one set of these plans in the arsenal and at the trial they were described as a 'design of great importance.'[9] Part of an anti-tank gun wrapped in a piece of paper with explanatory handwritten notes by Williams was also found. A third man, George Whomack, was accused of obtaining 'a plan of a naval gun calculated to be, or might be, or intended to be directly or indirectly useful to an enemy'. At the trial the Attorney-General, Sir

Donald Somervell, was keen to stress that 'the word "enemy" did not mean a country with whom we were at war. But a potential enemy.' When asked by the trial judge, Mr Justice Hawke, whether the accused had sought 'To supply people with information who might one day be at war with us?' the Attorney General replied: 'Yes, or information which might be useful to them now in preparation or in improving their own weapons.' [10]

Glading's plan according to the Attorney General had been 'to obtain secret documents from Woolwich Arsenal, have them photographed, and the originals returned to the place which they should never have left.' 'The criminal purpose,' he said, 'was brought to light by "Miss X" who has worked for some years under the direction of the Military Intelligence Department of the War Office' and had first come 'into contact with Glading some five years previously.' [11] In fact 'Miss X', real name Olga Gray, had been a 'sleeper' inside the CPGB for almost seven years, and had gained considerable insider knowledge of the activities of both Percy Glading and the CPGB's General Secretary, Harry Pollitt.

Olga Gray, a secretary working with the Automobile Association in Birmingham, had been recruited to the security service in 1931 by Maxwell Knight, former director of intelligence for Britain's first fascist organisation – British Fascists – from 1924 to 1927, and himself an MI5 agent since 1925. He told her that the requisite for all good spies was patience: 'she should be in no hurry to obtain results.' He arranged for her to move to London from her native Birmingham and to join the Friends of the Soviet Union (FSU) as a preliminary to joining the CPGB. [12]

Soon after her arrival in London 'Miss X' began working voluntarily for the FSU as a typist before moving to the offices of the British Section of Willi Münzenberg's League against Imperialism (LAI) in August 1932 where she met Percy Glading. He was then working as a paid secretary for the LAI, a post he held until March 1937. [13] In 1934 she switched to the London offices of the British Anti-war Movement and was introduced to Harry Pollitt. On 8 May 1934 Harry Pollitt and Percy Glading set her a test – 'carrying messages from here to other countries' – and in June she travelled to India with instructions and funding for the Indian Communist Party. When she arrived back in London on 28 July, 'having carried out her mission with great success', she was congratulated by Harry Pollitt, Percy Glading and other high-ranking members of the CPGB. Some months later, in February 1935, Harry Pollitt asked her to work as his personal secretary at Communist Party headquarters, 16 King Street, London, where she found herself in a unique position to gather information of critical importance on both the practices of the Comintern and the underground activities of the CPGB. As a result of over-work and nervous strain, however, she became ill, and told Maxwell Knight that she wanted to return to private work. Her resignation was accepted with the proviso that she maintain friendly relations with both Pollitt and Glading.[14] On 11 November she began working for an advertising firm and dropped all intelligence work for fourteen months. Then, on 17 February 1937, she telephoned Knight and told him that Glading had asked her to arrange for a safe house that could be used as a special meeting place for Communists. Glading would pay the rent, telephone and other incidental expenses. There were two conditions: the flat must not be in the Notting Hill area, and there must be no porter. It did not take her long to find a suitable flat at 82 Holland Road in north London, which she leased at an agreed rent of £100 per annum from 1 April 1937. Glading told her to have three sets of keys made, promising to warn her before anyone came to the flat.[15] On the night of 21 April 1937 he visited the flat with a 'Mr Peters', and stopped for about three-quarters of an hour. Nothing of any importance passed between them, and Olga Gray concluded that Mr Peters had come solely to check on her suitability for the task. Mr Peters was, in fact, the 'great illegal', Theodore Maly, and he was there to vet Olga Gray before making arrangements for Edith Tudor-Hart to supply a Leica camera and other equipment for photographing secret material at Holland Road.

Olga Gray met Mr Peters on a number of separate occasions and built up an interesting profile of him, which she passed to Maxwell Knight. She learnt from Glading that he was an Austrian who, at the beginning of the First World War, had been living in a monastery in Austria and had been taken prisoner by the Russians while acting as chaplain to an Austrian regiment. During the war he had fought with the Russian cavalry and had risen to the rank of captain before becoming a Communist and taking an active part in the Bolshevik Revolution. She described him as a fidgety man, whose manner, bearing and demeanour were somewhat striking:

From Miss 'X':

Description: Aged about 45; very tall, about 6' 4"; medium build, heavy enough not to look lanky; very dark hair; thinning along left and right partings; rather small eyes, dark possibly grey, rather heavy lids; straight nose but rather heavy; rather wide mouth, short upper lip, dark moustache, slightly cleft chin; typical shiny grey complexion of some Russians and Germans; teeth gold filled in front; hands with very long fingers, flat nails, strums with fingers on chair arm etc.; dressed in black suit, black shoes, dark tie. Spoke English very well, but slowly. Noticeable accent, but English correct. Has difficulty with 'w's, tries not to pronounce as 'v' but not very successful.

From Olga Gray's description, Maxwell Knight had little difficulty identifying her agent as Theodore Maly.[16] On 29 April Glading again visited Olga Gray, and told her of another man in connection with their work, describing him as 'a small man and rather bumptious in manner'. 'Glading', she said, 'dislikes him personally but he has to tolerate him for business reasons'.[17] This man was identified as Arnold Deutsch, Maly's principal agent inside the Lawn Road flats.

On 20 May Glading called on Olga Gray at 82 Holland Road and told her to enjoy a fortnight's holiday, for which he would pay. On her return she was to 'learn from another comrade something about photography' and would be given 'instruction in the photographing of documents with a miniature camera'. These documents, he informed her, would be 'borrowed' ones that would be delivered one evening and collected the next. She was to take and develop these photographs but she was not to print them. On average there would be some photographing to be done about once a week from papers and drawings of a very secret nature. Three weeks later, on 11 June, Glading called again, this time late at night, drunk and very worried. He made two significant remarks. One was, 'I am doing hardly any work for the Party now – it is mostly for the other people'. The second was that he had seen six of his ' "people" that evening'. He was not making sense and was obviously very, very agitated.[18]

Unbeknown to Glading a number of worrying episodes had recently threatened both the Woolwich Arsenal and Lawn Road networks. Earlier that month Arnold Deutsch had gone abroad to report that Edith Tudor-

Hart had lost a diary along with a folder containing a list of his expenses, including payment to his agents, which she had been given for safekeeping. As soon as Moscow Centre got wind of the missing folder they immediately closed down the Lawn Road flats network and ordered Arnold Deutsch to leave England. He had been abroad for three weeks when Edith Tudor-Hart, 'desperately searching her apartment for one last time, found the ill-fated folder tucked underneath the cushions of her sofa and rushed to tell Maly, who reported the good news to the Centre'.[19] These events must have taken place in June 1937 as Maly had received instructions to travel to Paris that month to arrange the murder of a defector, Ignace Reiss. He never returned to England. On 22 July, while still in Paris, he was ordered to Moscow, where he was reportedly interrogated and then shot for Trotskyite activities. Glading was told to expect a change of personnel.[20]

At the beginning of August Glading again called on Olga Gray at Holland Road and told her 'that in about a week's time some definite instructions would be given about the work to be done but that at the moment the necessary person was away. His actual words were "You know what it is – these blokes only go home about once in five years and when they do go there is no knowing how long they will stay at home. After all they live on a volcano the whole time they are over here and when they do go home you do not know if they will ever come back – or you may suddenly be confronted with someone else"'. He told her that he would be bringing a husband and wife team to the flat, and that the wife would carry out the photographic work: 'They do not think it would be safe for you to do it and so she will come round to your place to do it'.[21]

On 16 August 1937 Glading called at the flat accompanied by a man whom he introduced as 'Mr Stevens', the successor to Mr Peters 'who had gone "home"'. 'Mr Stevens' informed her that his wife would be coming 'to the flat about twice a month to do the necessary photographic work' and that the work would start in October. From Olga Gray's description of the couple Maxwell Knight was able to identify them as a Romanian-born Jewish couple, Willy and Marie Brandes, ostensibly French Canadians who had in fact obtained their passports by fraudulent means through a Russian spy-ring operating in Canada and the United States. Willy Brandes had arrived in London in 1937 as an agent of the aptly named Phantome

Red Cosmetics Company of New York with a large number of samples of Phantome face powder and as a photographer for another New York firm, the Charak Furniture Company.[22]

On 11 October 1937 Glading called at Holland Road and told Olga Gray that she needed to buy a long refectory table as the gate-legged table in the flat would not be steady enough for photographic work. On the 13th he arrived at the flat in a taxi with Mr and Mrs Stevens. They had with them a Leica camera and other photographic equipment. A further meeting was arranged for Monday 18 October, in order to test the photographic equipment in readiness for their first 'job' scheduled for Thursday the 21st at 7 p.m.

On the 18th Mr and Mrs Stevens called at the flat and experimented with a complete Leica copying outfit on maps of the London Underground for three and a half hours. Mrs Stevens was by no means an expert photographer and was apparently 'nervous about her ability to use the apparatus effectively without much practice'. Glading was not impressed and told 'Miss "X" to take a course in photography'.[23]

On 21 October Mrs Stevens arrived at the Holland Road flat with a large plan to be photographed in sections requiring forty-two exposures. After the films had been developed and hung up in the bathroom to dry Olga Gray was told to make a pot of tea. At 10.35 p.m. Mrs Stevens left the flat, taking the plan with her in a bundle of rolled-up newspapers. She was followed to Hyde Park Corner, where she was met by her husband and a gun examiner for the Inspector of Naval Ordnance at the Woolwich Arsenal, George Whomack. She handed over the plan to Whomack, who returned it to the Arsenal the following morning before anybody knew it had gone missing. That same day Glading and Olga Gray went to the Ford Motor Exhibition, returning to Holland Road at about 9.45 p.m. At 11.00 p.m. Glading left the flat, taking the negatives of the plan, which contained highly confidential information recently released by the War Office concerning a naval gun mounting, with him:

> The plan was identified, from a note made by Miss 'X', as that of a Naval gun mounting of which five copies only were in existence. They had been issued to Vickers, the Admiralty and the Ordnance Factory, Woolwich, during the week beginning 10th October. The

negatives of the photographs of the plan were collected from Miss 'X''s flat by Glading on 22nd October.[24]

There can be little doubt that the Russians had been waiting on this specific document's release, and had set up the Glading network to secure it. Whomack, who was thoroughly briefed on the nature of the document, smuggled it past the guards at the end of his evening shift on 21 October. Glading, who had a 'good contact at the War Office', had been given the exact date of the document's release to the Woolwich Arsenal.[25] The Woolwich Arsenal affair had been carefully planned. The spy network, established to solve the naval gun problem, was now expected to go quiet. On 2 November Glading called on Olga Gray and told her that the Brandes were leaving for Moscow almost at once because their daughter was ill, and that there would be no more work until after Christmas. Glading, however, was showing signs of unease, and told her that he was keen to get the business into his own hands:

> They [Glading and Gray] should 'continue to practice with the photographic apparatus in order to perfect their technique as he did not like being dependent upon the vagaries of foreigners'.[26]

Sometime afterwards Glading again visited Holland Road and took away the stand for the camera, saying that he had work to do at home and was unable to get the right stand. On 8 December he called and took the camera away with him, telling Olga Gray that his own would not fit the stand. He had a 'rush job' to do, he explained, and had been trying to balance his own camera on a pile of books. Glading was becoming a liability. He had bypassed the Russians and had embarked on a one-man spying odyssey. At a time when the Russians appeared to be desperately trying to dampen down their operations following the Edith Tudor-Hart scare, the recall of Arnold Deutsch and the execution of Maly, Glading had unilaterally decided to increase the flow of information. By now he considered himself an indispensable wheel in the Soviet intelligence machinery, not merely a cog, and informed Olga Gray that it was time 'to get the photographic end of the work into his own hands'. It was now time for the Communist Party to rein him in. On 12 November he received a letter from the CPGB signed by the Secretariat. It read:

Dear Comrade Glading,

It is now over a year since you informed us that you no longer desired to retain your membership of the Communist Party. You will remember that we immediately wrote to you then, asking that you should reconsider your decision. We again approach you to see if you have now changed your mind, and to see if you are prepared to rejoin our Party, of which you were such an active member.

We will be glad to hear from you and to consider any points you may have to make.

Yours fraternally,[27]

This was little more than a veiled instruction to sever connections with the 'secret' party and to rejoin the 'open' party organization. In other words he was to cease 'underground' activity immediately. Glading, however, was not to be denied. On 12 January 1938 he told Olga Gray that 'he had a special job' to do at his house on the weekend of 15–16 January and would have to photograph a secret book of 400 pages. On the 13th he told her that 'quite apart from the return of the Brandes, who would be coming back for about a week, a new man was expected who would be the administrative chief of the organisation'. What exactly Glading knew at this point is not clear. On 17 January he told Olga Gray that his overall 'aim and ambition' was to take control of 'the whole of the executive side of the work'. In this respect he 'did not like the Russians personally and regarded their employment over here as unnecessarily increasing the element of risk because they were foreigners and were nearly always illegally resident in this country'.[28]

On 20 January Glading telephoned Olga Gray at her office and invited her to have lunch with him the next day. He also asked her to leave the flat free for 'something important' tomorrow evening. She then telephoned Maxwell Knight and warned him that Glading was planning something big. On the 21st she lunched with Glading at the Windsor Castle bar and he told her to be back at her flat by 6.00 p.m. 'as there was some urgent photography to be done'. He then spent the rest of the afternoon transporting the photography equipment from his home in Warwick Avenue, South Harrow, back to the flat in Holland Road. It was a frantic afternoon. At 8.15 p.m. he was to collect the document to be photographed from his contact at Charing Cross railway station, photograph it and return it that same evening, a repeat run of the Brandes/Whomack operation. At 6.00 p.m., while he was setting up the camera, he told Olga Gray that 'he was very worried that neither Mr. Stevens nor the other man he was expecting had turned up. He was running short of money and was particularly anxious for the new man to arrive as he had got "stuff parked all over London". On being asked what he meant by this, he replied, "that he had got the negatives of the various documents he had photographed dumped at different houses".'[29]

At 7.30 p.m. Olga Gray telephoned Maxwell Knight and said that Glading had just left her flat for Charing Cross station, where at 8.15 p.m. he was to meet a man who would give him the material to be photographed. He said that he did not know what the material was himself, and he did not think that the man did. He referred to the man as an intermediary. From certain other remarks Olga Gray formed the impression that in the case of Mr and Mrs Brandes he had received instructions from Moscow as to what particular information was required. But this time he had simply instructed his sub-agents 'to get hold of anything they thought might be useful'. Up to the departure of the Brandes Glading had always been under the control and supervision of a resident foreign agent in this country; with the departure of the Brandes on 6 November this was no longer the case.

At about 8.15 p.m. on 21 January Glading was seen by a Special Branch officer of the Metropolitan Police at Charing Cross station, where at 8.20 p.m. he was joined by Albert Williams, an examiner in the Department of the Chief Inspector of Armaments, Royal Arsenal, Woolwich. The two men went to the station yard, where Williams handed Glading a brown-paper parcel. Special Branch officers immediately moved in and both Glading and Williams were arrested and taken to New Scotland Yard, where the parcel was opened in their presence and found to contain four blueprints showing the general arrangements and details of a pressure bar apparatus for testing detonators. When Glading's home was searched, two cameras and other photographic equipment were discovered along with invoices for a Leica camera and other photographic material supplied by Edith Tudor-Hart.[30] Spools of film found at Glading's house proved to be a copy of a textbook on explosives used in the services in 1925. The cover bore the inscription: 'The information given in this document is not to be communicated, either directly or indirectly, to the Press or to any person not holding any official position in His Majesty's Service.'[31] On the flyleaf was the date '18.2.1925'. Photographic plates found at the same time revealed five prints relating to the fuses designed for use by aeroplanes against submarines. During the search of Glading's living-room a Walker's Reform-Refill diary for 1937 was also found in the drawer of a sideboard. At the time of his arrest a similar diary for 1938, containing a variety of slips of paper, was found in Glading's inside pocket. On them were written two names and addresses, and a single address: 2 Station Terrace, Finchley, which was the address of Hilary and Melita Norwood.[32] The diary contained the following entry:

> Thursday, 13th January:- 1.O.L.Q.   One Lung.
>   Sirner.
>   Steadman.
>   Fink.
>   11.0. Davenport, Solicitors
>   Wintringham.

At first MI5 could make little sense of these entries and on 14 February, a month before the opening of the trial, they sent a photograph of the diary to the head of counter-espionage at MI6, Major Valentine Vivian, with the following covering letter:

> We would very much like to try and get some sense out of this before the trial on March 8th, but have not made much progress so far. ... We should be very grateful for any ideas you may be able to give us.[33]

The diary came back with 'Personal File 42480 Sirness' written next to Station Terrace, Finchley, which was bracketed, with an equals sign followed by 'Add. of Melita Sirness. Note for Personal File Norwood' (in 1999 Letty confirmed that 2 Station Terrace had been her address in 1937). For the diary entry on Thursday, 13 January the SIS officer had also bracketed '1.O.L.Q One Lung, Sirner, Steadman, and Fink' together, and wrote in ink alongside it, 'Noted in PF42405. Sirness, M.' (a mistake for PF42480). The surnames 'Sirner' and 'Steadman' were also bracketed separately under 'Note for Melita Sirness'. This could mean only one thing: that counter-espionage SIS had a Personal File active on Melita Norwood at the time of the Percy Glading affair, and were aware that Melita Norwood was involved with the Glading network. For some unexplained reason they decided against taking any action against her or her husband, Hilary.

On 14 March 1938, at the Old Bailey, Percy Glading, Albert Williams and George Whomack (who had been arrested eight days after the arrest of Glading and Williams) all pleaded guilty to charges framed under Section 1, Sub-section C of the Official Secrets Act of 1911, and were sentenced to six years, four years and eighteen months respectively. A fourth defendant, Charles Walter Munday, a laboratory assistant at the Woolwich Arsenal who pleaded not guilty, was acquitted. The indictment contained five counts of which only one, arguably the most important – that of 'obtaining a plan of a naval gun calculated to be, or might be, or intended to be directly or indirectly useful to an enemy' – involved Percy Glading and George Whomack. Of the remaining four offences, three – 'obtaining part of an anti-tank mine pistol; obtaining plans of an anti-submarine bomb fuse; and obtaining certain plans calculated to be useful to an enemy' – were committed by Percy Glading and Albert Williams. A fifth offence committed by Percy Glading and Charles Munday – obtaining information in a book relating to explosives – was later dropped. Over the course of the trial Glading and Williams bore the full weight of the legal process, yet the documents they stole from the Arsenal were neither solicited by Moscow nor were they classified as secret. The only document that was classified as secret and solicited by Moscow was the plan of a 14-inch (360 mm) naval gun 'of newest type', a drawing that Whomack had access to 'but no right to take out of the Arsenal'. It was, therefore, a grave error of judgement on the part of the Attorney-General when in response to a question from the trial judge, and despite knowing that the naval gun was 'highly secret', he described the crimes committed by Glading and Williams as being of a far more serious nature than those committed by Whomack.

Judge: If you can compute the relative importance of these things, how does that naval gun business compare in importance with the others?

Sir Donald: I should have said first the bomb fuse, with regard to which the greatest precaution would be taken.

Judge: That is not Whomack.

Sir Donald: The naval gun, I should say, came second. It was highly secret.[34]

There appeared to be a tacit agreement between the prosecution and the defence to divert attention away from George Whomack, despite the fact that he had been directly linked with foreign agents operating in this country. (On the day the Brandes left for the Continent they were carrying the complete plans for the 14-inch (360 mm) gun in their luggage.) This may well have been due to the skilful defence mounted by the leftwing lawyer Dennis Noel Pritt, long a thorn in the side of the legal authorities. Pritt's defence of the Woolwich Arsenal spies centred upon proving that what the defendants had done was 'almost ludicrously unimportant'. Every document or plan involved in the case was shown to be not of the secret or confidential class but only in the class 'for official use only' – which apparently included telephone directories. According to the evidence, the textbook on explosives was available to at least fifty people in the Arsenal. The prosecution needed to demonstrate unequivocally that the offences committed by the Woolwich Arsenal spies were as damaging to national security as was being claimed. The Attorney-General's response to Pritt was not convincing; as far as he was concerned the defendants were guilty of a heinous crime compounded by the fact that they were not foreigners but British subjects. Two of them were earning their livelihood as servants of the state. 'That aspect of the matter does not need any further words from me.' The involvement of a foreign power was of secondary importance:

> So far as the three men are concerned, Glading would at any rate appear to be the chief instigator. Williams certainly comes next in that the evidence shows that he was having photographs done in his own house. So far as Whomack is concerned, the evidence only connects him with the incident on October 21.
>
> He is connected in that incident by direct contact with Mr. and Mrs. Brandes, and he has handed to him a plan which was photographed on that day.[35]

In fact Whomack, who had been known to MI5 as a member of the underground Communist Party since 1929, was a significant catch for the authorities. He had first been brought to MI5's attention by Special

Branch in April 1927, when, as Chairman of Bexley Communist Party, he was placed under surveillance by Special Branch, who described him as a 'violent type of revolutionary'.[36] He had known Percy Glading since 1925, when both men were employed in the Department of Naval Ordinance at the Woolwich Arsenal. The two men had worked alongside one another until October 1928, when Glading had been dismissed from his position as a gun examiner in Shop D.15 of the Inspector of Naval Ordnance Department for membership of the Communist Party. Communists had been barred the previous year from employment at the Admiralty following a raid on the All Russian Co-operative Society (ARCOS) and the subsequent exposure of communist spies in the private armaments firms of Vickers-Armstrong and A. V. Roe. Many communists in the Admiralty and the Royal Dockyards had simply gone underground, and in March 1929 Special Branch reported that Whomack had denied being a member of the Communist Party to the Arsenal authorities.[37] The purge of communists in the Woolwich Arsenal, however, had done little to prevent a spy-ring developing around George Whomack inside the Arsenal for the simple reason that Whomack was no longer a member of the Communist Party. On the contrary, he was a member of the Labour Party and he was recruited as a spy by the Labour MP J. T. Walton Newbold.[38]

By the time of Whomack's recruitment his former colleague at the Arsenal, Percy Glading, was ready to play his part. After his dismissal from the Arsenal in October 1928 he had taken up temporary employment at the Marco Conveyor and Engineering Co. close to his home in Leytonstone before leaving to take up full-time Communist Party work in April the following year. In September he was elected a member of the party's Politburo, from where he monitored the Party's communist 'cells' employed by Soviet institutions in the UK. In September 1929 he was sent to the Lenin School in Moscow, returning to London in April 1930. His entry into the world of espionage was now virtually guaranteed. In 1932 MI5 reported that:

All the military espionage reports compiled in this country and intended for Moscow are sent to Glading. He is the paymaster for these reports. All secret reports from the British Colonies, it is said, are sent to 23, Great Ormond Street, where he has a nicely furnished office on the top floor. [39]

At some stage in 1935 Glading's contacts in the WO and Admiralty passed him information that the Royal Navy had a prototype of a 14-inch (360 mm) gun and that it was to be developed at the Woolwich Arsenal. This was a significant alteration to existing treaties limiting the size of naval guns. The Washington treaty of 1921 had reduced the scale of naval construction and had set the 13-inch (330 mm) gun as the absolute maximum. This was reaffirmed by the London treaty of 1930, but with Hitler's accession to power in January 1933 German rearmament plans threatened to render the Washington and London treaties worthless. At the Geneva disarmament talks in 1934 Germany and Japan, and to a lesser degree the Italians, pulled out of the negotiations, leading to a new and secret naval arms race. In order to avoid tonnage restrictions limiting the size of warships the German Navy adopted welding in naval construction. These ships were considerably lighter than riveted vessels, enabling Germany to build what were in effect quasi-battleships in the cruiser category. A 14-inch (360 mm) gun could not be fitted on a riveted cruiser because of the restrictions on the size of ship which tonnage agreements enforced. But a welded cruiser would effectively enable the German Navy to create a new category of warship, the battle cruiser, effectively a cruiser that could fire a 14-inch (360 mm) shell without going outside the terms of the London treaty. In terms of explosive power a 14-inch (360 mm) shell was a substantial increase on that of a 13-inch (330 mm) shell. The new technology involved in the construction of a 14-inch (360 mm) gun was far more advanced than navies had seen hitherto, and in turn advanced the technology in the field of range-finding. What this meant in practice was that the Soviet spy network was making its first foray into the world of analogue computing and precision shelling, then in its early stages.

At a time when sea power was axiomatic with world power status the Soviet Navy could not be allowed to fall behind in respect of new technology being developed by Germany and the UK. Ever since the humiliation at Port Arthur, when the Russian Navy was sent to the bottom of the Pacific Ocean by the Japanese Imperial Navy, Russia lived in fear of a naval disaster of similar proportions. It was therefore decided to send two agents, Willy and Mary Brandes, as illegals, to London to obtain the plans of the Royal Navy's projected 14-inch (360 mm) naval gun. The network was already in place – all they needed to do was to make contact with Maly, Glading and Whomack. At the beginning of 1937, however, at the height of the purges, Moscow Centre had already decided to withdraw Maly from London; Arnold Deutsch, too, was withdrawn once it became known that his cover might have been blown. Glading remained unaware of these decisions. He played his part well in the raid on the 14-inch (360 mm) naval gun plan, but failed to appreciate the dynamics unfolding around him. He thus compromised the networks, when, on his own initiative, he arranged to carry on spying from Olga Gray's flat in Holland Road, substituting Albert Williams for George Whomack. In all fairness, how was he to know that the safe house used during the entire 14-inch (360 mm) naval gun operation came courtesy of MI5? Others, however, had their suspicions, even if he did not.

During the trial Pritt complained of 'the mystery that had been spread round the case' that 'made it utterly impossible for any jury to have brought an impartial, blank, and fresh mind to bear'. He questioned the validity of Olga Gray's evidence, which had been given *in camera* and the withholding of her name from the press:

> It may sometimes be right for the Crown to ask the magistrate for a name to be withheld, but everybody knows that in this country, with a free press, the withholding of names fills everybody with sensational and dreadful thoughts. Another matter which would fill the mind of a jury, potential or actual, with the darkest and most terrible apprehension is the giving of evidence in camera.[40]

And yet all the defendants had pleaded guilty in line with instructions received from the CPGB, and relayed to the defendants by Pritt. On Friday 11 March M/7, one of MI5's agents inside the CPGB, met with the other defence lawyer involved in the case, Dudley Collard. Collard trusted M/7, and had no inkling of his MI5 status. He informed M/7 that 'he and Pritt had been trying to drive a bargain with the prosecution and that it was possible that they would all plead guilty save one'. He also 'expressed great satisfaction with the fact that the prosecution had refrained from bringing in the Communist Party as such'.[41] M/7 worked on the Communist Party's newspaper, the *Daily Worker*, and was presumably a solicitor, as Collard offered to put him up for membership of the leftwing lawyers' society, the Haldane Club. On another occasion over lunch he informed M/7 of Miss X's name and warned him that she had frequently taken down the minutes of *Daily Worker* staff meetings and that therefore his name (M/7's) was probably in the hands of MI5. He expressed his admiration for Olga Gray's craft, saying that he 'was greatly impressed with the fact that Miss "X" had been able to remain for six years amongst people with political opinions different from her own'. He made no secret of the fact that Glading was literally spying on behalf of Russia, and indicated his approval of such activities, remarking that 'the Party are exceedingly thankful that the Moscow aspect was kept fairly dark'. [42] In fact, at the trial Pritt had made much of this point, indicating to the jury that if it was a case of 'espionage carried out on behalf of some foreign power surely somewhere in the chain there would be somebody who knew something about what he wanted'. [43] Presumably the authorities, in seeking to wrap up the Woolwich Arsenal case so quickly, had not got to the bottom of the affair and had failed to prise open the parallel Soviet spy-ring then operating from Lawn Road. "If Glading had had stuff parked all over London', Pritt observed, 'it would be a strange thing indeed if some trace of it had not been found, and I ask you to assume in this case that nothing has been undiscovered of what the prisoners have done'. Asked if they had anything to say, each of the defendants replied 'nothing'. In passing sentence all reference to their communist beliefs was dismissed and the Moscow connection played down, as the judge expressed some sympathy in the case of Whomack. The judge told Whomack, 'You are the only one about whom I feel in difficulty, having regard to the comparatively small part you took in the case'. Glading and Williams received very different treatment. They, the judge said, had acted 'with the sole and vulgar motive of obtaining money'. [44]

So why did the authorities appear to get it so dramatically wrong? Fear of Stalin and Hitler undoubtedly played its part. In March 1938 Neville Chamberlain, the British Prime Minister, could not afford an open breach with the Soviet Union. On the day M/7 had learned that Collard and Pritt were 'trying to drive a bargain with the prosecution' the Wehrmacht had marched into Austria. The following day Hitler had announced Austria's incorporation within the German Reich. The British Foreign Minister, Lord Halifax, in response to Chancellor Kurt Schuschnigg of Austria's desperate pleas for help sent a telegram advising him that 'His Majesty's Government are unable to guarantee protection'. On 14 March Chamberlain told the House of Commons 'The hard fact is that nothing could have arrested what actually has happened – unless this country and other countries had been prepared to use force'.[45] In the same speech Chamberlain refused a British guarantee to Czechoslovakia. To the British left it appeared that Chamberlain was turning Hitler eastwards; to Stalin that the democracies were weak.

On 15 March Glading and his co-defendants were sentenced. During their first court appearance on January 29 the defendants had all entered a plea of not guilty. This changed over the course of three months, when it became apparent that an open breach with the Soviet Union had to be avoided at all costs. The greatest fear among Foreign Office officials was that Hitler would seek an agreement with Stalin. It was widely believed that since the onset of the Spanish Civil War in 1936 Stalin had regarded the Soviet Union as being in 'a war position'. The British FO's fear that Stalin would become so fixed on the destruction of the British empire that he would go to any lengths to achieve his object, including a military alliance with Hitler, appeared to be a very real one. The Soviet Union was regarded not as a country with which Britain was at war; but as a country that it might be at war with before too long. It was, therefore, against a backdrop of fear and suspicion that the charges of espionage against the Woolwich Arsenal spies were framed. But, as it was becoming increasingly obvious that Hitler was prepared to risk a general war in pursuit of his foreign policy aims, Chamberlain could not risk the Woolwich Arsenal case escalating into a full-blown diplomatic crisis. In 1927 an earlier spying incident had led to the ARCOS raid and the breaking off of diplomatic relations between Britain and the Soviet Union. A similar denouement in March 1938 was unthinkable. The Woolwich Arsenal case consequently received a good deal of press publicity that was intended as a firm warning to the Soviets to cease espionage activities in the UK. However, the British authorities stopped short of accusing the Russians of orchestrating these activities. Consequently, on 6 November 1937 MI5 officers had looked on helplessly as Mr and Mrs Brandes loaded their luggage containing the plan for the 14-inch (360 mm) gun into a taxi before driving off to Victoria Station to catch the boat-train. In order to maintain the fiction that the Woolwich spies had acted of their own free will a decision was also taken to play down the defendants' membership of the CPGB and to suggest that their motivation had been purely financial gain. Although attempts were made to establish the identity of Glading's War Office contact nothing came to light. The same was apparently true in respect of Melita Norwood.

During the investigations into the Woolwich Arsenal case, according to information smuggled out of Russia by the KGB archivist Vasili Mitrokhin, MI5 failed to detect clues to her 'identity contained in a notebook taken from the Communist ringleader, Percy Glading (codenamed GOT)', and in March 1938 the NKVD had decided to put her 'on ice' for a few months; she was reactivated in May 1938.[46] But this was not the case, as MI5 (along with counter-espionage MI6) had opened a file on Melita Sirnis sometime between 1934 and 1938, and had connected her with an address found in Percy Glading's diary. *The Mitrokhin Archive*, however, is clear that Melita Norwood, while falling under suspicion, was not identified during the investigations into the Woolwich Arsenal spies. If Mitrokhin is correct, then somebody involved with the case must have taken a decision to inform the Russians that her cover had not been blown. The MI5 officers who worked on the Woolwich Arsenal case were Guy Liddell and Jane Archer, who was then introducing Roger Hollis to the mysteries of counter-intelligence. It forces the question: how did the Russians know she was clean?

'The Centre', *The Mitrokhin Archive* continues, 'demonstrated its high opinion of Sirnis by maintaining contact with her for the next twenty-two months, at a time when the purge of foreign intelligence officers led it to lose touch with many other agents – including some of the Five. At the outbreak of the war it was clearly more interested in Sirnis than in Philby'.[47] Nevertheless, Moscow Centre continued to be deeply worried by the implications of the Woolwich Arsenal case, and in October 1942 Anthony Blunt was asked to send a detailed report outlining how MI5 got wind of the Woolwich Arsenal spy-ring down to the names of the surveillance team that had been involved. By October 1942, Moscow Centre may still have been 'more interested in Sirnis than in Philby', because by this time Sirnis (Melita Norwood) was providing valuable information on the Anglo-American atomic bomb project.

CHAPTER 9

'The Russian Danger Is Our Danger'

THE agreement between the British Prime Minister, Neville Chamberlain, and Adolf Hitler at Munich in September 1938, which led to the German invasion of Czechoslovakia, was arrived at without the participation of the Soviet Union, and led Stalin to conclude that Britain and France were leaving Germany a free hand against the USSR. Whether Stalin was right to draw this conclusion is a question that need not detain us; suffice it to say that he was wrong, because Hitler's intention was to attack first in the west. Nevertheless, Stalin, who had been involved in secret negotiations with Hitler since 1936, was convinced that Chamberlain, supported by the French government, was encouraging Germany to turn eastwards. Two days after the collapse of military talks between the USSR, France and Great Britain, Stalin and Hitler signed the Nazi–Soviet pact on 23 August 1939.

The signing of the pact demanded an intellectual leap on the part of the world communist movement, from one of outright opposition to fascism to one of open opposition to Western imperialism. On 24 August Moscow Centre withdrew its secret agents from Germany, and severed radio links with German nationals working for Soviet intelligence inside the Third Reich. The following day the German Communist Party issued a statement calling on communists to 'support the peace policy of the Soviet Union':

> The German working people, and especially the German workers, must support the peace policy of the Soviet Union, must place themselves at the side of all peoples which are oppressed and threatened by the Nazis, and must now take up the fight as never before to ensure that peace pacts in the spirit of the pact which has just been concluded between the Soviet Union and Germany are also made with Poland and Romania, with France and England, and with all peoples which have reason to feel themselves threatened by Hitler's policy of aggression.[1]

On 7 September Stalin told the Bulgarian communist Georgi Dimitrov, general secretary of the Comintern, what he expected of foreign Communist parties. 'They should denounce their governments' war plans as imperialistic and reduce anti-Fascist propaganda.' On the eleventh, with the war barely a week old, the Communist Party of the United States declared the war to be a conflict between 'imperialist' nations. On the 14th a broadcast from Soviet Russia announced that the war was an 'imperialist' one, and a 'predatory' conflict pursued by two aggressor nations.[2] On the 18th the General Secretary of the Communist Party of Great Britain, Harry Pollitt, published a pamphlet entitled *How to Win the War*. On the same day he received a Moscow press telegram with instructions that the war must be opposed. Under considerable pressure to conform to the new line he handed his responsibilities to a secretariat – a 'troika' – made up of the editor of the party's theoretical journal *Labour Monthly*, Rajani Palme Dutt, the new editor of the *Daily Worker*, William Rust, and David Springhall, the national party organizer.[3] At this point the troika began to anticipate hostilities rather than an alliance developing between Great Britain and the Soviet Union. Two days later, in accordance with a secret protocol of the Nazi–Soviet pact, Russian troops had crossed the eastern frontier of Poland at dawn and took up positions already agreed with Germany. On the 29th, the same day as the fall of Warsaw, a further German–Soviet treaty was signed, the German–Soviet boundary and friendship treaty, which defined in detail the limits of the respective occupations of Polish territory. In a joint declaration, issued on that date, the two governments claimed that they had 'definitively settled the problems arising from the collapse of the Polish State and have thereby created a sure foundation for a lasting peace in Eastern Europe'. Britain and France were called upon to recognize the boundary changes and a joint declaration issued that it would be in the interests of all nations to stop the war. A few days later the Communist International declared:

> The present war is an imperialist and unjust war for which the bourgeoisie of all the belligerent states bear equal responsibility. In no country can the working class or the Communist parties support the war. The bourgeoisie is not conducting war against fascism as Chamberlain and the leaders of the Labour Party pretend. War is

carried on between two groups of imperialist countries for world domination.[4]

On 11 October the CPGB announced that in view of differences of opinion within the party, Harry Pollitt had resigned as General Secretary. The Kuczynskis, the Norwoods, the Rothsteins and other foreign communists residing in Britain were said to be totally dismayed. Nevertheless, within a fortnight they had fallen into line. Robert Kuczynski's son, Jurgen, was the first German communist in Britain during the Second World War to come out openly in support of the Nazi–Soviet pact, condemning the war as an expression of Anglo-American imperialism disguised as a defence of democracy and freedom:

> The Stalinist Treaty policy with Germany is ... the only way of insuring a new and free Germany for the future. Europe must be prevented, above all, from coming under an English domination. In the same way it must be seen that Europe does not fall completely under the influence of the New York Stock Exchange. It is the duty of every revolutionary socialist to fight against the dictatorship of the financial magnates not excluding those who hide under the cloak of democracy.[5]

He began to call for acts of 'sabotage, strikes etc., in important war industries' in both Britain and Germany. As his statements became increasingly bellicose, anti-British, and pro-Stalin, MI5 began to monitor his activities more closely and on 23 November 1939 a Home Office Warrant (HOW) was granted allowing MI5 to open mail sent to his London address at 36 Upper Park Road, NW3. On 20 January 1940 he was interned by the Aliens Tribunal on the evidence that he was an alien and a communist:

> H.O. file K.4790 re Jurgen Kuczynski.
> 20.1.40. Interned. Met. Police Tribunal No. 11.
> Reasons: I think that this alien is a communist, and/or working in sympathy with that movement.[6]

An appeal was immediately launched for his release and a well-organized campaign got underway on his behalf led by the defence lawyer in the Woolwich Arsenal case, D. N. Pritt. On 22 January he sent a letter to the Home Office questioning the grounds on which Jurgen Kuczynski was interned.

On the 27th Lilian Bowes-Lyon and the president of the National Union of Railwaymen, John Marchbank, wrote separately to the HO demanding his release. Following further interventions on his behalf by the 'Red Dean' of Canterbury, Hewlett Johnson, and Harold Laski he was released from Warner's Camp, Seaton, Devon on 25 April on the grounds that membership of the KPD was not sufficient grounds for internment. Following his release he moved into number 6, Lawn Road flats.

On 16 July 1940, after his conquest of Western Europe, Hitler signed 'Directive No. 16 for Preparations of a Landing Operation against England [*sic*, i.e. Britain]'. At this stage of the war it was only the refusal of the British people to come to terms with Nazi Germany that stood between Hitler and fascist control of Europe. To force Britain's surrender Hitler ordered the German Air Force to draw up plans for a blitz offensive against London, and called on the German Navy to step up submarine warfare in the Atlantic. On 1 August he signed Directive No. 17, intensifying the air- and sea-war against Britain as the basis for her 'final subjugation'. The invasion of the British Isles – Operation Sealion – was planned for mid-September.

The offensive began on 13 August when German fighters appeared over southern England intent on sweeping the Royal Air Force from the skies. On the 17th, however, following a disastrous night for the Luftwaffe, Hitler accepted that the 'battle for the skies' had been lost, and changed his air strategy. Hitler had originally intended to unleash massive terror bombing of London as a prelude to Operation Sealion. He now brought that terror campaign forward. On the 24th, when a large number of German aircraft bombed London, the British replied with air-raids on Berlin. From 7 September to the middle of November night bombing became the norm. However, by the middle of November it was apparent that the attempt to bring about the collapse of British resolve by dislocating the capital had failed. Hitler, in pursuit of an alternative strategy to force Britain out of the war, turned to Fascism's main ideological purpose, the destruction of 'Jewish Bolshevism'. A true 'lightning war' against the Soviet Union would remove any remaining hopes Churchill entertained that Britain's salvation lay with Russia's entry into the war. Furthermore, a decisive victory against the Soviet Union would serve a double purpose. It would not only deprive Britain of the Soviet Union as a future ally; but once Russia had been delivered a knock-out blow, Germany's Japanese ally would be free to move against the British empire in the Far East, diverting America's attention to the Pacific.[7] Consequently, at four o'clock on the morning of 22 June 1941 German troops invaded the Soviet Union.

The invasion apparently took Stalin completely by surprise, despite the fact that he had received advance warning of the invasion from Great Britain and one of the GRU's 'great illegals' in Japan, Richard Sorge. Fearing a disinformation campaign aimed at embroiling him in a conflict with Hitler and the destruction of the Nazi–Soviet pact, Stalin simply refused to believe the intelligence reports arriving on his desk. The failure of the Soviet side to prepare for an invasion meant that the German attack was a rapid success. As Ian Kershaw argues, the scale of the invasion was immense, as over 3 million German troops invaded the Soviet Union's territory along a 1,800-mile front. Facing the invading armies, arrayed on the western frontiers of the USSR, were nearly 3 million Soviet soldiers, backed by tanks now estimated to have numbered as many as 14–15,000 (almost 2,000 of them the most modern designs), over 34,000 artillery pieces and 8-9,000 fighter planes. The scale of the conflict on the Russian front, as Kershaw rightly remarks, 'defies the imagination'.[8]

A few hours after the invasion of Russia began, British listeners to the BBC had their breakfast interrupted by this world-shattering news. Communists in Britain, who by now had managed to come to terms with the Nazi–Soviet pact, could hardly believe their ears. Only a few days earlier Andrew Rothstein through the TASS news agency 'had issued a statement maintaining that rumours, then current, of a coming German attack were without foundation' and were another example of the 'anti-Soviet dreams' of the 'British ruling class'.[9] As the Kuczynskis, the Rothsteins and the Norwoods sat down to breakfast on 22 June they listened to their radio sets with a dull sense of disbelief. All that day they went about their business with a sense of trepidation. Churchill, who had once remarked that if he had to choose between communism and fascism he would not choose communism, was expected to broadcast to the nation that evening.[10] At 9 p.m. communists turned on their radio sets with a sense of foreboding. Churchill, with his characteristic dry manner, would soon allay their fears:

No one has been a more persistent opponent of Communism than

I have for the last 25 years. I will unsay no word that I have spoken about it, but all this fades away before the spectacle which is now unfolding ... We have but one aim and one single irrevocable purpose. We are resolved to destroy Hitler and every vestige of the Nazi regime ... Any man or state who fights against Nazism will have our aid ... It follows, therefore, that we shall give whatever help we can to Russia and to the Russian people. We shall appeal to all our friends and allies in every part of the world to take the same course. The Russian danger is our danger ... just as the cause of any Russian fighting for his hearth and home is the cause of free men and free people in every quarter of the globe.[11]

The party's response was swift. The Communist MP for Fife, William Gallacher, stood up in the House of Commons and said that he was 'agreeably surprised' by Churchill's broadcast. He issued a press statement on 26 June saying he was adamant that the Communist Party would support the government in any steps it took to collaborate with the Soviet Union. On 4 July the Communist Party issued a manifesto under the title 'People's Victory over Fascism', declaring that 'the war was now a just war' and promising its full support for the government in giving assistance to the Soviet Union. Harry Pollitt, the Communist Party's Churchill – 'Harry's back' now mimicked the refrain 'Winnie's back'[12] – was restored to the leadership of the party. The spies also came back. The arrival of Jurgen Kuczynski's sister, Ursula Beurton (Sonya), from Switzerland in January 1941 (much to Jurgen's annoyance; he felt that her presence would compromise his own activities) would prove a turning-point in the history of Soviet espionage in Britain. For it was Sonya, more or less acting on her own initiative, who would co-ordinate Britain's atomic-bomb spies.

CHAPTER 10

Sonya

P ROFESSOR Robert Kuczynski's daughter Ursula, codename Sonya, nicknamed 'the Mouse' because of her small, pointed face and 'feverish inquisitiveness', was born in Berlin-Schlachtensee on 15 May 1907.[1] At the age of sixteen she joined the Communist Youth League before becoming a fully-fledged member of the KPD in May 1926 and leader of the KPD's Agitation and Propaganda Department (Agitprop) in Berlin's 10th District. Ursula, or Ruth as she preferred to be known, was a 'Red' Sally Bowles in a fading Weimar Republic:

> There's been a lot happening recently. A fancy dress party at the Academy of Arts which I enjoyed enormously. Theme: 'Beyond the Pale' My costume – bright red scanty shorts and tight-fitting shirt with stiff collar. There are those who say I kissed 20 boys, but without counting Rolf it can't have been more than 19.[2]

Dismissed from her job in 1928 for communist activities, she travelled to New York before returning to Berlin in 1929 to marry her childhood sweetheart, Rudolph (Rolf or Rudi) Hamburger, an architect with communist sympathies. She was twenty-two years of age and Rolf was twenty-six, and they talked constantly 'about seeing more of the world':

> We asked Walter, a good friend of Rolf's who represented a large German firm in China, to keep an eye open for us.
> One day a telegram arrived from Walter; according to a newspaper advertisement the Shanghai Municipal Council was looking for an architect. ... Rolf telegraphed his application. It was accepted – on condition that he must start at once.[3]

Shanghai was then virtually a state within a state, divided between the French Concession, the Anglo-American international settlement and the Chinese quarter. Before she left she visited KPD headquarters and informed the comrades of her 'wish to become active in China'. They greeted her offer with some surprise and incredulity. The city of Shanghai was in the grip of a 'White Terror' and China itself close to civil war.[4] Three years earlier a strike of Shanghai workers had been brutally suppressed by a Chinese warlord backed by French and British troops. Two hundred Chinese had been decapitated in the streets, their heads stuck on bamboo poles or displayed on kitchen platters; the Chinese Communist Party had been outlawed. Was she fully aware of the dangers involved? Looking back she could understand their incredulity:

> The comrades must have found it rather odd that I should bounce in and tell them naively what I wanted to do. So far I had not distinguished myself in any way. They spoke to me about the serious position in China, where party work was strictly clandestine and every communist, even by the smallest action, exposed to extreme danger.[5]

When she arrived in China she began vomiting daily and losing weight. The doctor put it down to the unsuitable climate until it became obvious that she was five months pregnant. She settled down to an uneventful life:

> Rolf held a respected position; we were frequently invited to parties and had to reciprocate. Various ladies called and expected me to return the visit – an alien world which I hated, a stark contrast to the life I had led until then. I did not protest; I knew that if I was ever to work here illegally as a communist, an outwardly bourgeois life-style would provide vital cover. Weeks and months passed while I waited for some word from the party.[6]

Her initial contact was the American journalist Agnes Smedley, a fluent German-speaker who had lived in Berlin during the Weimar period. An OMS agent working for the Comintern, she was the Far Eastern correspondent of the *Frankfurter Zeitung*, and a socialite who ran 'something of a salon in her various homes, providing a rendezvous for other journalists, communists and fellow-agents'.[7] A number of key figures in the world of espionage passed through her circle, among them the future head of MI5, Roger Hollis, then a young journalist and an employee of British American Tobacco.

It was Agnes Smedley who first introduced Ursula to Richard Sorge, perhaps the most famous of the GRU's 'great illegals'. Tall, well-built and handsome, his face scarred from previous fights, dressed in a new but already crumpled suit, he made an immediate impression on Ursula. Born in Baku in 1895 to a German father and a Russian mother, and a member of both the KPD and the Communist Party of the Soviet Union, he worked as an intelligence officer in China and Japan between 1929 and 1941. In Japan he formed the very effective 'Ramsay' group and established himself so securely in the German embassy in Tokyo 'that his position was second only to that of the ambassador himself. He was unofficial embassy adviser, with an office in the embassy building and full and free access to all the files.'[8] His most notable achievement was probably to send a top secret report to Moscow with the exact date of the German Army's planned attack on the Soviet Union.[9] His other major contribution to Soviet intelligence was the recruitment of Ursula Kuczynski, the only woman ever to be made an honorary colonel of the Red Army. In 1932, he arranged for her to undergo six months' professional training in Moscow, where she was instructed in wireless telegraphy and in the techniques of repairing and constructing 'music boxes' (radio transmitters); she was also given the codename Sonya. After completing her training she was sent to Manchuria in February 1934 to work undercover with a German comrade whom she referred to only as Ernst, and to whom she became romantically attached. She took her young son Micha with her; a difficult decision given the dangerous nature of the assignment and the fact that she would be working closely with communist partisans fighting occupying Japanese troops. In April 1935, following the arrest of a leading Chinese communist in the region, she was ordered immediately to leave for Beijing. Four months later she discovered that she was pregnant by Ernst, and decided to return to Europe with her husband, Rolf:

> Micha was now four years old and I yearned for a second child. In my line of business the time would never be right. If I was separated from Ernst, I might never be with anyone again from whom I would want a child. Now that it was on the way I wanted to keep it.
>
> The timing was particularly opportune. Within a few weeks Rolf, who had now completed five years in China, was to begin his home

leave in Europe. His English employers would be paying the fares for the whole family. Centre wanted me to use this opportunity to come to Moscow and discuss my work. Besides, I was glad at the chance to visit my family in London.[10]

Back in Moscow she was given instructions to prepare for an assignment in Poland. She went first to London, where she was met at the dockside by her parents and stayed with them at their 'dowdy three-roomed flat' in Lawn Road.[11] It was the first time that she had seen them since 1930. It was now 1936. Nine weeks later her daughter, Janina, was born in Warsaw.

After two years in Warsaw she was recalled to Moscow, travelling again via London, to learn how to build 'a more complicated transmitter, of a "push-pull" type', and was told that she had been promoted to the rank of major in the Red Army.[12] A decision was taken to send her to Switzerland, where she would establish a small group of anti-fascist activists 'prepared for illegal, dangerous work inside Germany'.[13] She requested that her recruits be drawn from members of the British Battalion of the International Brigade trained in sabotage techniques. Englishmen, she argued, were very well suited for the task that lay ahead:

> It was not unusual for the odd well-to-do Englishman to travel the world and settle for a while wherever he happened to feel like it, and if he felt inspired to choose Germany, then this was not at all out of keeping with the continental image of the eccentric Englishman. Centre agreed to my plan, but reiterated what I already knew: no contact with the British party. I kept to that.[14]

This was not strictly true. When Sonya arrived in England in late 1938 she approached an Austrian communist, Fred Uhlmann, a veteran of the Spanish Civil War, and asked him to recommend two English recruits for a Russian Intelligence Service sabotage group. Uhlmann approached David Springhall, a prominent figure in the International Brigade's British Battalion and the national organizer of the CPGB, who recommended an ex-Brigader, Alexander Foote. Uhlmann then interviewed Foote and dangled before him the prospect of a 'secret and dangerous' job abroad. His biographical details were passed to Sonya, who signalled them to

Moscow Centre, who in turn approved his recruitment, advising her to contact Foote before she departed for Geneva. Foote, however, was taken ill and the proposed meeting never took place. Contact was then made between Foote and Uhlmann at Communist Party headquarters in King Street and he was given the telephone number of Ursula's sister, Brigitte Kuczynski, now Bridget Lewis, then living in the Lawn Road flats. She invited him to lunch at the flats, where he was struck by the apparent incompatibility of his surroundings with the call to proletarian revolution. She told him that he had been given an assignment in Germany and issued him with a £10 note along with instructions on how to meet Sonya in Geneva:

> 'You will proceed to Geneva. There you will be contacted and further instructions will be given you.' The voice of my vis-à-vis was quiet and matter of fact, and the whole atmosphere of the flat was of complete middle class respectability. Nothing could have been more incongruous than the contrast between this epitome of bourgeois smugness and the work that was transacted in its midst.[15]

Foote's meeting with Sonya took place at the end of October 1938 and was remarkable for its bizarre amateur elaboration of introductory identification marks:

> Wear a white scarf and carry a leather belt in your hand. Sonya will be carrying an orange in one hand and a shopping net containing a green parcel in the other.[16]

When he met her he was struck by her calm demeanour. He was told to take lodgings in Munich, study German and to 'keep his eyes and ears open'. If possible, he was to 'establish connections with the Messerschmitt aeroplane factory'.[17] She asked him if he knew of others in Britain who would be willing to undertake anti-Nazi work and he suggested a rather quiet young man, Leon Charles Beurton, who had served alongside him in Spain. In the spring of 1939 Leon Beurton found himself taking lunch with Brigitte at the Lawn Road flats, and after receiving the customary £10 note, he was given instructions on how to make contact with Sonya. The meeting took place in Switzerland, outside the Uniprix shop in Vevey and it was love at first sight:

I met Len for the first time in January or February 1939 ... He was then twenty-five years old, had thick brown hair, eyebrows that met and clear hazel eyes. He was lean and athletic, strong and muscular. Half shy, half-aggressive, he gave the impression of boyish immaturity. Len was seven years younger than I was. Unlike Jim [Foote], he was not interested in material things and, again in contrast to Jim, he was extremely sensitive. When I told him that he had been chosen for dangerous work in Germany his face lit up ... Len was to settle in Frankfurt am Main and to make contact with personnel at the I.G. Farben chemical works.[18]

Foote and Beurton would often travel from Germany to Switzerland, rendezvous with Sonya in Geneva, and receive instructions in elementary sabotage techniques. She would often ask them for a list of suitable targets in Germany, and on one occasion Foote, half-jokingly, suggested Adolf Hitler. He told her of a time when he, along with Len, had dined at Hitler's favourite restaurant in the hope of catching a glimpse of the famous Führer. As luck would have it Hitler turned up:

> 'We didn't have to give the salute because we were British subjects, but we stood up like the rest!' At the moment of Hitler's entrance into the main restaurant BEURTON, who was facing him standing, put his hand inside his jacket to take out his cigarette case, but in appearance as though he were going to draw a revolver. F said his heart was in his mouth and he thought that he and BEURTON would be shot down by Hitler's escort. However nothing whatever happened and F commented to Sonya that if there was all this feeling against Hitler it was a wonder no-one tried to bump him off considering the lack of precautions taken on these informal occasions. He had pointed out, for example, that it would have been easy to put a bomb in a suitcase beneath the coats and hats which hung on the partition wall separating Hitler from the main restaurant. Then, said Foote, what did Sonya do but turn on me and say, what an excellent idea![19]

Sonya rented a small renovated farmhouse in the mountains of French Switzerland near the village of Caux along with her husband Rolf and their two children. Their marriage, however, was now one of convenience, and at the beginning of 1939 Rolf left Switzerland for Marseilles to train as a radio operator for an assignment in China. Moscow Centre sent instructions for the couple to divorce and for Sonya to enter into a pro-forma marriage with an Englishman in order to obtain a British passport. With war imminent it was decided to recall Beurton and Foote from Germany, and for Sonya to marry Foote. Foote, however, was reluctant and asked Sonya whether she wouldn't mind considering Beurton instead. An agreement was reached, and Sonya told Beurton that he could trust her to divorce him as soon as he wanted to. They were married on the birthday of the Red Army, 23 February 1940. The marriage lasted forty years.

In the late autumn of 1940 the Centre suggested that Sonya should move to England, alone if necessary:

> As a former member of the International Brigade, Len could not travel through Spain and had to stay in Geneva until we could find a different route for him.
>
> England could only be reached by the most improbable detours. At that time just one narrow road was open in France. This crossed the region 'governed' by the Nazi puppet General Petain, and led to the Spanish border. From there the route lay through Spain and Portugal. From Lisbon it was supposed to be possible to reach England by plane or ship.[20]

At the end of December 1940 Sonya journeyed to England, staying initially with friends of her father in Oxford before moving to the Oxfordshire village of Glympton. Beurton followed her in 1942. Foote took over from Sonya in Switzerland, where, under the leadership of the Hungarian Sandor Rado, the GRU's Rezident Direktor in the Swiss Confederation, he linked up with the *Rote Drei* (the Red Three), supplying Moscow with a stream of intelligence direct from the German High Command. Until the end of 1943 the *Rote Drei* sent thousands of radio messages detailing information on the Nazi war machine to Moscow Centre.[21] In England Sonya set about putting her transmitter at the service of the Kuczynski network, and rebuilding the GRU's damaged British connection.

1 'Find Three Policemen': Suffragette card inscribed 'Sasha to Gertrude. Xmas 1906'

(*opposite, above*) Alexander Sirnis with
[Tol]stoy's grandchildren, 'Lulu' (Ilya) and
[Ann]a, Tuckton House, 23 September 1907

(*opposite, below*) The Gardening Brigade,
[Tuck]ton House, 13 May 1907. Alexander
[Sirni]s is standing on the right.

(*right*) Tolstoy's manuscripts in the safe
[at Tu]ckton House

(*below*) The office, Tuckton House,
[1907]. Alexander Sirnis sits in front of the
[type]writer in foreground; Count Chertkov
[is st]anding, second from the right. The safe
[cont]aining Tolstoy's manuscripts is in the
[back]ground.

6 *(left)* Alexander Sirnis, 1909

7 *(below)* Tuckton Football Club, 1
an old photograph reproduced in
Christchurch Times, 3 September 1
Alexander Sirnis stands in the back
fourth from the right.

(right) Gertrude, Alexander and
[...]ed, aged 7, Christmas 1909

(below) Melita and Alexander Sirnis,
[...]os, 10 June 1915

(*opposite, top left*) Theodore Rothstein,
20

(*opposite, top right*) Jacob Miller in
cow, 1930s

(*opposite, below*) Take Three Spies –
ta, Gertrude and Gerty Stedman Sirnis,
Alfred Brandt, late 1920s

(*above*) Charlie Job, Communist Party
didate, Bexley, 1950 (photograph by
ry Norwood)

(*right*) Hilary Norwood, *c.* 1953

15 *(above)* Joint VOF–BSRP phila▮ exhibition, Moscow, 25–30 June 1976. Hil▮ Norwood sits in the centre.

16 *(left)* 'To Letty – Sonya Salutes You.'▮ card that 'Sonya' sent to Melita Norwc▮ with a copy of her memoirs.

CHAPTER 11

The American Bomb

WHEN Sonya arrived in England in January 1941 the surveillance of subversive movements in Britain by MI5 was carried out by B Division, which was then divided into four sections – B.1., B.4.a., B.4.b. and B.7., and had a total staff of seven. B.4.a., which was responsible for monitoring communists and Trotskyists, consisted solely of Roger Hollis as head, his assistant Miss H. Creedy and Miss W. Ogilvie. Miss Ogilvie had only joined the section, on 27 August 1939. During the war the section also began to monitor pacifists, and in April 1940 recruited a Mr Fulford to specialize in this side of the work.[1] The section known as B.4.b. (originally B.15) dealt specifically with enemy espionage through industry and commerce. It was particularly concerned with the possibility of espionage inside firms who had access to government departments and were either supplying or servicing goods to naval, military, or air establishments and factories engaged on government work. (In certain cases industrial and commercial spying was dealt with by B.1.c., usually because specific technical questions were involved.) Although Nazi Germany was the principal enemy during the Russo-Finnish war (November 1939 to March 1940) the Soviet Union came to be regarded as a major threat. As a result of Comintern instructions that the war should be opposed as a conflict between the imperialist powers, the CPGB found itself the target of much government hostility. A top secret plan was drawn up by Britain's Chiefs of Staff (Operation Pike) to launch a series of air strikes against Soviet oilfields in the Caucasus, and a joint Franco-British expeditionary force was assembled from among men already conscripted for the war against Germany.[2] At the same time a number of high-level espionage cases, linked with members of the USSR trade delegation from their offices in Hatton Garden, came to the fore. One such case, which had come to light in December 1939, was that of Alexsey Alexandrovich Doschenko, Director of engineering of the USSR trade delegation, who had attempted to gain secret information on gun turrets and the position, housing and release of bombs from a worker at an important aircraft factory. The following month Doschenko was deported. At the time of his deportation surveillance activities against members of the Soviet trade delegation were stepped up, causing considerable anxiety for the Soviet Embassy in London. In fact, by March 1940 Soviet espionage activity in British armaments factories after the Doschenko case, and the French raid on the USSR trade delegation in Paris that followed, was almost at a standstill. Information-gathering did continue at Metro-Vickers, where important government work was going on; but effectively Soviet agents had retreated to their embassy, and had closed down their residency.[3] A minute in the Doschenko file gives an indication of the extent of MI5's victory over Soviet espionage in Britain in the early stages of the war:

> Since the case of DOSCHENKO we have had no specific evidence against any members of the Trade Delegation. We know on very reliable evidence that it is common form for certain sections, particularly the Inspectorate, to engage in espionage activities. There are at the moment Russian Inspectors employed in the works of Metro-Vickers where important Government work is going on. They are engaged in taking delivery of Russian orders, but in the ordinary course of their work can and doubtless do pick up a certain amount of confidential information. As long as they are inside the factory it is impossible to control them. ...
>
> As regards the suggestion to raid the offices of the Trade Delegation, it seems doubtful whether at this stage any useful results would be obtained. It is known that owing to French action and to the Doschenko case, considerable anxiety prevails in Soviet circles here and it is almost certain therefore that any compromising documents have by now been housed in the Embassy.[4]

Given the uneasy stand-off between the Russian embassy and the British security services during the 'phoney' and Russo-Finnish wars, when the loyalty of British communists was in doubt, Moscow erred on the side of caution and all contact with Britain's spies, including Melita Norwood, was effectively stopped in March 1940. At the same time British counter-espionage was beefed up, and in August 1940, as a result of deepening suspicions about the loyalty of the Communist Party, section B.4.a. was expanded to seven members and the surveillance of Communist Party officials stepped up.

For over a year Melita Norwood enjoyed the routine of day-to-day war-time life in Cheshunt, Hertfordshire, where her husband, Hilary, worked as head of science at Cheshunt Modern School. They had moved there in March 1938 and had been fortunate on the outbreak of war to have the British Non-Ferrous Metals Research Association conveniently evacuated to the nearby Cooper Institute at Berkhamsted, close to G. L. Bailey's home in Boxmoor in Hertforshire. The Norwoods enjoyed suburban life, and played a full part in their local community, with Hilary, despite the Communist Party's opposition to the war (which according to Melita Norwood he privately disagreed with), volunteering his services as an air raid warden.[5] This was a position he obviously enjoyed:

> So I went along and was told what to do, and was told to get together several groups of three people at the school and pass on what I had been taught. I was also told that if you could organise a street party and provide yourself with equipment, well – why not? You would be protecting your own homes. So I trained a group of teachers and a group of school cleaners. And I went along my street, Carleton Road, and quickly found three people. We asked our landlord to provide the equipment to enable us to defend her property, and she paid for a stirrup pump, with which we practised.[6]

He made no secret of his Communist Party membership, and began coaching the local Air Training Corps (no. 1155, Cheshunt Squadron) in athletics.[7] Despite MI5 and the government's antipathy towards communism individual communists were not subject to public hostility. In fact, in the eight months since the announcement of the Nazi–Soviet pact in August 1939 and March 1940 Communist Party membership had risen from 18,000 to nearly 20,000; and in January 1940 the daily readership of the *Daily Worker* was 15,000 higher than it had been in January 1939, possibly because of the Communist Party's opposition to the war. Hilary Norwood's Communist Party membership did not adversely affect his standing in Cheshunt and, by all accounts, he was a popular teacher, despite his attempts to introduce his pupils to the dubious pleasures of double-digging as part of the government's 'Dig for Victory' campaign:

> I recruited them for three hours work digging on my allotment at the adult rate of 10d an hour, which gave them half-a-crown each for a morning's work. They started off alright, but after a while they started fooling around and I really began to get rather cross. Perhaps I did it the wrong way, and it didn't work. In the end it got rather ridiculous so I gave them their half-a-crowns and sent them packing.[8]

His position in the local community was further enhanced when he became a Gas Identification Officer and Incident Officer for the District. It was considered such an important position that a uniformed woman Army auxiliary would call on him each week and drive him to lectures. 'We had some interesting lectures, and one of the most useful I ever heard was by a physics teacher, Dr S. Gallin. It would have been wonderful for the public, but they were never given the information he gave us as a physicist. If you are out of doors when gas is around, where is the safest place? Many people thought that an open space was best, so that in a town you should stand in the middle of a crossroads. In fact it is the most dangerous, for wherever the gas is and whichever way the wind is blowing, you'll get some. The safest place is a narrow street; find the direction of the wind and go over to a wall on the lee side – but don't stand up against it, because such gas as does come over the wall will curve down and come up again. Your safest place is about half the height of the wall in front of it. All that sort of detail – and the public were never given this advice.'[9] Part of his training also included direct contact with gases in order to recognise them:

> There was a nerve gas we were supposed to take. When you first got a whiff of it, it didn't seem to affect you at all. Then very suddenly you'd feel the nose pinch with pain, the eyes would stream and you'd become pretty helpless. We were to go into a chamber and have this released; as soon as we felt the effects we were to put our gas masks on and get out, and we'd be alright. But this gas had after-effects, including severe depression; it had been known for people to commit suicide after quite a mild exposure. So we were told the week before we were to have this test to go home in pairs. There was an

antidote, we were told, which worked better for some people than others – alcohol. So, if we could find a pub that had got any spirits and have a stiff drink on the way home, so much the better. But on the day we were to have tried this gas the stuff hadn't arrived, so we never had this interesting test.[10]

When Sonya arrived in England in January 1941 the Norwoods were the epitome of bourgeois respectability, doing their bit for the war effort. Melita's return to spying in such circumstances was not difficult. When Sonya met Melita later that month they genuinely liked one another, partly because of the friendship between Letty's mother and the Kuczynski parents, but also because the two women trusted one another. This would prove invaluable later in the year, when Britain's atomic bomb project got underway and BN-FMRA acted in an advisory capacity to the Tube Alloys project, codename for the bomb.

Ever since H. G. Wells had forecast the release of nuclear energy in his book *The World Set Free*, the popular imagination had been haunted by the spectre of a weapon of mass destruction. Only five months before the outbreak of war readers of the *Sunday Express* had been frightened by rumours of a bomb with unimaginable destructive powers that recalled Orson Welles's American broadcast version of H. G. Wells's novel *The War of the Worlds* in October 1938:

Scientists Make an Amazing Discovery
Stumble on a Power 'Too Great To Trust Humanity With'
A Whole Country Might Be Wiped Out in One Second[11]

The *Express* correspondent claimed that 'a new way of producing energy in inconceivable quantities by splitting the atom of a rare metal, called uranium' was being investigated in 'the laboratories of Britain and certain other countries'. The *Sunday Express* claimed a scoop: 'This was the first news of it being published. ... It reads like H. G. Wells, but it is strictly authentic.'[12] The feasibility of an atomic bomb had been discussed in Britain as early as 1933, when the Hungarian physicist Leo Szilard, who had left Nazi Germany for Britain that year, gave an indication of exactly what might be the end result of nuclear fission. He was unaware that a chain reaction was possible in uranium but, nevertheless, remained 'sufficiently worried by the prospect of a nuclear chain reaction to take out a British patent in order to restrict the use that might be made of his idea.'[13] Szilard from the start had wanted to keep his research on nuclear fission secret, and had initially enjoyed some success. However, a paper published on 22 April 1939 by French scientists in the American scientific journal *Nature* had shown that neutrons were liberated when a uranium nucleus fissioned. The number of neutrons that had been emitted per fission was 3.5, making possible a chain reaction. One week later the alarmist report on the possibility of a nuclear bomb appeared in the *Sunday Express*, and on 3 May 1939 the British government produced a secret document on 'The Possibility of Producing an Atomic Bomb. A Review of the Position.'

An influential figure at the time impressing upon the government the possibility of an atomic bomb was Professor G. P. Thompson of Imperial College, London. He stressed the importance of preventing Germany obtaining access to the uranium held by the Union Minière company in Belgium.[14] This was seen to be particularly urgent, given that in March 1939 a German embargo had been placed on the sale of uranium from the Joachimsthal mines in the Sudetenland. The government paper on 'The Possibility of Producing an Atomic Bomb', while expressing incredulity on the prospect of such a weapon, was influenced by the fear that German physicists were working on a similar device. The 'issues at stake', it concluded, 'are too enormous to permit of a complacent attitude and even if there was a remote chance of bringing it off, the situation ought to be most closely watched and the present experiments given every encouragement. ... this country must keep in the forefront of the work and give it high priority.'[15] The project, it was felt, faced two major difficulties. First the critical size of the amount of pure uranium needed in order to set off a chain reaction, which physicists agreed 'might have to be one or more tons and not 1 lb. as depicted in the *Sunday Express*'.[16] Second there remained a lack of detailed knowledge of the fission process. It was unclear whether it was the main mass of the uranium element that reacted with neutrons setting off the detonation process or one of its isotopes present only in a relatively small proportion −uranium (235). If this were so it would be necessary to extract the isotope from the large quantities of Uranium ores which are available in various countries. The major stumbling block to the development of an atomic bomb, therefore, was the separation of the isotope uranium (235) from natural uranium. The breakthrough came in March 1940, when O. R. Frisch and R. Peierls of the University of Birmingham produced a strictly confidential report 'On the Construction of a "Superbomb", Based on a Nuclear Chain Reaction in Uranium'. They reported that:

fission observed with slow neutrons is to be ascribed to the rare isotope U235, and that this isotope has, on the whole, a much greater fission probability than the common isotope U238. Effective methods for the separation of isotopes have been developed recently. Of which the method of thermal diffusion is simple enough to permit separation on a fairly large scale.

This permits, in principle, the use of nearly pure U235 in such a bomb, a possibility which apparently has not so far been seriously considered. We have discussed this possibility and come to the conclusion that a moderate amount of U235 would indeed constitute an extremely efficient explosive.[17]

As a result of this memorandum the British government set up the Maud Committee to explore the possibility of manufacturing an atomic bomb. This committee completed its confidential report on 2 July 1941, and in its summary gave notice of a decision to 'make bombs to be dropped from the air which will produce explosions by the release of nuclear energy'. It was also agreed to pursue 'scientific methods of obtaining the sources of such nuclear energy, on an industrial scale ... with the support (on the industrial side) of Messrs. Imperial Chemical Industries Limited'.[18] The report also commented on the nature and extent of American involvement, which up until this point had been concerned with power generation:

We are informed that while the Americans are working on the uranium problem the bulk of their effort has been directed to the production of energy ... as a source of power, rather than to the production of a bomb. We are in fact co-operating with the United States to the extent of exchanging information, and they have undertaken one or two pieces of laboratory work for us. We feel that it is important and desirable that development work should proceed on both sides of the Atlantic.[19]

The decision to go ahead with the atomic bomb project was completed on 2 July, ten days after the German invasion of the Soviet Union on the 22 June 1941. Following that attack Winston Churchill had publicly promised Britain's full support for the Soviet Union; this, however, did not extend to inclusion in the atomic bomb project. On the contrary, such a shift in policy called forth a comparable shift within the security services that placed the Soviet ally on an equal footing with Nazi Germany. On 4 July MI5's B Division became F Division and broadened its scope to include Soviet intelligence activity in Britain. Roger Hollis found himself propelled to its helm, while his old department, B.4.a., was broken up into four separate sections: F.2.a., monitoring the CPGB; F.2.b., keeping an eye on the Comintern; F.2.c., countering Soviet espionage; and F-MA, preventing communist penetration of the armed forces. At the same time B.1, which dealt with industrial espionage, became F.1. Fulford's role in monitoring pacifists was upgraded, and a separate section was set up to deal with anti-war protestors.[20] Having tightened security, or so it was believed, Churchill now consented to further Anglo-US collaboration in the field of nuclear research, although at the time the US was not a wartime ally. Less than two months later information on the joint Anglo-American bomb project was landing on the desk of Lavrenti Beria, the head of the newly formed NKGB.

In September 1941 John Cairncross, the 'Fifth Man' among the Cambridge University spies recruited by Arnold Deutsch from the Lawn Road flats, began passing information to the Soviets on Anglo-American discussions to build an atomic bomb. The information was quite detailed and was evidently drawn from one of the meetings that the Defence Services Panel of the Cabinet Scientific Advisory Committee had held to discuss the Maud Committee's report. The information was passed through Anatoli Gorski (codename Vadim), the NKVD resident in London, who on 25 September 1941 transmitted to Moscow information to the effect that a uranium bomb could be developed within two years, and a fusing mechanism for the bomb could be designed within several months. That Cairncross was the source of this information seems pretty certain. In 1941 he was private secretary to Lord Hankey, Minister without Portfolio in the War Cabinet and chairman of the Cabinet Scientific Advisory Committee. Lord Hankey chaired the Defence Services Panel that had reviewed the work of the Maud Committee and would have had access to the material contained in Gorski's two reports.[21]

The Soviets, however, were very slow to respond to this information. This was partly due to the confused situation then prevailing in Moscow. When Cairncross's information arrived at NKVD headquarters at Moscow Centre it was less than a month before the great panic in the middle of October when most of the Soviet government was evacuated to Kuibyshev and thousands fled the city. For this reason it was not until March 1942 that the Soviet leaders responded to the information they were receiving from Britain. Beria, head of the NKVD, sent a memorandum to Stalin and the State Defence Committee recommending that work on the atomic question should be co-ordinated. He recommended that immediate steps be taken to integrate the 'research of all Soviet scientists and research establishments working on the question of the atomic energy of uranium'.[22] He suggested that 'an authoritative Scientific-Consultative body attached to the State Defence Committee' should be created consisting of eminent specialists that could be given access to the intelligence materials on a secret basis so that they could assess that information and respond appropriately.[23] Although this was a step in the right direction the proposal that 'eminent specialists' be granted access to intelligence material on the bomb project would suggest that as far as Beria was aware this information had not already, in some form or another, been made known to them. However, despite the fact that Moscow was in the grip of a panic in mid-October 1941, on 12 October the physicist Professor Piotr Kapitsa and other world-renowned Russian scientists had issued a veiled appeal for Soviet inclusion in the atomic bomb programme as a full member of the Grand Alliance. On 13 October, three months after the CPGB's change of policy and one month after the arrival of the contents of the Maud Committee's report in Moscow, the *Daily Telegraph* published a sympathetic article under the headline 'Soviet Call to World Science'. The article reported on an appeal issued by '20 world-famous Russian scientists' in Moscow on 12 October, which called on the 'scientists of the world to concentrate on discovering new methods of warfare to be used against Germany'. Quoting Kapitsa, the *Telegraph* discussed the possibility of the future development of an atomic bomb by the Allies, although the paper doubted that the bomb could be made soon enough to affect the outcome of the war. The article also referred to previous Soviet involvement in research into atomic science when Kapitsa had worked alongside Lord Rutherford at Cambridge:

A hint of a new explosive was given by Prof. Kapitza, who for many years worked on atomic problems with Lord Rutherford at Cambridge. The Royal Society honoured him by electing him an Honorary Fellow, the first such distinction to be given to a foreigner for 200 years.

'One of the principal weapons of modern warfare are explosives,' said Prof. Kapitza. 'In principle we can foresee another increase of the demolition power of explosives by about 100 per cent.

'New possibilities are also opening in that direction. Thus, for instance, the use of sub-atomic energy. I believe, however, that the chief difficulties in the use of this energy are to-day still so great that the probability of an atomic bomb being used in this war, unless it lasts a very long time, is small.

'It is worth while mentioning, however, that theoretical calculations prove that if the modern powerful bomb which can destroy to-day a whole district is replaced by an atomic bomb, it could really destroy a large capital with a population of several millions.'[24]

The *Telegraph* article, with its reference to 'theoretical calculations', would suggest that either Cairncross's information on the Maud Committee was finding its way through to scientists in Moscow; or they were receiving information from another source. It was quite possible that information on the proposed atomic bomb project in Britain was reaching Moscow from two separate sources, either from Sonya, working 'illegally' through Soviet Military Intelligence (GRU); or from Gorski, the NKVD 'legal' resident in London. In 1941 and 1942 Sonya was now controlling two of Britain's most important spies in the field of science and technology, Melita Norwood and the German-born physicist, Klaus Fuchs, a gifted scientist with degrees in mathematics and physics from the universities of Leipzig and Kiel. Fuchs was a committed communist, a KPD member since 1932, who had once been badly beaten up by student Brownshirts at Kiel University and thrown into the nearby river. On 28 February 1933, the day following the Reichstag fire, a warrant had been issued for his arrest and Fuchs had gone underground before fleeing to Paris and then to Britain.

'I was lucky', Fuchs recalled years later, 'because on the morning after the burning of the Reichstag I left my home very early to catch a train to Berlin for a conference of our student organisation (KPD), and that is the only reason why I escaped arrest. I remember clearly when I opened the newspaper in the train I immediately realized the significance and I knew that the underground struggle had started. I took the badge of the hammer and sickle from my lapel which I had carried until that time.' [25] He was ordered abroad by the KPD, and told to concentrate on his studies in preparation for the new communist Germany that they believed would follow the collapse of the Hitler regime. 'I was sent out by the Party, they said that I must finish my studies because after the revolution in Germany people would be required with technical knowledge to take part in the building up of the Communist Germany.' [26] He arrived in England on 24 September 1933, practically penniless, and was more or less adopted by Professor Neville Mott of the physics department at the University of Bristol, who arranged for him to enrol at the university to work on the electron theory of metals. In October he became Professor Mott's research student and was awarded the degree of PhD in December 1936 for a thesis on 'The Cohesive Forces of Copper and the Elastic Constants of Monovalent Metals'. He then went to the University of Edinburgh, where in 1939 he gained the degree of DSc for his thesis on 'Some Problems of Condensation, Quantum Dynamics and the Stability of the Nuclei'. [27]

On the outbreak of the war Fuchs's hitherto successful scientific career, however, came to an abrupt halt. Although he had been recognized by the tribunal for east Scotland as a refugee from Nazi oppression he was nevertheless interned on 12 May 1940 as part of the general internment of 'enemy aliens' in protected areas. An application for his release was made through the Royal Society, and on 11 January 1941 he was released and 'exempted by the Secretary of State from internment and from special restrictions applicable to enemy aliens'. In May 1941 he was invited by the German scientist Rudolf Peierls to come to the University of Birmingham to carry out research on the theory of the gaseous diffusion process of separating the uranium isotopes. The following month he signed the Official Secrets Act before starting work on Britain's secret atomic bomb project, codenamed Tube Alloys, evaluating the critical size and efficiency of an atomic bomb. Following Germany's invasion of the Soviet Union he contacted the KPD organiser in London, Jurgen Kuczynski, and asked for his help in passing to the Russians information he had learned while working on Tube Alloys. Kuczynski, who counted among his closest friends the Soviet ambassador in London, Ivan Maiski, himself no stranger to atomic espionage, arranged for him to introduce Fuchs to Simon Davidovich Kremer, a GRU officer at the London residency.[28] Kremer and Fuchs, however, could not get on, and in the summer of 1942 Fuchs was passed to Sonya, who since September 1941 had been receiving information from Melita Norwood on the behaviour of uranium – referred to in BN-FMRA as the 'X' metal – at high temperatures. The information provided by both Fuchs and Melita Norwood was important enough to keep the GRU abreast of research into atomic bomb design and the metallurgy of uranium, at a time when Stalin and the NKVD doubted the feasibility of a bomb.

Melita Norwood's contribution was particularly significant on two accounts. Not only did she have access to BN-FMRA documents but also she had access to documents from other leading industrial bodies linked with the Tube Alloys project, including Metro-Vickers and ICI, both of whom were associate members of the BN-FMRA. In the autumn of 1941, when the Tube Alloys project was in its infancy, Metro-Vickers had been given a contract for the design of a twenty-stage machine for isotope separation, and ICI had received a contract for the production of uranium hexafluoride. The production of uranium hexafluoride (UF 6) by ICI was essential to the Tube Alloys project as the separation of the isotope U(235) in any quantity – the production of 1 kg per day of U(235) involved the manufacture of between 450 and 650 kg per day of UF 6 – would mean production on a commercial scale. The process adopted by ICI was the one that had been used for the preparation of 3 kg of UF 6 for the Ministry of Aircraft Production (MAP) involving the direct reaction between fluorine and metallic uranium.[29] Despite production of U(235) being moved to the United States in July 1943, research being undertaken by BN-FMRA and ICI between 1941 and 1943, particularly on the corrosive nature of the fluoride gas on uranium metal, the secret reports on which Melita had access to, proved of immense value to Soviet scientists in their attempts to keep abreast of developments in Britain and the United States.

In the second half of 1943, however, this valuable source of information stopped when Melita left BN-FMRA to give birth to her daughter. Before leaving she asked her boss, G. L. Bailey, to donate the money collected for her to Mrs Churchill's Aid Russia Fund. After the birth of her daughter, Anita, she returned to work in 1944. G. L. Bailey, who had recently been appointed Director of BN-FMRA, called on her personally and insisted that she return to work as his secretary, agreeing to be flexible about her hours of work. The scientific and technical language of the BN-FMRA was apparently proving beyond the two secretaries employed in her absence. As Melita later explained, 'I was asked to return to work because I knew the ropes.' Her return to work could not have come at a more propitious time. As Director of the BN-FMRA, G. L. Bailey also sat on the advisory committee of the Tube Alloys project. He often held meetings in his house, where he kept the committee's papers in his personal safe. Melita would often stay overnight at his house in order to complete important work on the Tube Alloys project, and had access to his safe.

When Melita left BN-FMRA at the end of 1943 to have her baby Sonya's other atomic spy, Klaus Fuchs, who was by now a British citizen, was preparing to leave for the United States as part of the British team chosen to work on the Manhattan project, the American codename for the bomb programme. Cooperation between Britain and the US in this field had always been fraught with difficulty and had reflected concerns over security, both commercial and military. In the early stages of the war Britain had dominated this research and had hoped to maintain her advantage. The formation of the Maud Committee in June 1940 to co-ordinate all aspects of the physics and chemistry involved in the creation of a nuclear weapon had been intended to make Britain's lead in this field permanent. Under the chairmanship of G. P. Thomson the Maud Committee, working closely with the head of ICI, Lord Melchett, had intended to secure a monopoly of nuclear power production after the war. This scheme had run into difficulties early on in the project when committee members had accepted that at some stage research would need to be transferred either to the United States or to Canada. The huge amount of capital required, the vast technological resources needed and the danger of enemy bombing all militated against the building of a nuclear reactor in Britain, although at one point north Wales was seriously considered as a safe location. In October 1941 it was agreed by a majority of the Maud Committee that the world's first nuclear production plant should be built in the United States, not the UK. Lord Melchett raised objections about the valuable skills that would be lost if all research was allowed to migrate to America and argued that steps should be taken to safeguard British interests:

> If it be decided that the large scale development should take place in the United States or Canada, we believe that ICI in collaboration with nuclear physicists in this country should continue to work on the problem so as to be ready to exploit any successes in the national interest.
>
> ICI would hope to be able to influence DuPont ... in such a way that the future interests of the British Empire in this new source of power are safeguarded.[30]

Research into nuclear weapons, however, was developing at a faster pace in the USA than in the UK. In 1941 two American scientists, E. M. McMillan and P. H. Abelson, discovered the new radioactive, artificial element 94 by bombarding the isotope U(238) with fast neutrons. They found that 94, which was later named plutonium, was more fissionable than U(235), and offered an alternative route to the bomb without investing heavily in the large-scale separation of isotopes. The American government, however, was slow to realize the importance of McMillan's and Abelson's work, and it was not until 7 December 1941, the day before the attack on Pearl Harbor, that President Roosevelt authorized large-scale funding for research into the electromagnetic separation of isotopes and for reactor materials. Even then the first step towards the construction of an actual pilot plant to test production processes was not taken until the summer of 1942, when Vannevar Bush, director of the Office of Scientific Research Development, convinced the President that such plants should be built.

The second step followed on 17 September, when Brigadier-General Leslie Groves, who had vast experience of construction and project management, was placed in charge of the Manhattan Project. The third step was taken on 2 December in Chicago, when Enrico Fermi, using purified graphite as a moderator in the form of bricks, which he interspersed with sealed cans containing uranium oxide powder and uranium blocks, achieved the world's first controlled, self-sustaining chain reaction. The fourth and final step was taken on 28 December, when President Roosevelt approved the construction of full size reactors, thereby committing the US to the wholesale manufacture of atomic bombs. This decision effectively guaranteed US dominance in the field of nuclear weapons and as a consequence this aspect of US relations with Great Britain, despite America's entry into the war, became strained. There were a number of prickly issues to be resolved, not least the question of future ownership of any post-war nuclear weapons and nuclear power industry. On taking charge of the Manhattan Project Groves had openly expressed US concerns about Wallace Akers, the research director of ICI, and his assistant, Michael Perrin, suggesting that they were playing a powerful dual role in both ICI and Tube Alloys. The question of security was also raised. The US was highly suspicious of Great Britain and feared a leak of nuclear secrets. Roosevelt simply did not share Churchill's enthusiasm for a nuclear partnership. In late 1942, when Churchill again proposed a free exchange of atomic bomb research material, Roosevelt approved only a 'restricted interchange' of information.[31] In part this was caused by conflicting views on who was to be the bomb's main target – Nazi Germany, Japan or Soviet Russia? Within two weeks of taking charge of the Manhattan Project General Groves, while not a politician, claimed that he was quite clear 'that Russia was our enemy and that the project was conducted on that basis'.[32] Almost contemporaneously with these remarks Britain and Russia signed an agreement for the exchange of technical information whereby both countries were to 'furnish to each other specifications, plans, etc. relating to weapons, devices, or processes which at present are, or in future may be, employed by them for the prosecution of the war against the common enemy'.[33] Although under the terms of the agreement signed on 29 September 1942 there was a get-out clause allowing either country to withhold specific information as long as good cause was given, Henry Stimson, the US Secretary of War, argued that the agreement had created a 'very serious situation; sharing information with Great Britain could well mean that the Soviets would have access to American secrets'.[34]

Roosevelt was thus cautious when Churchill again proposed in June 1943 that 'exchange of information on Tube Alloys should be resumed'. This situation, however, soon changed under the exigencies of war and a secret Agreement Relating to Atomic Energy was signed by Roosevelt and Churchill at Quebec on 19 August 1943. Under the terms of this both countries agreed not to 'communicate any information about Tube Alloys to third parties except by mutual consent'. This would have important implications for security. Not only did the Quebec agreement lead to the inclusion of Fuchs in the Manhattan Project but it also led to the involvement of Canada through the newly created Combined Policy Committee (CPC) in the atomic bomb project. Canada was to prove important for a number of reasons. Apart from the vast deposits of uranium at Great Bear Lake, the uranium refining plant at Port Hope, Ontario and the nuclear laboratory at Montreal, the first reactor outside the United States would be built in Ontario, at Chalk River. Chalk River was the experimental tool around which Britain's post-war nuclear work grew – 'pursued partly in the hope of producing a second string to the nuclear bow in the form of plutonium'.[35] Because of this Chalk River became a key target for Soviet agents seeking nuclear secrets.

Before Fuchs sailed for America in December 1943, he passed critical information to Sonya on the gaseous diffusion method of separating the uranium isotope U(235), as well as the mathematical methods being deployed for evaluating the critical size and efficiency of an atomic bomb. He also reported that similar work was being done in the USA and that there was collaboration between the two countries. She gave him 'explicit instructions' concerning Harry Gold, his future contact in New York, who would make himself known to Fuchs sometime in February or March 1944. His contact, she told him, would arrive holding a pair of gloves in one hand and a green-covered book in the other, while he was to be carrying a handball. By this time Sonya had come under suspicion following the arrest of her ex-husband Rolf Hamburger in Iran. The Chief Constable of Oxford, Charles Fox, was instructed by F Division to keep Sonya under close surveillance. Fox reported back that a 'large wireless set' was known to be in her possession 'with a special pole erected for use for the aerial'. However, his suggestion that 'you may think this is worthy of further enquiry' for some inexplicable reason was ignored, and a decision taken that 'no further action' should follow. This was an error of some magnitude. As 1943 drew to a close both Melita Norwood and Klaus Fuchs were taken away from the Kuczynski circle, but the damage had already been done. The information they had supplied to Sonya on Britain's atomic bomb programme had found a direct route to the scientific director of the Soviet nuclear project, Igor Kurchatov. It was invaluable material, and the following year the NKGB issued instructions to its residencies in Britain and the United States that all information on atomic research must come direct to them. The GRU had been forced to give way to its more powerful 'neighbour'.[36]

CHAPTER 12

Hiroshima and Nagasaki

T HERE can be little doubt that the GRU had regarded Sonya's partnership with Melita Norwood as critical, enabling them to secure vital information on the metallurgy of uranium and nuclear reactor design. When Melita was first exposed by Vasili Mitrokhin and Christopher Andrew in 1999 some doubt was raised by commentators as to her actual significance as a spy. Some questioned whether the GRU would have put such an important spy as Sonya at risk by allowing her to work with an agent of such little significance as Melita Norwood. The notes taken from Melita Norwood's file by Mitrokhin are also cautious on this point. They 'record that she was controlled from 1941 to 1944 by an unidentified "head agent" codenamed FIR. The fact that FIR was also "involved in the Klaus Fuchs case" and was questioned after the war by MI5 strongly suggest, but do not quite prove, that FIR was the Centre's codename for SONYA of the GRU.'[1] Sonya's address, The Firs, Oxford, would suggest that FIR was indeed Sonya. This has been more or less verified by the Russians in an official history of the GRU published in 2004, which states that Letty 'began passing information on the Tube Alloys project to her controller ("*veroyatno, eto bila Ursula Kuchinski*" (probably, this was Ursula Kuzcinski)) from September 1941'. (*Veroyatno* can be taken as GRU-speak for *nesomnenno*, which translates as 'undoubtedly'.)[2] That Melita was crucial to the development of the Soviet atomic project from 1941 onwards is also suggested by the steps taken to shelter her from detection.

Hitherto, it has been thought that when in 1944 Melita was moved from Sonya's control back to the Centre it was solely because of the fierce rivalry between the GRU and the NKVD. Beria, the head of the NKVD, had only recently been told by Stalin to gather all his atomic agents under one roof. However, the GRU's official history points to an agreement between Moscow Centre and the GRU regarding Sonya. Both were concerned at this time that she had been compromised following the arrest of her first husband Rolf Hamburger by the Americans in Iran in April 1943. The Americans had informed the British that Hamburger had been actively engaged in espionage and sabotage. 'On two occasions', they said, 'he was known to have bought information on railway and military installations – principally British – in Persia.'[3] During his interrogation Hamburger had maintained that he was not working against the Allies but was merely collecting information for his 'Group', the particulars of which he resolutely refused to disclose. The Russians were undoubtedly worried by Hamburger's arrest and quickly came forward to claim him as one of their own, demanding that the Americans hand him over to them. Hamburger, too, informed the Americans that he had been a professional agent working with the Russians for some time, and would continue doing so. He said his interest in the Persian railway system was to discover if the Allies were really doing their best to send supplies to Russia (at that time Iran was seen as an alternative route to the Arctic Convoy). Although Hamburger knew nothing about Sonya's British operations he knew enough about her role as a spy in Switzerland to compromise her under interrogation. In 1943 Sonya was undoubtedly one of the Soviet Union's leading female controllers at the height of her career. She would not have been asked to handle Melita if Melita's's information was of only minor importance; similarly Fuchs would not have been endangered by allowing Sonya to handle a minor spy. Once Moscow Centre believed it necessary to move Sonya's two most important agents, Klaus Fuchs and Melita Norwood, to a more secure environment, the GRU had no alternative but to concur.

In February 1944 Klaus Fuchs was transferred to Anatoli Yakovlev of the NKGB. He was then working on the calculations for the gaseous diffusion plant under construction at Oak Ridge, Tennessee for the production of fissionable uranium. He was asked to develop a theory of control, especially the mathematical hydrodynamics explaining the flow of uranium hexafluoride through metal barriers made of sintered nickel powder – a key element in the diffusion process.[4] This caused specific problems, as uranium hexafluoride has a corrosive effect on uranium metal. To find a solution to this problem British scientists turned to the BN-FMRA, which had been working on the development of a theory of corrosion for uranium metal since 1941. In March 1945 BN-FMRA was officially co-opted on to the Tube Alloys project, and from this moment the NKGB file on

Melita Norwood describes her as supplying 'many valuable materials on the top secret Tube Alloys project to build the first atomic bomb'.[5] According to the *Mitrokhin Archive* she would remove the Tube Alloy files from her boss's safe, photograph their contents and pass the photographs to her NKGB controller, who warned her not to tell her husband about her atomic espionage. As Bailey's secretary she had ample opportunity to make copies of documents:

> Sometimes, if I was typing something, I typed an extra copy. I passed on copies by arrangement, left them somewhere or met somebody, not a regular weekly, monthly thing. I didn't know them, names or anything, didn't spend time chatting with them. Papers were sent to Committee members from various firms, they weren't marked secret. It never seemed like pressure when I was gathering information; it wasn't a major part of my life. What with the washing, shopping and the kid I had other things to worry about. I was very conservative in my habits. Sometimes I stayed with friends of the Baileys further up the road who worked at the Coopers jam factory. Various committees had been set up to study various aspects of corrosion. Copies of the Reports were produced after Committee meetings, typed and duplicated, with spares to go to committee members and staff. Sometimes, if I was typing something I would type an extra copy. I made a carbon copy. I would have photographed a bit of stuff.[6]

In August 1945 Fuchs was transferred to the newly built bomb assembly and design laboratory at Los Alamos, New Mexico, a secret town protected by barbed wire fences and guards situated on a 7,000-foot mesa in the Jemez Mountains north of Santa Fe. The location provided breathtaking views of the surrounding mountains and desert and had been chosen for its remoteness and security.[7] It was at Los Alamos that Fuchs first came to realize the full nature and magnitude of the American atomic energy programme and the importance of plutonium as an alternative to U(235). He wrote a report summarizing the problems involved in making an atomic bomb, including a statement of the special difficulties that would have to be overcome in the production of a plutonium bomb, which he passed to the Soviets. His report drew attention to the high spontaneous fission rate of plutonium, and the deduction that a plutonium bomb would have to be detonated by using the implosion method rather than the relatively simple gun method, which could be used with U(235). Fuchs's theoretical knowledge of the implosion device for a plutonium bomb and his earlier work on gaseous diffusion completely transformed the work of the bomb group working alongside the Russian scientist in charge of the Soviet bomb project, Igor Kurchatov. Fuchs was informative when it came to the explosive design of the American bomb, while the technical problems encountered by Russian scientists working on the construction of a nuclear pile remained outside his area of expertise. There were considerable gaps in their knowledge in two important areas. First, they knew very little about the creep properties of uranium and had yet to develop a fully coherent theory of corrosion of non-ferrous metals critical to the design of a nuclear reactor. Without a solution to those problems Fuchs's theoretical knowledge of the bomb had no practical application.

In America work on creep and corrosion of non-ferrous metals was then being carried out at the University of Chicago and the Massachusetts Institute of Technology. In Britain similar work was being undertaken by the BN-FMRA. American and British scientists did not co-ordinate their research in this area for the very simple reason that by 1944 Britain had begun to accept the need to move towards an independent British atomic energy and atomic bomb programme. The BN-FMRA was, therefore, at the forefront of British research into the atomic bomb. The results of their experiments were finding their way to Moscow courtesy of Melita Norwood, and would advance the Soviet atomic bomb programme by several years.

MI5's own assessment of the damage caused by Melita's spying activities, published in June 2000 by the Intelligence and Security Committee (ISC), while reluctant to admit that Melita Norwood had been an invaluable Soviet spy, was clear on two points. First, that 'elements' of 'BN-FMRA's classified work was related to fuel performance (e.g. spectrographic analysis of uranium) and post-irradiation corrosion resistance'. And second, that the main research was connected with the choice of fuel cladding, otherwise known as 'canning'.[8] Combating post-irradiation corrosion resistance, however, was not as straightforward as the ISC would have us believe. The canning process (the development of a metal sleeve to encase the uranium fuel) was essentially a protective sheath to protect uranium from water corrosion, to keep fission products out of the water, to transmit heat from the uranium to the water and to prevent absorption of too many neutrons. The ISC's report was misleading on a number of points in respect of canning. The argument that the Soviet scientists adopted the US method of using aluminium jackets to seal the fuel rods in their reactors fails to mention that British scientists, advised by BN-FMRA, also used aluminium jackets.[9] Those scientists in Britain who worked on this problem at the BN-FMRA had all been required to sign the Official Secrets Act. All the support staff, including Melita Norwood, were also required to sign the Act. The Department of Scientific and Industrial Research, which controlled the Tube Alloys project, could not have been clearer on this point. Prior to the BN-FMRA securing a contract on the Tube Alloys project a letter from the Director of the Tube Alloys project to G. L. Bailey, stamped SECRET, stressed the importance of information being shared solely on a 'need to know' basis.

> The investigation is secret and full precautions will be taken to ensure that no unauthorized person obtains information about its nature or results. Authorized persons will be yourself, such other employees of the Association as this Department may approve and such persons as the Secretary of the Department or the Director of Tube Alloys may authorize from time to time ... Every such person, having been approved by the Department, will be warned of the secret nature of the work and that the provisions of the Official Secrets Acts apply thereto.[10]

In his reply Bailey stated that 'such clerical staff and others as have access to confidential matter have been required to sign a statement to the effect that they have read certain extracts from the Official Secrets Acts. The extracts are the obvious ones which matter and frankly I feel nothing but harm could be done by making them read all three Official Secrets Acts in full. I am sure that reading the Acts in full (as I have myself done once) would result in a state of complete confusion.'[11] In March 1945 Melita was asked to read the relevant extracts and to sign the required statement of the Official Secrets Act before being allowed to continue accessing secret information from the investigations being conducted by the BN-FMRA for the Tube Alloys project.

At this time the Americans were pursuing both the plutonium and U(235) routes to the atomic bomb. A huge gaseous diffusion plant had been built at Oak Ridge and was producing U(235), while two pairs of chemical separation plants had been constructed at Hanford, Washington to separate plutonium from the irradiated uranium. Despite the fact that British scientists were employed on the US atomic bomb project, Britain was not party to American technological knowledge, particularly in the area of canning, which was regarded by American scientists as 'the last major problem to be solved on the Hanford project'.[12] Between March 1945, the month that BN-FMRA secured its contract with Tube Alloys, and the atom bomb attack on Hiroshima on August 6, Britain's contribution to the Manhattan project had been essentially limited to work on the diffusion process and the implosion method for assembling a plutonium bomb. The problem of canning was barely touched upon. At the time of the atomic bomb attack on Hiroshima the experiments being undertaken at the BN-FMRA anticipated Britain's own nuclear programme, not that of the Americans. Churchill had in fact notified Roosevelt six months earlier that Britain intended to build its own nuclear weapon.[13] Although the new British Prime Minister, Clement Attlee, had consented to the nuclear bombing of Japan, American cooperation on technical matters had already been withdrawn. Both Roosevelt and Harry Truman, President since April 1945, were well aware that Britain coveted an atomic bomb not as a deterrent but as a symbol of world power. Hiroshima highlighted the one-sided nature of the 'special relationship' and demonstrated America's willingness to use the bomb.

The explosive yield of the bomb dropped on Hiroshima was equivalent to about 13 kilotons of TNT. The destruction was frightening; virtually everything within a radius of 500 metres of the explosion was incinerated. 'Buildings as far as 3 kilometers away were set ablaze. A thick cloud of smoke mushroomed into the sky to a height of 12,000 meters. Death was instantaneous for some; for others it was much slower. By the end of the year 145,000 people are estimated to have died from the effects of that one bomb; five years later the number of deaths resulting from the bomb had reached 200,000.'[14] Three days later the United States exploded a plutonium bomb over Nagasaki. In this instance the explosive yield was the equivalent of 21 kilotons of TNT and by the end of the year over

70,000 people had died from that one bomb. In Moscow people's spirits plummeted. 'It was clearly realized', Alexander Werth, *Sunday Times* correspondent in Moscow from 1941 to 1948, wrote, 'that this was a New Fact in the world's power politics, that the bomb constituted a threat to Russia, and some Russian pessimists I talked to that day dismally remarked that Russia's desperately hard victory over Germany was now "as good as wasted".'[15] An independent Soviet atomic bomb programme became an overwhelming priority.

CHAPTER 13

Proliferation

A T 8 p.m. on 5 September 1945 Igor Gouzenko, principal cipher clerk to Colonel Nikolai Zabotin, the military attaché at the Soviet embassy in Ottawa, Canada, defected. Over the previous few weeks he had removed from the embassy a number of documents marked 'Top secret. Burn after reading'. In total there were more than a hundred carefully selected secret documents detailing a vast Soviet network operating in the United States and Canada, among them a member of the British high commissioner's staff, Kathleen Wilsher, codenamed 'Ellie'. The British high commissioner, Malcolm MacDonald, was informed of the case and it was decided that Ellie should be placed under observation. MacDonald then agreed to serve on a small informal committee made up of Canadian intelligence officers, the Canadian Prime Minister, Mackenzie King, and the Canadian Permanent Secretary for External Affairs, Norman Robertson, to investigate the extent of Soviet espionage in Canada. MacDonald's membership of this committee was regarded as essential, since Mackenzie King 'wished to share all the secrets with his colleagues in London'.[1]

As more and more of the Gouzenko material was translated it became clear that the reach of the Soviet spy networks in the US and Canada was bigger than had first been anticipated and included the Canadian National Research Council. Within the first few days of Gouzenko's defection four agents working for the council were exposed as spies. These were Durnford Smith, E. W. Mazerall, Dr Raymond Boyer and a fourth agent identified only by his codename 'Alek', known to be closely associated with the manufacture of the atomic bomb. There was also a fifth man, Israel Halperin, whose level of involvement remained hidden. The identity of Alek, however, was discovered after a telegram from Nikolai Zabotin to Moscow Centre was intercepted, revealing that Alek would soon be taking up an appointment as a lecturer at the University of London:

Alek will work in King's College, Strand. It will be possible to find him there through the telephone book. Meetings: October 7, 17 and 27 on the street in front of the British Museum. The time, 11 o'clock in the evening ... At the beginning of September he must fly to London.[2]

Further investigations by the Canadians revealed that Alek was Dr Allan Nunn May, a British nuclear physicist and a known communist sympathizer. Nunn May's involvement with Russian spies in England had a long history. His Austrian-born wife, Dr Hildegarde Broda, was the sister of Engelbert Broda, a nuclear physicist working in the Cavendish Laboratories at the University of Cambridge, and the lover of Edith Tudor-Hart. Both Brodas were members of the Austrian Communist Party and were known to the British security services. MI5 kept a detailed file on Engelbert Broda, and knew of his relationship with Edith Tudor-Hart, one of the Lawn Road Flats inner circle and the supplier of photographic material to the Woolwich Arsenal spies. Until 1943 Nunn May had been controlled by Sonya.

In January 1945 Nunn May had been invited to Canada as part of the Anglo-Canadian research team working under Professor Cockroft, director of the Atomic Energy Research Council in Montreal. Some months later he was contacted by Lieutenant Pavel Angelov of the Soviet military attaché's office, who recruited him to 'the net', as the Russian espionage system in Canada was then known. According to Gouzenko's testimony Alek knew all there was to know about atomic weapons research in Canada and America and had handed a sample of U-(235) to Lieutenant Angelov in Nikolai Zabotin's office. Zabotin had considered these samples so important that he had immediately dispatched them to Moscow.

On 8 September, three days after Gouzenko's defection, Peter Dwyer of MI6 and Roger Hollis of MI5 arrived in Canada to interview Gouzenko. During his interrogation Gouzenko told Hollis of the existence of a Soviet mole in MI5 who had such high-level access inside the intelligence services that his reports were sometimes taken directly to Stalin himself. In his report back to MI5, for some reason, Hollis failed to make any mention of this 'mole', and set out to discredit Gouzenko's information by suggesting that he knew very little about British intelligence.[3] The interrogation itself was brief and Hollis, Gouzenko later recalled, didn't bother to take any notes:

> We were standing. We did not even sit down. It was very short. He just listened. He didn't write one word. Maybe he asked me one or two questions.[4]

On 23 September 1945 Mackenzie King, met with several Canadian and British intelligence officials, including Roger Hollis, to discuss how best to handle Nunn May. The next day Mackenzie King dictated a short account of their meeting:

> The first question discussed was the alternative methods re security. One was to allow everything to be hushed up and not proceeded with further; another was to take action at once and let the British and US Governments know the situation with a view to taking what steps might be taken to prevent further developments. The third was adopting a course which would make the whole thing public, immediate arrests made and getting additional information at trials, etc. ...
>
> My own view was that the second course was the appropriate one, and I found that was the view that appeared to be generally held.[5]

The following week Mackenzie King travelled to Washington for talks with President Truman to discuss 'preventive steps' to put a stop to spying. The British connection was also discussed.

Towards the end of the war the BN-FMRA, anticipating Britain's future independent nuclear programme, had made preparations to move back into its Euston headquarters at 1–6 Reynart Buildings, which had been damaged by enemy bombing in 1940. Partly because of the revenue generated by the Tube Alloys project, and partly as a result of the knowledge that this project was set to continue, the BN-FMRA had purchased the lease of 14–22 Euston Buildings adjacent to Reynart Buildings and adapted three floors of 18–20 Euston Buildings to house the specialist equipment that had been moved out to Berkhamsted during the war.[6] In September 1945 the BN-FMRA was transferred to the Ministry of Supply and was contracted to the ministry's newly created Atomic Energy Department. All existing staff who had worked on Tube Alloys were again asked to sign the Official Secrets Act, including Melita Norwood. As Bailey's secretary, however, given the recent Gouzenko revelations and G. L. Bailey's connections with the Chalk River plant, she was to be interviewed by an MI5 officer. The only employee, in fact, to be interviewed privately:

> When I was vetted by M.I.5 I asked for it to take place in the Director's office at Euston, and he was there. Nice chap he was. I forget what I was asked. I would in any case have denied being a member of the Communist Party. Quite a pleasant interview I recall. I can't remember the exact date ... I had to take a couple of aspirins before the interview ... I knew there was going to be an outside person. It was well-announced. ... It was a friendly interview, but if you want the truth from somebody it is best to be that way.[7]

Melita Norwood was now meeting with her NKGB controller in London on a regular basis. Three sharp blows down the telephone line signalled a meeting for the following day. At these meetings she would be congratulated and informed that the documents she was supplying were of the utmost importance. Moscow Centre took the added precaution of issuing her with an additional codename, TINA. Her position was more precarious than was thought. In 1945 the US Army Security Agency (SIGINT) had begun decrypting some of the wartime messages exchanged between Moscow Centre and its American residencies, and had accidentally stumbled on TINA's existence, although they were unable to discover her identity.[8] According to these decrypts TINA, nearly six weeks after the atomic bomb attacks on Hiroshima and Nagasaki, was known to be supplying vital information on atomic intelligence linked to the Allied atomic bomb programme:

> We agree with your proposal about working with 'TINA'. At the next meeting tell her that her documentary material on 'ENORMOUS [ENORMOZ]' [Atomic Energy Project] is of interest and represents a valuable contribution to the development of the work in this field ... instruct her not to discuss her work with her husband and not to say anything to him about the nature of the documentary material which is being obtained by her.[9]

At the end of the war revelations about the extent of Soviet espionage in the United States, Canada and the United Kingdom were beginning to have a negative effect, and were preventing the three powers from reaching a common policy on the bomb. On 1 October Mackenzie King sailed for Britain to discuss the Anglo-American and Canadian positions on the atomic bomb *vis-à-vis* the United Nations with Clement Attlee. During these discussions the Nunn May affair came up and the two men agreed that the whole business should be hushed up while investigations on both sides of the Atlantic continued. When the British Foreign Secretary, Ernest Bevin, met with Mackenzie King, however, he strongly disagreed, arguing that an arrest or two would serve as a warning to the Russians. Those who wanted the investigations to be allowed to continue were further disappointed when Nunn May, who had been allowed to leave Canada and take up his appointment at the University of London, failed to keep any of his proposed meetings with his Russian controller outside the British Museum. Nor was there any sign of this contact.[10]

In October 1945 Clement Attlee informed parliament that an 'atomic energy research establishment' would be set up at Harwell and at other locations. The real goal, though, was a plutonium bomb and the target date was 1952. Britain's independent nuclear weapons programme was underway. 'An air-cooled research reactor began operating at Harwell under the auspices of the United Kingdom Advisory Committee on Atomic Energy. Plutonium production reactors were constructed at Windscale, and a gaseous diffusion plant to make U(235) was built at Capenhurst in Cheshire. Aldermaston was to be the weapons design centre.'[11]

Secrecy was paramount, and the British parliament was not informed. In fact, the bomb programme was so secret that apart from the scientists involved, only Clement Attlee, Ernest Bevin and perhaps half a dozen members of Attlee's Cabinet Committee on Atomic Energy knew that Britain was building an atomic bomb. There were, of course, others who knew, not least an unassuming housewife from the Home Counties, Melita Norwood, and her Soviet handlers.

On 3 November 1945 Mackenzie King sailed from Southampton for New York and travelled overnight to Washington by train. He arrived at the same time as Attlee, who had flown from London. On the 15th President Truman announced to the world 'that the three government heads had agreed on the need for international action, under the auspices of the

United Nations, for the provision of controls over atomic energy to ensure its use for peaceful purposes only.' 'We agree', he added, 'that there should be full and effective co-operation in the field of atomic energy between the United States, the United Kingdom and Canada.'[12]

The race to build a bomb before international controls were agreed by the UN now became priority for the Soviet Union. On Christmas Day 1945, under conditions of the utmost secrecy, an experimental reactor in the Soviet Union went critical. In January 1946 work was started on the design of a production reactor. On the 24th the United Nations General Assembly adopted a resolution setting up an Atomic Energy Commission to make recommendations on the following four issues. First, the exchange of basic scientific information; second, the control of atomic energy to ensure its use for peaceful purposes; third, the elimination of atomic weapons; and fourth, to put in place 'effective safeguards by way of inspection and other means to protect complying States against the hazards of violations and evasion'. The head of the US delegation, Bernard Baruch, set out the basic American position. This called for the placing of all dangerous activities, which they defined as any activity that offered a solution to 'one of the three major problems of making atomic weapons', under an international agency. Those three major problems were listed as the supply of raw materials, the production in suitable quality and quantity of plutonium and uranium(235) and the use of those materials to make atomic weapons. Safe activities, such as research and the peaceful uses of atomic energy, were to be left under the control of individual states. The American position also called for the punishment of any state that contravened the agreement on international control of 'dangerous activities'. But most controversially the Americans argued that the right of veto possessed by permanent members of the Security Council should not 'protect those who violate their solemn agreements not to develop or use atomic energy for destructive purposes'. This was unacceptable to the Soviets. 'If the veto were removed, as Baruch proposed, the United Nations would have the right to take action against the Soviet Union if it believed the Soviet Union was infringing the ban on nuclear weapons.'[13] Instead the Soviets called for an international convention banning the production, stockpiling and use of atomic weapons and the dismantling of all bombs within three months of the conclusion of this convention. The two sides could not have been further apart. The

Soviet proposal called on the US to ban their bomb but would not agree to the creation of an international agency to guarantee that they themselves were not building a bomb. The US, on the other hand, wanted an international inspection agency put in place to monitor the Soviet Union's nuclear energy programme. Only then would they consider the destruction of their own nuclear arsenal. The United Kingdom, of course, was subject to the same strictures as the Soviet Union, despite Truman's declaration on 15 November that 'full and effective co-operation in the field of atomic energy between the United States, the United Kingdom and Canada', had been agreed. The arrest of Nunn May on 4 March 1946 virtually put an end to all cooperation.

Nunn May was charged on 5 March with having communicated 'information which was calculated to be or might be useful to an enemy' contrary to the Official Secrets Act 1911. He was remanded in custody for a fortnight, and was brought before Bow Street Magistrates Court on 20 March. He pleaded not guilty, and a trial date was set for 1 May. By this time he had changed his plea to guilty and the proceedings were concluded on the same day. In his summing up Mr Justice Oliver was in no doubt that spying was nothing less than treachery. The defence's argument that the Russians should have been included in the Allied atomic bomb research from the outset was not acceptable:

> How any man in your position could have had the crass conceit, let alone the wickedness, to arrogate to himself the decision of a matter of this sort, when you yourself had given your written undertaking not to do it and knew it was one of the country's most precious secrets, when you yourself had drawn and were drawing pay for years to keep your own bargain with your country – that you could have done this, is a dreadful thing.[14]

'The sentence upon you', Mr Justice Oliver concluded, 'is one of ten years' penal servitude.' Sir Wallace Akers, who had been in charge of the Tube Alloys project, was said to be 'flabbergasted' both by the sentence, which he regarded as too severe, and by the general attitude of the judge.[15] In Canada, where a Royal Commission had been set up to investigate the Gouzenko affair in February, the sentence was greeted with a sense of relief. Throughout the trial there were fears that the Royal Commission's inquiry, if leaked, might prejudice proceedings. In fact its deliberations were kept secret until 15 July.[16] In America, on 1 August 1946, the US Congress responded to the passing of the McMahon Act by prohibiting the exchange of nuclear information between America and other countries, encouraging Britain to press ahead with the development of its own atomic bomb programme. Everything was in place. Under Sir John Cockroft, an air-cooled research reactor began operating at Harwell, a virtual military base on the Berkshire Downs, while Canada's nuclear reactor at Chalk River became the experimental tool around which Britain's post-war nuclear work grew, still working towards a target date for a British bomb of 1952.

The British government's desire for the bomb could not have been more urgent. Margaret Gowing, the official historian of Britain's atomic bomb programme, pointed out that the British decision to build an independent nuclear deterrent was taken for a variety of reasons, mainly strategic, but it was also determined by the question of status and the nature of Britain's changed relationship with the United States. It was a strategic deterrent because the only answer to an atomic bomb was the readiness to use one in retaliation, and Britain could not rely on the United States to threaten the use of atomic bombs to serve British interests. Status was involved because 'an atomic bomb would present the world at last with the real possibility of an international police force. Britain and America together might be able to police the world.'[17] A British atomic bomb, therefore, would restore to Britain the power and prestige it had lost with the collapse of empire and guarantee Britain's place at the top table; British scientists with experience of the Manhattan Project were now at a premium.

In the summer of 1946 Klaus Fuchs returned to England to begin work at Harwell, where he had been appointed head of the theoretical physics division. He was a very popular man, said to be 'friendly with the entire staff, including the chief security officer, Henry Arnold, who became his next-door neighbour'. In August 1946 'he gave his first scientific report on the properties of fast reactors, and predicted that all power stations would be using nuclear fuel by the 1980's.'[18] Some months after his arrival in England he attempted to re-establish contact with Jurgen Kuczynski. Jurgen, however, had left Britain in November 1945 and was now living in the American sector of Berlin, where he had taken up a post at Berlin

University. Before leaving, Jurgen had visited Gertrude Sirnis. Why he did so has never been established, but when he left Gertrude gave him her husband's papers, requesting only that he publish an article showing how Alexander Sirnis was the first to translate Lenin into English.[19]

Unable to establish contact with the Kuczynskis, Fuchs then approached a British communist, Angela Pilley, and asked her for the address of the German communist who had first introduced him to Jurgen Kuczynski in London in 1941, Johanna Klopstech. Pilley told him that the British Communist Party would not supply her present address as there was 'nothing doing because they didn't do things that way'. Fuchs, however, was able to obtain the address through Jurgen Kuczynski's wife, Marguerite, who was still living in England.[20] This was a reckless act and Fuchs was lucky not to have been arrested. In 1946 MI5 considered Klopstech 'dangerous', and had included her in a list of twenty-one subversives supplied to the American embassy in London on Boxing Day that year. Nevertheless Fuchs received instructions, via the British Communist Party, to rendezvous with a Russian agent at the Nag's Head, Wood Green: 'FUCHS should enter the public house carrying a copy of the *Tribune* and sit on a certain bench in the saloon bar. His contact would carry a red book.' Further meetings were held at the Nag's Head and at the Spotted Horse, Putney, at two-monthly intervals.[21] If for any reason a rendezvous broke down, Fuchs was to re-establish contact by throwing a copy of the magazine *Men Only* over the wall of 166 Kew Road with a message on the tenth page giving details of an alternative place and date. The message was not to contain any technical information. The address 166 Kew Road was then occupied by Charles John Moody, his wife, Gertrude, and Clara Isaacs. Both Gertrude Moody and Clara Isaacs were already under investigation by MI5 for distributing communist literature to members of the armed forces in 1935, and Charles Moody had been linked with Percy Glading in 1936.[22]

In 1947 Fuchs appeared to be living a charmed life. Three months after the 1946 Canadian Royal Commission on Espionage reported, the security officer at Harwell, Henry Arnold, triggered a new security check on Fuchs that would last for five months when he informed MI5 that one of the staff members was a German who had been naturalized during the war. Thus at the same time that Fuchs was re-establishing contact with the Russians via Marguerite Kuczynski, Johanna Klopstech and 166 Kew Road, he was actively being investigated by MI5. And yet, amazingly, the only piece of information that MI5 could come up with when they investigated Fuchs was an old 1934 Gestapo report detailing his communist activities in pre-war Germany. Hollis, who was in charge of the investigation, went through the MI5 file on Fuchs for the sixth time and once more cleared him for secret work.

In November 1947 the Ministry of Supply asked for Fuchs to be vetted again before his promotion to a permanent civil service post at Harwell. He was again cleared, with disastrous consequences. At this time Fuchs suspected the existence of another atomic spy in Britain who was passing information to the Soviets on nuclear reactor technology. In 1948 the Russians had asked him how the uranium rods in use at Harwell had been fabricated. Following his arrest in 1950 he told his interrogator that he did not give them this information and had expressed his surprise 'that this one specific detail had been asked for while there were no questions about the recovery of uranium from its ore, the preparation of pure uranium compounds or metal, canning techniques, dimensions of uranium rods or the preparation, purity and dimensions of graphite. ... It suggested to him that the Russians were getting information from other sources.'[23] This, of course, was the secret work then being undertaken by researchers at the BN-FMRA, which Melita Norwood copied and passed to the Russians.

An atomic industry in Russia had existed since Christmas Day 1945, when, under conditions of the utmost secrecy, an experimental reactor in the Soviet Union had gone critical. However, in January 1946 early work on the design of a production reactor had run into a number of difficulties, among the most urgent being the problem caused by corrosion. The Soviets' first production reactor was, like the experimental reactor, a uranium-graphite system which had to be cooled when in operation. The decision to use water as the coolant meant that pipes had to be inserted into the reactor to channel the water to where it was needed. In order to separate plutonium for a bomb the uranium fuel had first to be removed from the reactor. It was, therefore, decided to manufacture uranium fuel slugs that would easily pass through the moderator.[24] In order to protect these slugs from corrosion they would have to be sealed in some way against direct contact with the water so it was decided to seal or 'can' them in aluminium jackets. This was difficult. In early 1946 30,000 copies of a

Russian translation of the US Army's *Atomic Energy for Military Purposes* had been published. Although there was no information on the canning process the report identified the 'canning problem' as being 'one of the most difficult'. In order to overcome this problem, at the beginning of 1946 the Russians carried out research in four different institutes on methods of sealing the fuel rods before a solution could be found.[25] Work undertaken by the BN-FMRA for the reactors at Harwell and Chalk River on this precise problem was copied by Melita Norwood and passed to her controller, who forwarded it to Moscow Centre for distribution to these research institutes. But even then difficulties continued. The first Soviet production reactor would be built in the Urals about 80 kilometres north-west of the industrial city of Cheliabinsk. Assembly of the reactor took three months and was completed by the end of May 1948. Now came the time to test the instruments for monitoring the reactor, and the mechanisms for controlling it. At the beginning of June 1948 water was let into the pipes, and the uranium slugs were loaded into the fuel channels. On 7 June the emergency rods were withdrawn and the flow of water into the reactor was stopped. The reactor went critical that evening and reached a power output of 10 kilowatts in the early hours of 8 June. In July the reactor was operating according to the plan for plutonium production.

However, unexpected problems arose. The aluminium canning on the fuel slugs suffered severe corrosion and was replaced by aluminium oxidized in a different way. But more seriously, the fuel slugs swelled up (creep) and wrinkles and lumps developed on the surface of the uranium (pitting), causing the slugs to become stuck in the discharge pipes. The reactor had to be shut down and the uranium taken out and studied, and the plutonium that had been built up extracted.[26] Again, research carried out by the BN-FMRA dealt with these precise problems. When the Tube Alloys project closed at the end of the war and was moved from the Department of Scientific and Industrial Research to the Ministry of Supply, G. L. Bailey had been appointed a full member of the Metals Research Panel at the Directorate of Atomic Energy. From 1946 onwards Bailey was engaged in research on the corrosion and creep properties of aluminium alloys, particularly regarding corrosion resistance to water when the design of a British reactor was still in its early stages, and issued a 'very full and complete report' to the designers of the British plant. At Chalk River

scientists had discovered that the purity of the water was the most important factor affecting corrosion resistance, and Bailey was asked to produce
a statement dealing specifically with water-cooled reactors.[27] He was also
asked for detailed information on oxide 'inclusions' and aluminium alloys
in respect of the canning stage and the problem of embrittlement caused
by reduction of oxides. In short the technological problems experienced
at Cheliabinsk were the same as those experienced by reactor designers in the UK and Canada. Melita Norwood, who had access to research
undertaken by the BN-FMRA into the canning problem (all reports were
stamped SECRET), passed those documents to the Russians. This enabled
Soviet metallurgists and Soviet scientists to develop a theory of corrosion,
solve the dual problems of creep and pitting, successfully overcome the
'canning' problem and test an atomic bomb in 1949. This was three years
before the British test in 1952, and much sooner than the United States had
expected. US and UK intelligence estimates had placed the most probable
date for a Soviet atomic bomb test at mid-1953.

At the end of the Second World War British and American code-break-
ers began sifting through mounds of intercepted Soviet traffic, including
wartime messages to Moscow from the Soviet consulate in New York. By
the summer of 1949 the Soviet code and cipher system had been broken.
In the process a report on the Manhattan Project written by Klaus Fuchs
while he was working at Los Alamos, and later despatched to Moscow
via the diplomatic bag, was unearthed. Other FBI intercepts pointing to
Fuchs's identity were discovered. A scientist whose sister was believed to
have attended an American university, for example, was identified as an
active Soviet agent. Further investigations showed that Fuchs's sister, Kristel Heineman, had attended Swarthmore College in the 1930s and was then
living in Cambridge, Massachusetts. Moreover, the names of Klaus Fuchs
and his sister had both appeared in a notebook taken from a suspected
Canadian atomic spy, Dr Isaac Halperin. At the time of his arrest in September 1945, following the Gouzenko defection, two notebooks containing 436 addresses were seized by officers of the Royal Canadian Mounted
Police (RCMP), of which 163 were to be found in the US, 150 in Canada
and five in Britain, including that of Klaus Fuchs. The RCMP then began
'thorough investigations' into the 150 Canadian names and addresses,
and passed on details of the American and British names to the security

representatives of those countries. At MI5, Hollis, however, chose not to investigate any of the five British names given to him by the RCMP. Not surprisingly, when this came to light in 1950 following Fuchs's arrest, there were heated exchanges between the Canadians and the British. The Canadians were understandably upset at accusations that they had failed to pass on relevant information:

> Canada had 'very carefully investigated' the Canadians whose names were found in the book, an ordinary small 'alphabetically indexed' address book that contained addresses and phone numbers. The owner of the book had been 'interviewed' about them all.
>
> The five United Kingdom names, together with all pertinent information, were given to a British official [Hollis] in Ottawa in 1946. He was allowed to attend hearings of the Royal Commission on Espionage and to look at the wealth of evidence that taxed the capacity of a large room. ...
>
> Surely when we had 150 to investigate, it was Britain's responsibility to investigate the five in their country including Fuchs.[28]

In 1946, unbeknown to Hollis, the FBI had sent their agents to interview Kristel Heineman, and as a result instructions were issued to FBI offices in New York, El Paso, Knoxville and Washington to initiate a thorough investigation of Fuchs. The FBI, of course, had a vested interest in preventing Fuchs working for the British nuclear programme; Hollis did not. Nevertheless, although the information obtained by the FBI was 'sketchy', it was considered important enough to be passed to the British intelligence team in Washington, which at the time included Kim Philby. In 1949 the FBI agent in charge of the investigation, Robert Lamphere, sent a top secret memorandum to the British embassy in Washington, detailing FBI suspicions and drawing attention to the inclusion of Fuchs's name in the Halperin notebook. The memorandum was sent to Sir Stuart Menzies, the head of MI6 in London, who sought advice from a senior MI5 officer, Dick White, and Michael Perrin, principal research assistant to Wallace Akers at ICI, working on Britain's atomic bomb project. On 6 September 1949 Perrin informed Menzies that 'it looks very much as if Fuchs of Harwell is working for the Russians.' Attlee gave Scotland Yard the go-ahead to interrogate Fuchs, with instruction to persuade him to confess to information that had already been gleaned from deciphered Soviet codes. Without his confession the British would not be able to arrest him without letting Moscow know that their codes had been broken.

The noose was beginning to tighten. As a result of the spy Alexander Foote's defection in July 1947 with specific information that he had worked with Ursula Beurton (Sonya) in Switzerland, and that she remained a Russian spy, MI5 decided to interview her at her home in Great Rollright, Oxfordshire. During the interview it became quite clear that Sonya had indeed been working for the Russians for a number of years:

> She made it quite clear from the start of our interview that she did not 'think that she could co-operate' and stated she did not intend to tell lies and therefore preferred not to answer questions. It is fair to say right away that by the stand she took she tacitly admitted that she had worked for Soviet Intelligence. The manner in which she did so was a credit to her earlier training, every possible piece of cajolery, artifice and guile that could be used was employed, without any success whatsoever. She made no denial whatever, sheltering always behind the rock of 'non-cooperation' ... As a result of this interrogation, we regard ourselves as confirmed in our beliefs, and take FOOTE's story to be substantially true.[29]

Incredibly, two days later, on 15 September, and the day before this report was filed, HOWs endorsing letter checks at Sonya's Great Rollright address and at 12 Lawn Road, the former address of her parents and now the address of her sister Barbara, were suspended. So too were letter checks for 62a Belsize Park Gardens, the address of her sister Brigitte, and at Brigitte's former address at the Lawn Road flats. MI5 appeared very reluctant to bring the Kuczynski family to book.[30]

At the beginning of 1948 Alexander Foote had apparently bumped into Brigitte quite by chance in St John's Wood. Not knowing that Foote had defected she told him that MI5 had recently interviewed Sonya and that Sonya had been very upset by this visit and was quite scared. So much so that 'she had been obliged to break off and not go to a most important rendez-vous which she was due to attend the next day.'[31] In May 1950 Foote gave MI5 the details of this meeting and a decision was taken to reinstate the HOW on The Firs, Great Rollright, as a preliminary to questioning both Sonya and Brigitte.[32] The recent arrest of Fuchs, on 2 February 1950, had much to do with their decision. During interrogation Fuchs had refused to identify Sonya as his controller in the UK but had identified Jurgen Kuczynski as his initial contact with the Russians. On 31 February 1950 Fuchs was shown a number of photographs of people suspected of spying for the Russians. When he was shown Sonya's photo he simply shook his head.[33] By this time Sonya was safely out of the country, having fled to Czechoslovakia with her two children and there applying for a military permit to visit her brother in Berlin.

Following the arrest of Fuchs, British intelligence informed the Americans about Jurgen Kuczynski's communist past, and a HOW was set up for his home address in Berlin-Zehlendorf West, Klopstockstrasse 34 (US sector), as well as his place of work, Berlin University, Berlin C.2., Spandauer Strasse 1. In June 1950 British intelligence asked the Americans to make him 'available for questioning'. Somebody tipped him off, and he moved to Berlin-Weissensee in the Russian sector. Sonya visited him there some weeks later and remained in East Berlin. Her husband, Leon Beurton, who had broken his leg in a motoring accident and had stayed behind in Great Rollright, joined her there in July 1950. The Kuczynskis had got away.

MI5 now decided against interviewing Brigitte Lewis or other members of the Kuczynski circle in England for the following good reason: 'If we do interrogate Brigitte Lewis, we are I think bound to disclose that we really know very little about what is going on.'[34] Fuchs, secure in the knowledge that Sonya was safe, on 1 December 1950 identified her to MI5 as his controller:

> In placing this photograph of Ursula Beurton before Fuchs I said to him: 'This is a photograph which I have already shown to you earlier' and he immediately said, 'That is the woman at Banbury.' I went into the matter very carefully with him since I did not want him to be identifying merely a photograph which he had seen before, but his identification was quite positive though he would have expected to find the woman rather more dishevelled than this photograph portrays. In this connection I entirely agree with him, for Beurton had a very untidy mop of hair. [35]

In February 1951 a memo arrived on the desk of Guy Liddell, deputy director-general of MI5, stating that it 'would be of great interest to ascertain the identity of any other contacts of the Kuczynskis and the Beurtons in the UK'.[36] This was discreetly passed to the waste-paper bin. In 1949, when the intelligence services were closing in on the Kuczynskis and Klaus Fuchs, Letty Norwood had been quietly removed from her post as director's secretary at the BN-FMRA. They were on to her, as she knew only too well:

> The Director's [new] secretary was very reliable. I remember asking for a file and it was refused. I knew there was something going on but it wasn't common knowledge in the office. I accepted it. Didn't go into it. I didn't know what it was, wouldn't have understood it. Got on with my work. Had enough work to do. Yes, I asked if I could borrow a file. Can't remember putting it as strongly as that. They might have been using me as bait to find out who I contacted and dah de dah de dah.[37]

On 29 August 1949 the Soviet Union successfully tested an atomic bomb. Sir Henry Tizard, chief scientific adviser to the Ministry of Defence and chairman of the Defence Research Policy Committee, could only believe that the Russians had stolen some plutonium.

CHAPTER 14

'Sonya Salutes You'

IN 1947 the Norwoods had moved from Cheshunt to the London suburb of Bexleyheath, following Hilary's appointment as head of science at Erith County Grammar School. Bexleyheath was then the very epitome of post-war smugness in an age of austerity, boasting houses with fake Tudor beams, spacious parks and golf courses. It was middle country, middle class, middle management and middlebrow. Melita was thirty-eight years of age and Hilary was approaching his fortieth birthday. They were a middle-aged professional couple with a fixed mortgage, presumably beyond reproach. Melita would drop off her seven-year-old daughter, Anita, at the local primary school before commuting to London. At weekends they could be seen tending their spacious back garden, 200 feet in length, boasting fruit trees, herb border and kitchen garden. Their front garden was positively resplendent in the summer months, with several varieties of well-tended rose bushes in bloom. Bexleyheath at this time was just beginning to get back to normality after the Second World War. The general election of 1950, greeted across the country as the harbinger of better times to come, caused a great deal of local excitement. The promising young Conservative candidate, Edward Heath, was standing against his long-standing adversary from his student days at Balliol College, Oxford, Ashley Bramall. For Bexleyheath, it was a highly charged, passionate affair. After the votes were counted it was announced that the Conservatives had received 25,854 votes to the Labour Party's 25,721, a majority of only 133. There was uproar among Labour Party supporters in the Town Hall once it became clear that the Communists had polled more than Heath's majority and had gifted Heath the seat. The following year Heath was again elected, and the constituency of Old Bexley and Sidcup became synonymous with the name of Ted Heath.

1949, the year of the Soviet atomic bomb test, had been a critical year for the West. The Soviet test was simultaneous with the revolution in

China and the coming to power of the communists under Mao Zhedong. In London a strike by dockworkers – the Canadian seamen's strike – which Attlee was increasingly disposed to explain in terms of 'malignant orchestration', led to charges that communists were seeking to take over the London docks and posed a threat to national security. In the background were accelerating security problems in the colonies, with heavy demands being made on MI5 by riots and insurgencies in the Middle East, Egypt, the Gold Coast and Malaya.[1] Attlee, although reluctant to sanction a security arm of the state that he feared would import many of the unwelcome features of the Gestapo into British politics, found himself under pressure to extend the powers of the security services. During the election campaign of June 1945 there had been a heated exchange between Churchill and Attlee over the dangers of the creation of a post-war Gestapo in Britain. At that time the US was withholding full exchange of information on both atomic and political matters, awaiting evidence of improved security in the UK. Attlee, pressed by the security services, was persuaded to tighten security. Although he resisted the imposition of positive vetting, security procedures were tightened in a general clamp-down on what information passed across civil servants' desks. In 1949 the Technical Intelligence Committee system operated by MI5 was abandoned in favour of a Director of Scientific Intelligence as part of an overall revamping of the security services.[2] Melita now found that she no longer had access to classified documents. This, however, was not because she had begun to arouse suspicion but because the classified contract BN-FMRA held with the Atomic Energy Authority had been closed.

According to Alex Cibula, director of BN-FMRA between 1958 and 1972, between 1945 and 1948 a total of five BN-FMRA staff, including assistants, had been working on creep and corrosion and the structure of uranium metal. This was an interim arrangement until the work (but not the staff) was transferred to the newly completed Harwell laboratories. Uranium was openly referred to within the BN-FMRA, and the codename 'Tube ALLOYS' had been dropped. Research now concentrated on reactor design for power generation:

> Service staff in microscopy and the workshop who prepared or examined specimens knew the material as uranium for power generation.

BN-FMRA staff were not aware of the intention to extract plutonium for other purposes.[3]

Nevertheless, plutonium was extracted 'for other purposes', and Harwell was a burgeoning top secret government research centre working on Britain's own atomic bomb. When Calder Hall in Cumbria was opened by the queen in 1956 it was heralded as the world's first commercial producer of electricity from nuclear power. However, Calder Hall was primarily a military reactor designed to produce plutonium for Britain's nuclear weapons' programme. It was only after Britain had extracted enough plutonium for its needs that Calder Hall was gradually run more and more for electricity production. In fact it was not until the 1990s that Calder Hall ceased to be used for defence purposes.[4] Margaret Gowing, the official historian of the Atomic Energy Authority, was in no doubt that Britain had been determined to build a 'home grown, home-made' independent nuclear deterrent, and that 'she simply wanted full exchange of information with the Americans, plus some scarce materials.'[5] In late 1949 that belief was modified, not thrown over, once it became 'clear that the Americans' technological lead was increasing as they built up industrial factory production of more efficient weapons, while Britain was still struggling to produce one laboratory, Nagasaki-type bomb'.[6] By the end of 1949, she concluded, Britain was left with no other choice but to open talks with the Americans about 'a much deeper collaboration' where Britain would be permitted to produce some plutonium but would be expected to send it to the United States, which alone would produce nuclear weapons. In return the US would provide Britain with a stockpile of weapons for her own use. Ernest Bevin was unhappy and, harking back to the situation in the summer of 1940, objected to placing British capacity for atomic energy production unreservedly in American hands:

> If war should break out, it might be a matter of life and death for the British to use atomic weapons but their supply might be denied by American delays or disapproval of British policy. Bevin greatly feared that the Americans would control Britain's industrial development of peaceful atomic power. Britain, he said, should make no sacrifice which would impair her ability to deal with the United States on equal terms.[7]

These were brave words; gaping holes in British security would soon put an end to all such hopes.

Alexander Foote, who had been recruited by one member of the Kuczynski family and worked for another, published his memoirs, *A Handbook for Spies*, in 1949. A spy for eleven years, he concluded that 'The only excitement that a spy is likely to have is his last, when he is finally run to earth – a similar emotion to that experienced by the fox.'[8] During the first two decades of the Cold War the number of major Russian spies who were 'finally run to earth' ran into double figures worldwide and caused deep concern inside intelligence communities. The first inkling that British security had failed to put its house in order came in 1951 with the disappearance of the diplomats Guy Burgess and Donald Maclean and their reappearance in Moscow. The Korean War was then at its height, and Britain's rearmament programme was underway. Melita Norwood, by now comfortably settled in Bexleyheath, was working within the 'legal' residency operating from inside the Soviet embassy. The nature of that work is difficult to assess as she no longer had access to classified information. Nevertheless, the Soviets continued to think highly of her, and in 1958 she was awarded the Order of the Red Banner, one of the highest decorations in the Soviet Union.[9] Later that year she was switched from the 'legal' residency to one of the Soviet Union's great post-war 'illegals', Gordon Lonsdale.

Born in 1922, the son of two Soviet scientists, Lonsdale's real name was Konan Trofimovich Molody. He had been earmarked for training as a foreign intelligence officer at the age of ten, and had been sent to live with an aunt in California in order to learn English. He returned to Moscow in 1938, and was recruited by the NKVD the following year. During the Second World War he gained 'a degree in Chinese and worked as a Chinese language instructor before training as an "illegal" in 1951'.[10] In March 1955 he was given the identity of a 'dead double', a Canadian who had died in infancy, Gordon Arnold Lonsdale, and was posted to Britain. Before arrival he was given details of several important targets in the UK, including the Germ Warfare Centre at Porton Down, where the Russians believed a number of ex-Nazi scientists had been redeployed.[11] His partnership with Melita Norwood, however, produced very little in the way of results, although in his autobiography he mentions directing his attention at Britain's nuclear industry.[12] He was introduced to Melita on 23

December 1958; she was safely back inside the 'legal' London residency by February 1959.

After the crushing of the Hungarian national uprising in November 1956 Moscow Centre found it difficult to recruit spies from within the British Communist Party. New recruits were now more likely to be people who had either been compromised or were seeking financial gain. It was a totally different spying world from the one Percy Glading and Sonya inhabited in the 1930s and 1940s. Lonsdale came across as a Russian playboy in the Western world – the director of several companies operating jukeboxes, vending machines and one-armed bandits, pursuing a succession of glamorous girls attracted by his easy money and good looks.[13] Melita Norwood simply could not abide him.[14] This was fortuitous, as in March 1960 Lonsdale came under intensive MI5 surveillance when his office in Wardour Street and his flat in the White House, Regents Park, were both bugged. The Lonsdale network, unlike the Kuczynski network, was very quickly closed down by MI5.

Apart from Melita Norwood, Lonsdale's network ran two other agents: Harry Houghton and his mistress, Ethel Gee. Houghton, a civilian clerk in the Underwater Weapons Establishment at Portland, and Gee, a filing clerk at the base, had access to top secret information on anti-submarine warfare and nuclear submarines.[15] In 1961, after being identified as a spy by the Polish defector Michal Goleniewski, Houghton was put under MI5 surveillance and was followed to a meeting with Lonsdale, who led them to a home in Ruislip, where a powerful high-speed radio transmitter used for communications with Moscow Centre and a short-wave radio used for receiving messages on high-frequency bands were found under the kitchen floor. The house was a veritable treasure trove of spying equipment: one-time cipher pads hidden in flashlights and a cigarette lighter, a microdot reader concealed in a box of face powder, equipment for microdot construction, a storage jar containing magnetic iron oxide used for printing high-speed Morse messages on to tape, thousands of pounds, dollars and travellers' cheques and seven passports were uncovered. At their trial in March 1961 Lonsdale was sentenced to twenty-five years in prison, the owners of the house to twenty, Houghton and Gee to fifteen.[16]

Two months later George Blake was convicted under the Official Secrets Act, and was handed down a record sentence of forty-two years' imprisonment. At Blake's appeal his barrister, Jeremy Hutchinson QC, commanded some public support when he expressed his abhorrence at the length of the sentence: 'This sentence is so inhuman that it is alien to all the principles on which a civilized country would treat its subjects.'[17] The risks involved in Cold War spying could not have been more dramatically illustrated. Fuchs, who had been convicted on four counts of passing atomic bomb secrets to the Soviet Union, had been sentenced only to a maximum of fourteen years. Blake's sentence, with the exception of Lonsdale's, was unprecedented, and marked the first time in modern British criminal history since 1887 that a sentence of more than twenty years had been handed down for any crime. In his summing up the Attorney-General, Sir Reginald Manningham-Buller QC, MP, stressed that 'although he [Blake] held responsible positions, his employment fortunately did not give him access to any information relating to secret weapons or nuclear or atomic energy, but it is the case that he has done most serious damage to the interests of the country.'[18] The gravity of Melita Norwood's crime was that she had done exactly that, and handed over information on all three areas deemed essential to national security – secret weapons, nuclear power and atomic energy.

The sentencing of John Vassall in September 1962 to eighteen years' imprisonment for handing over thousands of highly classified documents on weapons development and NATO and British naval policy was further proof of the government's determination to stamp out spying during the hot Cold War of the early 1960s. If Melita Norwood had been 'outed' in 1962 there can be little doubt that she would have received a lengthy prison sentence. She was vetted in 1962, and once again refused clearance. At the end of the year Britain signed the Nassau agreement and paved the way for the purchase of Polaris missiles for Royal Navy submarines from the United States. Such Anglo-American nuclear collaboration was unprecedented, and national security, including protection from espionage, was seen as critical. Nevertheless, a series of spy scandals continued to harm the nuclear relationship. The defection of Kim Philby on 23 January 1963, the fall-out from the Profumo affair later that year and the confession of Anthony Blunt to spying on 25 April 1964 all had to be carefully managed by the British intelligence community if the Americans were to remain wedded to the nuclear 'special relationship', particularly in the light of

negotiations then taking place to update the 1955 Civil Bilateral agreement
due to expire on 20 July 1965.[19] Under this agreement, in order to guarantee Britain's nuclear status, Britain and America had to circumvent IAEA
safeguards:

> United States officials have explained to the Embassy that they need
> to demonstrate to Congress and to other countries that they have
> good and sufficient reasons for not including in the new Agree-
> ment provision for the immediate application of International
> Atomic Energy Agency (I.A.E.A.) safeguards to supplies of United
> States materials for our civil nuclear programme, and that the
> absence of such provision does not indicate any weakening in the
> United States Government's general policy of support for I.A.E.A.
> safeguards.[20]

In order to get round IAEA safeguards the United States government
proposed an 'Exchange of Letters' with the IAEA stating that 'the application of Agency safeguards ... would not be of practical significance. Our
principal reason for coming to this conclusion is that, under arrangements
concluded in 1958 and 1959, the United States and the United Kingdom are
exchanging large quantities of material for defence purposes. If circumstances were to change with respect to these changes, a re-examination
of the current civil agreement under the terms of Article _____ would
be appropriate'. The British government, however, fearing that the IAEA
would raise objections proposed a change in the wording, and substituted
the following: 'our principal reason for coming to this conclusion is that,
under arrangements concluded in 1958 and 1959, the United States and the
United Kingdom are actively co-operating for defence purposes. If this cooperation were to cease, the United States and the United Kingdom would
consult each other under the terms of Article _____ of the revised Civil
Agreement'.[21] Clearly, the last thing the Labour government of the time
wanted, in the midst of protracted and difficult negotiations over the Civil
Agreement, was the exposure of yet another atomic spy.

For this reason when MI5 launched 'an extended investigation' into Mrs
Norwood in 1965, concluding that while she had been a spy in the 1940s,
there 'was no usable evidence to support the view', her liberty was never
at risk. The Home Secretary of the day, the Rt Hon. Sir Frank Soskice QC,

whose Russian-born father had once worked alongside Theodore Rothstein and had also been on friendly terms with Mrs Norwood's parents,
Gertrude and Alexander Sirnis, was informed of the security service's suspicions. A decision was taken 'not to interview her because that would
have revealed the Service's knowledge which was relevant to other sensitive investigations then underway'.[22] Nevertheless, she continued working
for Moscow Centre, and in 1967 she recruited a civil servant to the KGB
known only by the codename HUNT. When pressed on this matter in 2002,
she refused to comment: 'A bloke called Hunt. I wonder if he had another
name? No comment on Hunt. I am not going to deny it. But memory being
what it is – no comment on Hunt. I don't want to involve anybody else. I
take complete responsibility and blame'.[23] In fact, Hunt proved to be a very
valuable KGB asset:

> In the fourteen years after HUNT's recruitment in 1967, he provided
> S & T and intelligence on British arms sales (on which no further
> evidence is available). In the late 1970s the London residency gave
> him £9,000 to found a small business, probably in the hope that he
> could use it to supply embargoed technology.[24]

In 1965, therefore, when Sir Frank Soskice took the decision not to pursue the investigation of Mrs Norwood, she was still an important spy, and
although MI5 did not know that she was still active, she remained so until
her retirement in 1972.

In September 1979, at the age of sixty-seven, she travelled to Russia for
the first time. At a small ceremony in Moscow she was presented with
the Order of the Red Banner, and was told that she would receive a KGB
pension. She later stopped it; but for a while it came regularly through the
post: 'It didn't go on for long. Cash through the post. I told them I had
enough to live on and turned it down'.[25]

At this time Hilary Norwood was a frequent visitor to the Soviet Union.
In October 1964 he had been elected a member of the British Society of
Russian Philately (BSRP), and, as a fluent Russian speaker, he travelled
regularly to Russia to liaise with officials of the All-Union Society of Phila-
telists (VOF). In 1976 he became the BSRP's press officer, and in June of
that year helped to organize a joint exhibition of the BSRP and VOF in
Moscow, where he was awarded a silver medal for his exhibits of Russian

stamps. Between 1974 and 1983 he was the Stanley Gibbons consultant on Russian stamps, and in 1985 he was elected president of the BSRP. He died in October 1986, aged seventy-five, and an obituary, written by the Russian playwright Viktor Rozov, appeared in the Soviet journal *Filateliya SSSR*. Viktor Rozov had known the Norwoods very well, and had made four visits to London to meet with Andrew Rothstein, each time staying at the Norwoods' house. 'It was literally drowned in roses', he later wrote, 'enormous bushes in every garden, of all colours including violet. I had never seen violet-coloured roses before.'[26]

When the Soviet Union collapsed in 1991 Melita Norwood's world changed dramatically. She was then seventy-nine years of age and the Union of Soviet Socialist Republics, or more correctly her 'myth image' of it, had been the dominant feature of her life. The following year the KGB archivist, Vasili Mitrokhin, defected to the West bringing with him several files copied from the KGB's foreign intelligence archives. Among those files was one on agent HOLA detailing a spying career spanning nearly forty years. This file was passed to a MI5 case officer pending a decision on whether she should be questioned about her spying activities. During 1992 and the early months of 1993, amid growing concerns for Mitrokhin's safety and the need to keep secret the international investigations then underway into secret agents identified by the files, it was decided not to interview Melita Norwood but to review her case internally. The review concluded that it was not in anybody's interest to investigate her further as she was now more than eighty years old, and her spying career had ended some time ago. MI5, however, failed to consult with law officers before reaching this conclusion and was, therefore, in breach of process. Failure to either interview Melita Norwood or gather evidence at this stage meant that any future prosecution was now impossible. This would later cause MI5 some embarrassment once it became clear that the decision not to investigate Mrs Norwood had been taken at a junior, as opposed to a senior, level.

On 13 September 1999, following publication in *The Times* of extracts from *The Mitrokhin Archive* detailing some of Melita Norwood's activities as a spy, the Labour Home Secretary, Jack Straw, was put in the embarrassing situation of having to face down Tory MPs' calls for her prosecution, which he knew to be out of the question. To avoid further embarrassment he announced the setting up of an Intelligence and Security Committee

(ISC) inquiry to look into the intelligence agencies' handling of Mitrokhin's material, under the chairmanship of former Defence Secretary Sir Tom King MP. The inquiry uncovered an extraordinary series of events leading up to Melita Norwood's 'outing' as a spy in 1999.

The Director-General of MI5 in 1993, Dame Stella Rimmington, told the committee that she had never been briefed about the case and that the decision not to prosecute Mrs Norwood could not, therefore, have been taken at a senior level. The security services then excused themselves to the committee by suggesting that Melita Norwood had simply 'slipped out of sight' until her name reappeared in the draft of the book on the Mitrokhin material being written by Professor Christopher Andrew. This was an amazing admission, given the fact that *The Mitrokhin Archive* was not published until 1999, and that Melita and her husband had been the subject of a two-page article by the Russian playwright, Viktor Rozov, in 1994 published in the Russian-language journal *Zavtra*, a journal known to have close ties with the old KGB. The article was full of nostalgia for communism and the former Soviet Union, and recounted a time when Hilary Norwood had taken him (Rozov) to meet Andrew Rothstein, 'an old man, who when five years old had sat on Lenin's knee. Andrew's father, Theodore Rothstein had known Lenin very well.'[27]

The article was published again in February 1995 in the second issue of a quarterly glossy Russian-language magazine, *Zhurnal 'Voskrecen'e: Novaya Rossiya'* along with a photograph of Letty, Hilary, Anita and her husband spread across almost half a page. *Zhurnal 'Voskrecen'e: Novaya Russia'* (Resurrection: New Russia) was advertised as the successor to Maxim Gorky's 1930s journal of the same name. It was an expensive, large format, coffee-table magazine with a limited print run aimed specifically at Russia's *nouveaux riches*. Russia-watchers and readers of the Russian press in the British security services should really have noticed this article about Hilary and Melita Norwood in *Resurrection. New Russia* and asked themselves a series of questions. Was the Russian Foreign Intelligence Service, the *Sluzhba Vneshnei Razvedki* (SVR), the successor to the KGB, happy with the 'outing' of Mrs Norwood? Was it aware of the content of Mitrokhin's material? Could this 'archival' material, in fact, be manipulated so as to create a positive image of the Russian secret service, a vindication of its past record? Was it an attempt to draw a line under its KGB past, to shed past spies? Was Mitrokhin's material an attempt to embarrass key Western political figures by spreading misinformation about their past? Was Melita Norwood to be used as evidence of the truth of the Mitrokhin files when spreading these falsehoods? This is all conjecture; but the fact that the Norwoods were featuring in the Russian press at the same time as Mrs Norwood's case was being reviewed by MI5 should have convinced them that she was important enough to be interviewed.

According to the evidence given to the ISC when a SIS interview team interviewed Mitrokhin he told them that the reason for compiling the archive and smuggling it out to the West was to have it published. But he later told the committee that he was unhappy with the way SIS had developed the book. He had wanted the material to be published in full, with an editor to craft it for the Western market, and he made his displeasure perfectly clear when he told the committee that 'he wished that he had had full control over the handling of the material.'[28]

When it was first agreed to publish Mitrokhin's material the then Conservative government under John Major and the British intelligence services put in place a strategy that would allow them to oversee the publication project, and to thereby prevent the publication of any material they believed to be unfit for public consumption. In 1995 they approached a Cambridge historian, Professor Christopher Andrew, and 'invited him to participate in the publication project'. There were a number of reasons for this decision, not least the fact that Professor Andrew was a distinguished academic who specialized in intelligence history:

> The SIS regarded Professor Andrew as a safe pair of hands, who had worked previously * * * on the Gordievsky books. Professor Andrew was also security cleared and had signed the Official Secrets Act. Professor Andrew agreed to complete the project, knowing that ministerial approval would be required before the book could be published. The SIS nominated Professor Andrew as the editor for the book in the 6 March 1996 submission to Malcolm Rifkind, the Foreign Secretary.[29]

Under what became known as the Rifkind criteria the Foreign Secretary agreed to endorse the project, first setting down certain guidelines governing publication. 'The names of the people the KGB had targeted for recruitment or attempted to influence could not be made public unless they had been prosecuted and convicted or they had agreed to the release of their names.'[30] In other words Malcolm Rifkind made it quite clear that he did not want the intelligence services to decide whether names should be released into the public domain without clearance from the FCO or Home Office. Michael Howard, as Home Secretary, was then 'made aware' of the project and an interdepartmental working group was formed under the chairmanship of the Intelligence Co-ordinator, with representatives from the SIS, FCO, Home Office and security services. The working group met in July 1996, November 1996 and March 1997. It did not meet again until 1999. Following the election of a Labour government on 2 May 1997 it became the Intelligence Co-ordinator's responsibility to inform the incoming government of the publication project and of the Rifkind criteria that all concerned, including the book's publishers, had accepted. However, because Whitehall civil servants had not worked with a Labour government since the 1970s, communication between civil servants and ministers during the first few months of the new government was not good. So it was not until 23 October 1997 that the incoming Foreign Secretary, Robin Cook, received a note from Sir John Kerr, the Parliamentary Under-Secretary in the FCO, informing him about Mitrokhin's material and the publication project. Kerr's note was brief, and in his evidence to the ISC Kerr 'agreed' that this note 'could have said more' and could have been 'more felicitously drafted'. But this admission masked the fact that Kerr had failed to inform Cook about the restrictions placed on the project by the Rifkind criteria.[31]

The new Home Secretary, Jack Straw, fared little better. He was not informed of the project until 10 December 1998, although in this instance the ISC's report was less critical of the intelligence services. 'The submission and accompanying note from SIS were informative and contained some detail about ongoing Security Service investigations.'[32] Moreover, Straw was also informed that the security service was considering recommending the prosecution of an eighty-six-year-old spy, but did not mention Melita Norwood by name. To stop Straw worrying he was also informed that the Prime Minister, Tony Blair, and Foreign Minister, Robin Cook, had both been made aware of the project. In fact Blair, as Leader of the Opposition, had been briefed on the Mitrokhin material as early as January 1995. However, despite Blair being brought up to date, and the

Cabinet ministers concerned being brought into the loop, by now the Rifkind criteria were a lame duck. Labour politicians had been sidelined while the Home Office and FCO's control over the project had been overtaken by Whitehall civil servants and representatives of the intelligence services. Although the interdepartmental working group was to meet four times in 1999 (January, June, July and September) the FCO, Home Office, SIS and security service representatives on the group did not pass on information about the group's work and decisions to ministers and senior officials. This led to a situation where both Jack Straw and Robin Cook simply did not know what was going on around them. The ISC report was quite clear on this point: 'There were two significant occasions when the group agreed a course of action that was subsequently not carried out by the Home Office. One concerned the failure to consult the Home Secretary on interviewing Mrs. Norwood and the second that the working group agreed in January 1999 that the book would need to be cleared by the Home Secretary.'[33] In fact, the FCO told Robin Cook that Jack Straw was clearing the UK-related material, when he was not. The situation was further complicated by a decision taken by the SIS to make available material from Professor Andrew's and Vasili Mitrokhin's book, *The Mitrokhin Archive*, to the journalist David Rose, who was making a television documentary, 'The Spying Game'. This decision effectively drove a horse and cart through what was left of the Rifkind criteria. Among the material passed to David Rose was the identity of agent HOLA. Rose informed the publishers of *The Mitrokhin Archive* that he would be naming her in his documentary. Once the publishers had this information they persuaded the working group that they should be allowed to publish her name in *The Mitrokhin Archive*, in breach of the Rifkind criteria, as the ISC noted:

> Whether or not aided by material from *The Mitrokhin Archive* or from other sources, David Rose identified HOLA as Mrs. Norwood and told the book's publisher that he would be including her in his documentary. In the light of this the working group was persuaded by the book's publisher to include the names of Mrs Norwood and Mr Symonds. The Committee notes that this was technically in breach of the Rifkind criteria.[34]

The decision to pass information to David Rose, including the identity of agent HOLA, was taken by John Scarlett, head of MI6. In an article criticising David Rose's 'adulatory feature' in the *Observer* following John Scarlett's appointment as 'C' (head of SIS), *Private Eye* claimed that Scarlett had been the source responsible for placing Mrs Norwood's name in the public domain thereby scuppering the Rifkind criteria:

> In 1999 ... David Rose made a BBC documentary about Soviet defector Vasili Mitrokhin, the KGB's former archivist, which revealed inter alia that a British woman called Melita Norwood had spied for Russia while working at the British Non-Ferrous Metals Association ... who was the generous spook who provided Rose with details of the Mitrokhin dossier? Though the source was never identified, it was in fact ... John Scarlett.[35]

The question that leaps to mind is, of course, why would John Scarlett have wanted to release Melita Norwood's name to the media and so undermine the Rifkind criteria? Despite the fact that the working group was made up of representatives from the FCO, Home Office, SIS and the security service there were significant differences between them. Where Melita Norwood was concerned SIS wanted a prosecution, while the security service did not. Scarlett, in particular, no doubt had reasons to raise his profile. But the main stumbling block to reaching an agreement appears to be the lack of experience across the group in publication and media matters as they struggled to produce a media strategy. According to the ISC report, Jack Straw 'saw the press lines in the week prior to the HOLA story appearing in *The Times*. The Foreign Secretary did not see them.' Thus the report concluded: 'Once the story broke Ministers were unable to use the prepared press lines because they were inadequate.'[36] This was significant as SIS and the security service had devised rival media strategies. The SIS view was that Melita Norwood had been a major spy and should be prosecuted, while the security service played down her significance as a spy and was happy with a media strategy that portrayed her as rather a dotty old lady. What happened next was that the story hit the headlines in a sensationalist manner when the original 'objective of the publication project', under Malcolm Rifkind, had been 'to place Mr Mitrokhin's material in the public domain in a controlled and unsensational manner':

In the submission to Malcolm Rifkind the SIS stated that the project would provide 'an important insight into the internal workings of the KGB while documenting the external subversive and espionage activities of the former communist state, most of which was unknown not only within Russia but even within the current Russian intelligence service. [The work] would describe a significant and usually hidden part of the 20th century history which, to be properly understood, needs detailed, unsensational, scholarly exegesis.'[37]

An element within SIS appeared to be unhappy with this strategy, and chose instead to leak material to the press. Thus when the story broke headlines portrayed Melita Norwood as a Mata Hari – the great-grandmother spy who had given the Soviets a blueprint of the atomic bomb that threatened the security of the West. The fact that she prepared homemade chutney, drank tea from a Che Guevara mug, shopped at the Co-op for ideological reasons, supported CND, enjoyed gardening and did a delivery round for the *Morning Star* at the age of eighty-seven only added to the excitement. 'Revealed: The Quiet Woman Who Betrayed Britain For 40 Years. The Spy Who Came In From The Co-op' was *The Times* headline on 11 September 1999. 'The Mole Who Came Into The Garden', was preferred by the *Independent*. The *Sunday Telegraph* quoted her as saying 'I would do everything again.' One Sunday newspaper told the story of a recent spy convention at the former NATO listening station on Teufelsberg, near Berlin, where retired members of the CIA, KGB and MI5 raised their glasses to the little old lady from Bexleyheath. 'Cold War Club Welcomes A New Member', smiled the headline:

> To absent friends they raised their glasses: to George Blake, who sent greetings from Moscow, and then to the pensioner whose name they didn't know, unmasked as one of their own for more than 40 years. ...
>
> 'I never had heard of this lady before,' Major General Oleg Kalugin, formerly of the KGB and latterly engaged in the creation of a computer game called Spycraft, informed the *Independent on Sunday*. 'But I knew from some sources that there was a lady involved in atomic espionage. ... I think there is a tendency here to overstate the efficiency of Western intelligence, and underestimate the

achievements of the KGB,' he said. 'Certainly in the late 1940s, we were the best outfit in the world.'[38]

The working group's media strategy was not working, and was in danger of spinning out of control. If it had been SIS's intention in publishing *The Mitrokhin Archive* to expose the worst practices of the KGB then it was ill-advised to put Melita Norwood's name into the public domain. The British have a peculiar attitude towards spies ranging from fascination and approval to extreme horror. The day after Melita's exposure as a spy an editorial in the *Independent on Sunday* described her story as 'classically British ... in more ways than one.'

> The 87-year old great-grandmother, whose wispy grey-haired exterior masks a life of studied betrayal, was for 40 years one of Russia's most effective Cold War spies. There has been a characteristically British touch of ambivalence in the reaction to the news: the old lady is simultaneously dubbed a 'great' spy to rank with the 'Magnificent Five' of Burgess, Maclean, Philby, Blunt and Cairncross, and yet there are calls for her prosecution on the grounds that 'treachery is never forgivable.'[39]

Foremost among those calling for her prosecution was the shadow Home Secretary, Anne Widdicombe, who knew even less about what was going on than Jack Straw. Badly briefed before his statement to the Commons on 13 September, and somewhat rattled by the ferocity of Anne Widdicombe's attack, Jack Straw fumbled his press lines and failed to put across MI5's view that Mrs Norwood had been a spy of little consequence. This was a point of view that had very little grounding in fact. Jack Straw told the House of Commons on 13 September:

> There is no reason to doubt the detail of the material drawn from Mr. Mitrokhin, nor that the KGB regarded Mrs. Norwood as an important spy. She was one of a number of spies in this country and the United States who passed information to the Soviet Union about the development of the atom bomb during the 1940s. ...
>
> When Mitrokhin's notes of the KGB archive material became available to British Intelligence in 1992, they confirmed suspicions about Mrs. Norwood's role. The view was taken by the service that

this material did not on its own provide evidence that could be put to a UK court. Moreover, a judgement was made by the agencies that material should remain secret for some years as there were many leads to more recent espionage to be followed up, particularly in the countries of a number of our close allies. It was also judged that interviewing Mrs. Norwood, which might have proved admissible evidence, could have jeopardised exploitation of those leads. These decisions were made by the agencies. Ministers of the day, including law officers, were not consulted.[40]

In fact when the security services did consult the law officers to see if they could mount a prosecution under the Official Secrets Act in March 1999 they were told by Sir John Morris, the Attorney-General, 'that there was no decision for him to take as 1992 had represented the last opportunity for any prosecution'.[41] Because the authorities had known about Mrs Norwood's espionage activities for some considerable time, and had not taken any action against her earlier, any prosecution would now be regarded as abuse of process. Jack Straw was not consulted. Stephen Lander, the Director-General of the security service, in giving evidence to the ISC defended the security service's decision by claiming that 'the decision to interview Mrs. Norwood was an operational matter, and therefore it was for him to make and not the Home Secretary.'[42] As far as he was concerned there was nothing to be gained from such an interview. Melita's age, the fact that the offences were committed fifty years ago and the lack of hard evidence meant that any interview would not be in the public interest. However, the failure to refer Melita's case to the law officers in mid-1993 was heavily criticized by the ISC, who regarded this as proof positive that the decision whether to prosecute Mrs Norwood was taken solely by the security service. Was MI5 engaged in a cover-up? Whatever the reasons MI5, no doubt in collaboration with the Home Office, now took evasive action and sought to portray Melita Norwood as a somewhat daft old lady who simply did not have a clue about what she was supposed to have done. An article by Philip Knightley appeared on 13 December 1999 in the *New Statesman* arguing that Melita Norwood could not have been where *The Mitrokhin Archive* had placed her in the 1940s. A report in Home Office files, he claimed, showed that she had left the BN-FMRA in 1943, and did not return until 1946.

Unfortunately, that Home Office report never existed. What did exist was a letter sent to the Home Office on 12 September by Alex Cibula, who had joined the BN-FMRA in 1947 and who had been Melita's boss between 1958 and 1972, pointing out that none of their documents at that time was classified. Incidentally, in his letter he claimed, 'I was never informed that Letty [Melita] did not have security clearance – it was not significant by that time; even though some of our work was of interest to defence industries, it was not specifically military.' Cibula's letter was passed by the Home Office to Knightley who in his *New Statesman* article elevated it to the status of a Home Office document. Clearly the Home Office was engaged in yet another media strategy to obscure the true nature of Mrs Norwood's spying activities. But there can be little doubt that Melita Norwood had been a spy of some importance, and that MI5 over a sixty-five-year period, despite having numerous clues to her identity and espionage activities, failed to stop her. In September 1999 Melita received a copy of Sonya's autobiography, *Sonya's Report*, through the post; inside was a photo bearing the simple inscription:

To Letty
'Sonya' salutes you and 'Reni' sends her love. Enjoy the pictures and captions and lend it to your family – ask them to give you a summary!!

Sonya, who died in Berlin on 7 July 2003 at the age of ninety-three, was one of the few people alive in 1999 who could comment on Letty's life as a spy, apart from Letty herself. When Letty did finally begin to talk about her past she gave the impression that she was doing so with Sonya's tacit approval, as if the arrival of Sonya's autobiography through the post was one last call to arms. What struck me most while I sat listening to her story on those Sunday afternoons was how Letty's spying career had bridged two very different eras of communism. Here was a woman who had spent her childhood among an eclectic mixture of anarchists, suffragettes, Tolstoyans and the pioneers of British socialism, who had eagerly embraced the ideals of Lenin's October Revolution. Their Utopianism remained with her throughout her life and blinded her to the worst excesses of Stalinism.

Her role as an atom spy cannot be excused but it can be explained. When the Second World War ended, the United States had emerged as the sole atomic power with the political will to drop the bomb. US intelligence at the end of the war predicted that it would take between five and ten years for the Soviet Union to develop a bomb. In fact it took them four. The contribution of Britain's atomic spies had greatly reduced the time-scale for a Russian atomic bomb. Melita, an unassuming housewife from Ted Heath's old fiefdom of Bexleyheath, had made history. By helping to create an armed stand-off between two nuclear superpowers Melita Norwood had played a significant part in ushering in the era of détente and its counterpart, Mutually Assured Destruction (MAD). For that millions of Russian people probably owe her their lives. Melita Norwood finally came in from the Co-op on 2 June 2005, when she died aged ninety-three.

Notes

Sources

Records held at The National Archive of England and Wales, Kew, London (TNA).

AB1 *Department of Scientific and Industrial Research and related bodies: Directorate of Tube Alloys and related bodies: War of 1939–45, Correspondence and Papers*

AB1/8 Maud Committee – Minutes of Meetings 1940–1.

AB1/9 Maud Committee – Papers relating to Atomic Bomb 1939–41.

AB1/10 Maud Committee – Various Scientific papers and reports 1940.

AB1/325 Canadian Organization Technical Committee on Radiological Research 1942–4.

AB1/682 Tube Alloys Project: organization in United Kingdom 1941–5.

AB16 *Ministry of Supply and United Kingdom Atomic Energy Division and London Office: Files 1939–78*

AB16/105 Corrosion and anti-corrosion protective measures (water treatment sheathing) 1946.

AB16/155 Spectrographic sources 1946.

AB16/181 Extra-mural research, universities, firms, etc.: British Non-Ferrous Metals Research Association.

CAB *Cabinet Reports*

CAB24/97 Revolutionaries and the Need for Legislation 2 February 1920.

CAB24/111 A Monthly Review of Revolutionary Movements in British Dominions, Overseas and Foreign Countries 21 July 1920.

FO *Foreign Office*

FO371/3347 Russia 1918.

FO371/11029 Russia 1925.

KV2 *The Security Service: Personal (PF Series) Files*

KV2/483 Aleksey Alexandrovich Doschenko.

KV2/512 Samuel Henry Cohen, instructor at the Comintern's Wilson School, Moscow.

KV2/573 Leonid Krassine.

KV2/777 Pyotr Leonydovitch Kapitza.

KV2/817 Brian Goold-Verschoyle.

KV2/1004–1007 Willy and Mary Brandes.

KV2/1008–1009 Theodore Maly.

KV2/1012–1014 Edith Tudor-Hart.

KV2/1020–1023 Percy Eded Glading.

KV2/1034–1047 Harry Pollitt.

KV2/1062–1066 Denis Nowell Pritt.

KV2/1108–1115 ROSTA (Russian Telegraph Service/TASS).

KV2/1237–1238 George and Edith Whomack.

KV2/1245–1270 Klaus Fuchs.

KV2/1575–1584 Andrew and Theodore Rothstein.

KV2/1611–1616 Alexander Foote.

KV2/1871–1880 Jurgen and Marguerite Kuczynski.

KV4 *The Security Service: Policy (Pol F Series) Files*

KV4/56 Report on the operations of F2A in connection with Communism, Trotskyism and other British leftwing subversive activities (1 January 1945–31 December 1945).

KV6 *The Security Service: List (L Series) Files*

KV6/41–45 Ursula Kuczynski; Ruth Werner (Sonya).

PREM *Records of the Prime Minister's Office*

PREM8/1280 Fuchs Case: parliamentary statement by P.M. and Lord Chancellor; Canadian government material.

PREM13/128 Nuclear safeguards: inspection of Central Electricity Generating Board station at Bradwell; UK–US agreement on civil uses of nuclear energy April–December 1965.

WO *War Office*

WO32/9304 Military Press Control: History of the work of MI7 1914–19.

CHAPTER 1
The Secret Life of Melita Norwood

1 The first Soviet was set up in St Petersburg in October 1905 as an improvised organ of workers' self-government. It was non-party in composition although during the course of the 1917 October Revolution the Bolsheviks substituted the authority of the party for soviet constitutionalism.

2 Colin Holmes, 'Immigrants, Refugees and Revolutionaries', in *From the Other Shore: Russian Political Emigrants in Britain, 1880–1917*, ed. J. Slatter (London: Frank Cass, 1984), p. 8.

3 Peter Verigen leader of the Doukhobors, Paul Birukoff friend and biographer of Tolstoy.

4 Stanley Carlyle Potter, 'Reminiscences of Tchertkoff and Tuckton's Russian Colony', *Christchurch Times* 15 March 1963.

5 Melita Norwood Papers, currently in the possession of the author.

6 'Straw's Statement – The Full Text', *The Times*, 14 September 1999.

7 Philip Knightley, 'Norwood: The Spy Who Never Was', *New Statesman*, 13 December 1999.

8 Melita Norwood, interview with the author, 13 January 2000.

9 Allen Weinstein and Alexander Vassiliev, *The Haunted Wood: Soviet Espionage in America – The Stalin Era* (New York: The Modern Library, 2000), p. 19.

10 Ibid., p. 19.

11 See David Holloway, *Stalin and the Bomb* (New Haven and London: Yale University Press, 1994), pp. 161–6.

12 Ibid., p. 173.

CHAPTER 2
'Is This Well?'

1 *Bournemouth Echo*, 14 February 1943.

2 *Sussex Genealogies* (publisher not given, n.d.) Melita Norwood's uncle, Thomas Stedman, wrote the chapter on the Stedman family.

3 *Bournemouth Echo*, 14 February 1943.

4 Wilfrid Blunt, *Married to a Single Life* (Salisbury: Michael Russell (Publishing) Ltd, 1983), p. 2.

5 Correspondence: Andrew Rothstein to David Burke, 23 April 1983.

6 Correspondence: Hyndman to Marx, 29 October 1881, quoted in Henry Pelling, *Popular Politics and Society in Late Victorian Britain* (London: Macmillan,1968), p. 14.

7 This article formed the basis of Lenin's system later set out in his pamphlet *What Is to Be Done?*, published in March 1902. In this essay Lenin argued the case for a centralized, disciplined party, which would lead the workers' movement, and not follow in its wake.

8 Wilfrid Scawen Blunt, *My Diaries. Part 2 1900–1914* (London: Martin Secker, 1919), entry for 28 October 1910.

9 Ibid.

10 M. A. Cooke, 'The Friends of Leo Tolstoy', *Millgate Monthly* February 1909.

CHAPTER 3
'Neither the Saint nor the Revolutionary'

1 'Neither the saint nor the revolutionary can save us; only the synthesis of the two.' Arthur Koestler, *The Yogi and the Commissar and Other Essays* (London: Cape, 1945), p. 256.

2 The Free Age Press (English Branch). Joint Editors: V. Tchertkoff, A. C. Fifield. Manager: A. C. Fifield. '1900–1902, A brief statement of its work', by A. C. Fifield, 1933 (copy of first page). Melita Norwood Papers.

3 Correspondence: Aunt Theresa to Melita Norwood, 27 March 1968; Melita Norwood to Alfred Brandt, 1 May 1968. Melita Norwood Papers.

4 Thomas Preston, *Before the Curtain* (London: John Murray, 1950), pp. 9–10.

5 See for example Bart Kennedy, "The Wandering Romanoff", *Evening News*, 21 August 1900; William Le Queux, *Strange Tales of a Nihilist* (London 1892; reprinted London 1894); Oscar Wilde, *Vera, or the Nihilists* (London, 1880) and *Lord Arthur Savile's Crime* (London, 1891).

6 Hansard (Commons), 4H, 18, c.891, 14 November 1893.

7 Minute by G. Lushington, 6 April 1983 on TNA Kew HO 144/587/2840c item 21c. 'The situation at that time was aggravated by a new American Immigration Act (1891), and an extradition treaty between America and Russia, ratified in 1893, which removed the exemption in favour of political assassination.' Bernard Porter, 'The British Government and Political Refugees, c. 1880–1914', in Slatter, *From the Other Shore*, p. 41.

8 Preston, *Before the Curtain*, p. 10.

9 Ibid., p. 11.

10 Ibid.

11 Melita Norwood, handwritten notes, n.d.; Correspondence: Melita Norwood to Professor Valentine Steinberg, 3 December 1986, 'I should point out that my aunt (Mrs. Theresa Valois (nee Stedman) – my mother's sister) never met Tolstoy – he had returned to Russia earlier. It was Vladimir Tchertkoff whom she knew at Tuckton House. She did tell me and others that Tchertkoff had invited her on one occasion to have tea with him and Kropotkin.' Melita Norwood Papers.

12 Preston, *Before the Curtain*, p. 13.

13 Ibid., p. 16.

14 'Recollections of Russian Tuckton', *Christchurch Times*, 3 September 1971.

15 Henri Troyat, *Tolstoy* (Harmondsworth: Penguin Books, 1970), p. 853; Notes by Alfred Brandt (about 1948), 'Conversations with his Mother, Mrs. Gertrude Elisabeth Gurney Sirnis, widow of Peter Alexander Sirnis'. Melita Norwood Papers.

16 Cooke, 'The Friend of Leo Tolstoy'.

17 Michael J. de K. Holman, 'Translating Tolstoy for the Free Age Press: Vladimir Chertkov and His English Manager Arthur Fifield', *Slavonic and East European Review* 66, 2 (April 1988), 184–97.

18 Correspondence: Alfred Brandt to Melita Norwood, 30 April 1974. Melita Norwood Papers.

19 'Alfred Brandt's notes on a conversation with Stanley Carlyle Potter (February 1948), the last surviving member of the Tolstoyan Group at Tuckton House, who died 25th December 1973 aged 90.' Melita Norwood Papers.

20 'The Team of the Year', *Christchurch Times*, 3 September 1971.

21 Bernard Pares, *Russia* (Harmondsworth: Penguin Books, 1940), p. 84.

22 For Sirnis's membership of the RS-DLP see Partarkhiv pri TsK KP Latvii, f.2, op. 1, d.16, l.54. (Instityt istorii AN LatvSSR), cited Shteinberg, V. A. and Straume, M. F., 'Latviya: L. N. Tolstoi i "Tolstovstbo" (Konets XIX–Nachalo XX v.), *Izvestiya Akademii Nauk Latviiskoi SSR* 1978, no. 10 (375), 18–29. ['Latvia: L. N. Tolstoy and "Tolstoyism" (at the end of the nineteenth–beginning of the twentieth century', *Newsletter of the Latvian Academy of Science* 1978, 10 (375)].

23 Troyat, *Tolstoy*, p. 820.

24 'Notes by Alfred Brandt (circa. 1948)'. Melita Norwood Papers.

25 Correspondence: Alfred Brandt to Melita Norwood, 30 April 1968. Melita Norwood Papers.

26 'Wanders had been working on T.B. for many years. (Ovaltine was their first success in this direction) but they had not then discovered PAS etc. They founded the chair of physiology at £100,000 at London University. They don't seem to be doing so well now. Taxation etc. has stopped their researches and they have been taken over by another, larger Swiss firm. The *New Statesman* vilification of the pharmaceutical industry makes me sick. "The Drug Racket" etc. Packed with lies. Mugs (like you?!) lap it up.' Correpondence: Alfred Brandt to Melita Norwood, 30 April 1968; Melita Norwood Notes n.d. (Alfred did not share Letty's views). Melita Norwood Papers.

27 'Peter Alexander Sirnis. Notes by his eldest daughter, Melita Stedman Norwood, age 66, October 1978.' Melita Norwood Papers.

28 'Notes by Alfred Brandt (circa. 1948)'. Melita Norwood Papers.

29 Thomas Gurney Stedman to Wilfrid Scawen Blunt, 16 July 1914, Blunt MSS Box 55, West Sussex Record Office.

30 Ibid., 7 August 1914.

31 Arthur Marwick, *The Deluge: British Society and the First World War* (Harmondsworth: Penguin Books, 1967), p. 30.

32 Ibid.

33 *Daily Mail*, 5 August 1914, cited Marwick, *The Deluge*, p. 31.

34 A. J. P. Taylor, *The Struggle for Mastery in Europe 1848–1918* (Oxford: Oxford University Press, 1954), p. 530.

35 Donald Sassoon, *One Hundred Years of Socialism: The West European Left in the Twentieth Century* (London: Fontana Press, 1997), p. 27.

36 'Notes by Alfred Brandt (circa. 1948)'. Melita Norwood Papers.

CHAPTER 4

Lenin's First Secret Agent

1 In 1908 as a result of an increase in membership the SDF transformed itself into the Social-Democratic Party, and became the British Socialist Party in 1912.

2 The leading members of this group were Albert and H. W. Inkpin, E. C. Fairchild, Joe Fineberg and Zelda Kahan.

3 The National Archives, Kew (hereafter TNA Kew) WO 32/9304.

4 Ibid.

5 Ibid.

6 Ibid.

7 Correspondence: Andrew Rothstein to David Burke, 13 January 1981.

8 TNA Kew FO371/3347/179551.

9 Ibid.

10 TNA Kew KV2/1575 Theodore Rothstein. The British Secret Service responsible for counter-espionage at this time was MO5g. In the War Office reorganization of January 1916 MO5g acquired its modern name MI5. Foreign espionage was the responsibility of the Special Intelligence Bureau, the forerunner of SIS or MI6.

11 Ibid.

12 Ibid.

13 Ibid.

14 Andrew Rothstein, 'So whose were these initials? Mozart! Father passionately loved classical German music.' See V. V. Al'tman, *Imperializm i borba rabochevo klassa: Pamyati Akademika F. A. Rotshteina* [Imperialism and the Struggle of the Working Class. Essays in Memory of Theodore Rothstein] (Moscow, 1960), pp. 51 and 70.

15 Entry in Alexander Sirnis's diary 16 March 1917. Melita Norwood Papers.

16 TNA Kew KV2/1575 Theodore Rothstein.

17 Ibid.

18 Both were Marxist political parties. The SLP put more faith in industrial organization and the efficacy of the General Strike as an instrument of revolutionary advance, and was often accused of syndicalism, while the BSP remained affiliated to the Labour Party and believed in 'parliamentarianism' – the efficacy of parliament as an instrument of revolutionary advance.

19 Correspondence: Socialist Labour Party to Sirnis, December 1917, Jurgen Kuczynski Papers, Berlin, hereafter JK Papers, Berlin. (The JK Papers are in the possession of Jurgen's son, Thomas Kuczynski, Weisensee, Berlin.)

20 Socialist Labour Party to Sirnis, January 1918, JK Papers. Berlin.

21 Correspondence: W. R. Stoker to Sirnis, n.d., JK papers, Berlin.

22 Correpondence: Sirnis to W. R. Stoker, n.d., JK papers, Berlin.

23 'William Paul stayed with us at least twice at "The Pines" (Westend) but he called himself "Maxton" (but not "James Maxton"). "Arnold" was probably one of his other pseudonyms. He was at that time on the dodge from Army Call-up. Mum accompanied him on the piano. Another chap, also on the run, stayed with us on

one occasion when "Maxton" was there.' Melita Norwood, 'Notes, 5 November 1973'. Melita Norwood Papers.

24 Correspondence: W. R. Stoker to Sirnis, 7 February 1918, JK Papers, Berlin.

25 Correspondence: Paul to Sirnis, n.d. (penciled explanatory note from Gertrude Sirnis that Wm. Paul, who was on the run at the time from the authorities, signed himself Miss Elizabeth Coyle). JK Papers, Berlin.

26 Correspondence: Thomas Bell to Sirnis, 23 August 1918. JK Papers, Berlin.

27 Correspondence: Stoker to Sirnis, 17 July 1918. JK Papers Berlin.

28 Leonard Woolf, *Downhill All the Way: An Autobiography of the Years 1919–1939* (London: Harcourt Brace Jovanovich, 1960), p. 27.

29 Robert Bruce Lockhart, *Memoirs of a British Agent* (Harmondsworth: Penguin Books, 1950; first published 1932), p. 198.

30 Ibid.

31 Ibid., p. 200.

32 *The Call*, 14 July 1918.

33 Correspondence: Stoker to Sirnis, 31 August 1918. JK Papers, Berlin.

CHAPTER 5
Rothstein and the Formation of the Communist Party of Great Britain

1 Woolf, *Downhill All the* Way, p. 20.

2 Ibid.

3 John Buchan, *Mr. Standfast* (London: Pan Books, 1964; first published 1919), p. 51.

4 TNA Kew FO371/3347/179551 29 October 1918.

5 Ibid.

6 Ibid.

7 Ibid.

8 Francis Meynell, *My Lives* (London: Bodley Head, 1971), p. 125.

9 Ibid., p. 128.

10 TNA Kew CAB24/97 'Revolutionaries and the Need for Legislation 2nd February 1920', p. 6.

11 TNA Kew CAB24/111/1804 'A Monthly Review of Revolutionary Movements in British Dominions, Overseas and Foreign Countries', 21 July 1920.

12 TNA Kew KV2/573/64.

13 Meynell, *My Lives*, p. 125.

14 'When in London he resides at his mother's house at 53 Whitehall Park, Highgate, but he also occupies a converted Pullman car at Tophill, Windermere. His son, a Brackenbury scholar at Balliol College, Oxford, assists him.' TNA Kew CAB24/97/544.

15 TNA Kew CAB24/97, p. 5.

16 V. I. Lenin to Theodore Rothstein 27 Oct. 1919; V. I. Lenin to G. V. Chicherin 4 Jan. 1920. V. I. Lenin, *Collected Works*, 4th edn (London: Lawrence & Wishart, 1960),

vol. 44, pp. 304, 325–7. See Tom Quelch, 'Parliamentarianism, Lenin and the BSP', *The Call*, 22 January 1920; Lenin's 'reply to a leading English Communist' [Sylvia Pankhurst], in *Kommunisticheskii Internatsional* September 1920. (The full text of Sylvia Pankhurst's letter to Lenin written on 16 July 1919 was not published in English until 2 April 1920 in *The Call*.)

17   TNA Kew CAB24/97 'Revolutionaries and the Need for Legislation', 2 February 1920.

18   TNA Kew CAB24/111.

19   Ibid.

20   V. I. Lenin k F. A. Rotshteiny, 15 iyulya 1920g, V. I. Lenin *pol'noe sobranie sochinenii, izdanie pyatoe tom 51 pic'ma iyul' 1919–noyabr' 1920*. Institute marksizma-leninizma pri TsK KPCC, izdatel'stvo politicheskoi literature Moskva, 1965, p. 239. (V. I. Lenin to F. A. Rothstein, 15 July 1920, in V. I. Lenin *Collected Works*, vol. 51: *Letters July 1919–November 1920* (Moscow: Institute of Marxism-Leninism, 1965).) English translation in Lenin, *Collected Works*, 4th edn (London: Lawrence & Wishart, 1960), vol. 44, pp. 403–4. An alternative version of these events is given by Andrew Rothstein, who in a letter to the author dated 13 August 1981 stated that his father returned to Moscow simply at his own request. He asked to accompany Milyutin of the Russian trading delegation, who was returning 'to report on progress in the peace talks with Lloyd George ... TR specifically asked to be allowed to go, not having been back for 29 years. In fact there is a letter from Lenin which missed him, pressing him not to go, because the British Government might play some dirty trick on him!' Lenin's letter to Theodore Rothstein dated 15 July 1920 reads: 'I am not against your coming "to take a look" at Russia, but I am afraid that to quit Britain is harmful for the work.'

CHAPTER 6
Recruitment

1   Melita Norwood, interview 31 October 2000.

2   'A Brief History of the family of Mrs. Letty Norwood (explaining her beliefs), March 2000.' Melita Norwood Papers.

3   The house itself was sold in 1929 and became a maternity home but was finally demolished in 1965. For Holah (Letty's codename) see Brotherton Library, University of Leeds, Tuckton House MS 1381, Correspondence F & J Holah 1916–17.

4   TNA Kew KV2/1111/ 146a.

5   Ibid.

6   TNA Kew FO371/11029 ROTHSTEIN, Andrew F.

7   TNA Kew KV2/1576 Defence Security Intelligence Report (DSIR) Subject ANDREW ROTHSTEIN, 23 May 1922.

8   TNA Kew FO371/11209.

9   TNA Kew KV2/1576 M.I.5/B 23, November 1920.

10   TNA Kew KV2/1576 Secret Communist Organisation, 29 February 1926.

11   TNA Kew KV2/1580.

12 TNA Kew FO371/11029 'C. M. Roebuck', 2 November 1925.

13 TNA Kew KV2/1582 Top Secret Andrew Rothstein August 1946.

14 Noreen Branson, *History of the Communist Party of Great Britain 1927–1941* (London: Lawrence & Wishart, 1985), p. 5.

15 The line of 'Class against Class' had disastrous consequences in Germany. By defining social democrats as 'social-fascists' and as 'the main enemy' the Comintern made a broad anti-Nazi front impossible. See Sassoon, *One Hundred Years of Socialism*, p. 38.

16 TNA Kew KV2/1582 Top Secret Andrew Rothstein August 1946. On his return to Moscow Theodore Rothstein was appointed Soviet ambassador to Teheran. He was recalled in 1922 to assume a higher position in the Commissariat of Foreign Affairs as chief of the Anglo-American department. Between 1924 and 1925 he headed the World Economic and Political Institute. Between 1925 and 1939 he was Press Director of the Commissariat and also wrote for the Comintern press under the name Iranski. He was spared during the purges and in 1939 was elected a member of the Soviet Academy of Science. He died in 1953.

17 Melita Norwood, interview 12 December 1999.

18 Ibid.; Klaus Munther, interview 11 July 2001.

19 Melita Norwood, interview 12 December 1999.

20 John Goodey (Hilary's schoolfriend), 'Recollections of Bronislaw Nussbaum', 1986. Melita Norwood Papers.

21 Jack Gaster (1907–2007). Jack Gaster was the twelfth of 13 children of Dr Moses Gaster, expelled from Romania in 1885 and chief rabbi of the Sephardic community in Britain. After Jack Gaster joined the Communist Party in 1935 he became a member of the secret legal group of the Communist Party, and advised the leaders on the legal (or illegal) aspects of their activities.

22 BN-FMRA 11th Annual Meeting, London 8th June 1931. (BN-FMRA papers are held in the British Library, London.)

23 BN-FMRA 12th Annual Meeting 1932.

24 TNA Kew KV2/777/79A; 80A; 82.

25 Interview with Melita Norwood, 31 October 2000.

26 Jacob Miller (1912–2000). Born in Sheffield, the seventh of eight children of Jewish immigrants from Lithuania, he won a scholarship to Sheffield University to read economics and Russian language, literature and history. Between May 1936 and September 1937 he was attached to the Economic Research Institute of Gosplan in Moscow. This unique experience was made possible by strong recommendations to V. I. Mezhlauk, the enlightened head of Gosplan, from Sidney Webb and (on behalf of the CPGB) by R. Page Arnot. In 1945 he went on to pioneer Soviet Studies at the University of Glasgow.

27 Robin Page Arnot 1890–1986. Born in Greenock, the son of the editor of the *Greenock Telegraph* and *Clyde Shipping Gazette*. Secretary of the Fabian Research Department 1914–26. Imprisoned as a conscientious objector 1916–18. A founder member of the Communist Party in 1920 and a member of the Central Committee. He was arrested under the 1797 Incitement to Mutiny Act in 1925 and spent several months in gaol. Between 1949 and 1975 he wrote a famous six-volume series on the history of the miners of Great Britain. That he was known to

Gertrude Sirnis would have meant that she was seen as having some importance by King Street.

28 Robin Page Arnot to Harry Pollitt. Comintern Archives 495/100/943. I am indebted to Dr John McIlroy of the University of Manchester for this reference.

29 Jacob Miller, unpublished autobiography. Manuscript in the possession of David Burke.

30 TNA Kew KV2/512/49a.

31 Dorothea Miller to David Burke, 17 May 2002.

CHAPTER 7
The Lawn Road Flats

1 AWCS Annual Delegates Conference Reports, 10 March 1934 and 30 March 1935. AWCS Papers, Working Class Movement Library, Salford.

2 See Hugh Thomas, *The Spanish Civil War* (Harmondsworth: Penguin Books, 1965), p. 288.

3 Ibid., p. 292.

4 Interview with Melita Norwood, 13 January 2000.

5 The British Committee for the Relief of the Victims of Fascism received many donations simply labelled 'Spain'. The money was used to set up the British Medical Aid Committee by leftwing doctors under the leadership of Kenneth Sinclair Loutitt, a contemporary of Philby's at Cambridge. The value of this small unit was considerable, since nearly all the army doctors in Spain were supporters of Franco.

6 Robert Chadwell Williams, *Klaus Fuchs, Atom Spy* (Cambridge, MA, and London: Harvard University Press, 1987), p. 25. For further information on British and German intelligence collaboration against the KPD see TNA Kew KV4/110 'Policy on Liaison between Metropolitan Police Special Branch and German (Prussian) Ministry of the Interior, concerning communism' (1930); and TNA Kew KV4/111 'Liaison with German Political Police and Nazi Authorities 1933 – Visit of Captain Liddell to Berlin: "I attach herewith a report ['The Liquidation of Communism, Left-Wing Socialism & Pacifism in Germany'] on Captain Liddell's visit to Berlin, the object of which was to establish contact with the German Political Police, and if possible to examine documents obtained in the recent Communist raids."'

7 As for little-known communist activists, they were often executed by beheading; see the case of Edgar (Etkar) Andre, who was beheaded by axe in Hamburg on 4 November 1936. He had been arrested on 5 March 1933 for fighting against the SA. (Cited in Jean-Michel Palmier, *Weimar in Exile: The Anti-Fascist Emigration in Europe and America* (London: Verso, 2006), pp. 18, 275, 305, 746.)

8 Interview with Melita Norwood, 12 December 1999, and TNA Kew KV6/42.

9 The house numbers in Lawn Road do not follow the normal English pattern of odd numbers on one side of a road and even numbers on the other. Hence Goold-Verschoyle and Charlotte Moos lived practically next door to the Kuczynskis.

10 TNA Kew KV2/817.

11 Ibid.

12 Ibid.

13 Ibid.

14 Wells Coates to Jack Pritchard, 15 July 1930, published in Laura Cohn, *The Door to a Secret Room: A Portrait of Wells Coates* (London: Lund Humphries, 1999), p. 135.

15 Christopher Andrew and Vasili Mitrokhin, *The Mitrokhin Archive* (Harmondsworth: Penguin Books, 1999), p. 75.

16 TNA Kew KV2/1012.

17 Ibid.

18 Andrew and Mitrokhin, *The Mitrokhin Archive*, p. 76.

19 Bruce Leitch, David Page and Philip Knightley, *Philby: The Spy Who Betrayed a Generation* (London: Sphere Books, 1977).

20 Ibid.

21 TNA Kew KV2/1012.

22 TNA Kew KV2/817.

23 Ibid.

24 Walter Krivitsky, *I Was Stalin's Agent* (London: Hamish Hamilton, 1939).

25 *The Times*, 11 August 1997, obituary of Professor Jurgen Kuczynski; TNA Kew KV6/42.

CHAPTER 8
The Woolwich Arsenal Case

1 TNA Kew KV2/1020/19A 'Government employees sacked for politics'.

2 TNA Kew KV2/1020 'Copy of statement by Percy Glading to Arsenal Authorities, October 3rd 1928'.

3 TNA Kew KV2/1022/244 'Percy Eden GLADING'.

4 TNA Kew KV2/1022/243a 'Percy GLADING. Notes which might be useful in cross-examination'.

5 'B.1.' was accessing crucial information. Thurlbeck's wife, Beattie Marks, was Harry Pollitt's secretary.

6 TNA Kew KV2/1035/89a B.a. Report 'B.1.' 3 July 1931.

7 Ibid.

8 Jurgen Rohwer and Mikhail S. Monakov, *Stalin's Ocean-Going Fleet: Soviet Naval Strategy and Shipbuilding Programmes 1935–1953* (London: Routledge, 2001), p. 223.

9 TNA Kew KV2/1022/245a; *Manchester Guardian*, 15 March 1938.

10 Ibid.

11 Ibid.

12 TNA Kew KV2/1022 'Statement of "X" the Informant in this case'.

13 Ibid.

14 TNA Kew KV2/1022 'Statement of "X" the Informant in this case'.

15 TNA Kew KV2/1022; KV2/1023.

16 TNA Kew KV2/1008; KV2/1022; KV2/1023.

17 TNA Kew KV2/1022.

18 Ibid.

19 Igor Damaskin, with Geoffrey Elliott, *Kitty Harris: The Spy with Seventeen Names* (London: St Ermin's Press, 2001), p. 150.

20 TNA Kew KV2/1023.

21 TNA Kew KV2/1008; KV2/1023.

22 TNA Kew KV2/1004; KV2/1022; KV2/1023.

23 TNA Kew KV2/1022; KV2/1023.

24 TNA Kew KV2/1023.

25 TNA Kew KV2/1021/192a, re Percy Glading, 6 May 1936.

26 TNA Kew KV2/1022; KV2/1023.

27 TNA Kew KV2/1022.

28 Ibid.

29 Ibid.

30 TNA Kew KV2/1013; KV2/1022/235B.

31 Ibid.

32 TNA Kew KV2/1022/235B.

33 TNA Kew KV2/1022/240A.

34 TNA Kew KV2/1022/245a; *Manchester Guardian*, 15 March 1938.

35 TNA Kew KV2/1062/77B.

36 TNA Kew KV2/1237/26A.

37 TNA Kew KV2/1037/57B.

38 TNA Kew KV2/1037/62B.

39 TNA Kew KV2/1020/52a.

40 TNA Kew KV2/1022/245a; *Manchester Guardian*, 15 March 1938.

41 TNA Kew KV2/1062/145a.

42 TNA Kew KV2/1062/145B.

43 TNA Kew KV2/1022/245a; *Manchester Guardian*, 15 March 1938.

44 Ibid.

45 Quoted in Alan Bullock, *Hitler: A Study in Tyranny* (Harmondsworth: Pelican Books, 1962), p. 436.

46 Andrew and Mitrokhin, *The Mitrokhin Archive*, p. 153.

47 Ibid.

CHAPTER 9

'The Russian Danger Is Our Danger'

1 Allan Merson, *Communist Resistance in Nazi Germany* (London: Lawrence & Wishart, 1985), p. 213.

2 Branson, *History of the Communist Party of Great Britain*, p. 256.

3 Francis Beckett, *Enemy Within: The Rise and Fall of the British Communist Party* (London: John Murray, 1995), pp. 90–3.

4 Branson, *History of the Communist Party*, p. 268.

5 TNA Kew KV2/1872/128a.

6 TNA Kew KV2/1871/68.

7 See Ian Kershaw *Hitler 1936–1945, Nemesis* (Harmondsworth: Penguin Books, 2000), pp. 307–10.

8 Ibid. p. 393.

9 Branson, *History of the Communist Party of Great Britain*, p. 329.

10 See *Industrial and General Information*, 27 June 1941, cited in Branson, *History of the Communist Party of Great Britain*, p. 331 and p. 338, n. 5.

11 *The Times*, 23 June 1941. Quoted in Branson, *History of the Communist Party of Great Britain*, p. 331.

12 The chant 'Winnie's back' greeted Churchill's replacement of Chamberlain on 10 May 1940.

CHAPTER 10
Sonya

1 Roger Faligot and Remi Kauffer, *The Chinese Secret Service* (London: Headline, 1989), p. 247.

2 Ruth Werner, *Sonya's Report* (London: Chatto & Windus, 1991), p. 17. Ursula Ruth Kuczynski (Sonya) wrote under the pen name Ruth Werner.

3 Ibid., p. 22.

4 On 'White' Russian involvement in the Chinese Terror see Alexander Millar's research into the Noulens case, 'British Intelligence and the Comintern: The Noulens Case' (MPhil thesis, Faculty of History, University of Cambridge, 2006).

5 Werner, *Sonya's Report*, p. 22.

6 Ibid., p. 24.

7 Chapman Pincher, *Too Secret Too Long* (London: Sidgwick & Jackson, 1984), p. 12.

8 Philip Knightley, *The Second Oldest Profession: Spies and Spying in the Twentieth Century* (London: Pimlico, 2003), p. 202.

9 Sorge was arrested along with his fellow conspirator Ozaki in 1941. Ozaki, a Japanese specialist on Eastern Asia and a close friend of Sorge, had been co-opted to Prince Konoe's Cabinet as a Chinese specialist. Both men were executed on 7 November 1944. Other members of the Ramsay group received long prison sentences.

10 Werner, *Sonya's Report*, p. 49.

11 Ibid., p. 154.

12 Ibid., p. 177.

13 Ibid., p. 189.

14 Ibid., p. 188.

15 Alexander Foote, *Handbook for Spies* (London: Museum Press, 1949) p. 10. See also TNA Kew KV6/42/151b; KV2/1612.

16 TNA Kew KV2/1613.

17 Ibid.

18 Werner, *Sonya's Report*, p. 221.

19 TNA Kew KV6/41.

20 Werner, *Sonya's Report*, p. 228.

21 The *Rote Drei* was arguably the Soviet Union's most important wartime agent network, with access to sources inside Germany operating in Switzerland. See Christopher Andrew and Oleg Gordievsky, *KGB: The Inside Story of Its Foreign Relations from Lenin to Gorbachev* (London: Hodder & Stoughton, 1990), p. 224.

CHAPTER 11
The American Bomb

1 TNA Kew KV4/56/85150.

2 Branson, *History of the Communist Party of Great Britain*, pp. 277–81. See also Calder Walton, 'British Intelligence and Threats to National Security, *c.* 1941–1951' (PhD thesis, Faculty of History, University of Cambridge, 2006).

3 TNA Kew KV2/483/77a.

4 Ibid.

5 Melita Norwood, interview, 16 July 2001.

6 Peter Rooke, *Cheshunt at War 1939–1945* (Published by the author, 1989), p. 14. Interview with Hilary Norwood.

7 Hilary Norwood, 'Application for Post as Chemistry Master, High Wycombe Grammar School 16 December 1946'. Melita Norwood Papers.

8 Rooke, *Cheshunt at War*, p. 76. Interview with Hilary Norwood.

9 Rooke, *Cheshunt at War*, p. 19.

10 Ibid.

11 *Sunday Express*, April 1939.

12 Ibid.

13 Holloway, *Stalin and the Bomb*, p. 56.

14 Ibid., p. 57.

15 TNA Kew AB1/9 'The Possibility of Producing an Atomic Bomb. A Review of the Position', 3 May 1939, p. 2.

16 Ibid., p. 4.

17 TNA Kew AB1/9 'On the construction of a "super-bomb", based on a nuclear chain reaction in uranium'.

18 TNA Kew AB1/10 Maud Summary.

19 TNA Kew AB1/8 'Report by Maud Committee on the use of Uranium for a Bomb', p. 4.

20 TNA Kew KV4/56.

21 Holloway, *Stalin and the Bomb*, pp. 82–3.

22 Ibid., p. 84.

23 Ibid.

24 *Daily Telegraph*, 13 October 1941.

25 Williams, *Klaus Fuchs*, p. 15.

26 Ibid., p. 17.

27 Ibid., p. 29.

28 In 1931 Maiski, along with Andrew Rothstein, had been making regular trips to the University of Cambridge's Cavendish Laboratory to meet secretly with Piotr Kapitsa.

29 TNA Kew AB1/682.

30 TNA Kew AB/1/8.

31 Williams, *Klaus Fuchs*, pp. 65–7.

32 Ronald. W Clark, *The Greatest Power on Earth: The Story of Nuclear Fission* (London: Sidgwick & Jackson, 1980), p. 133.

33 Ibid., p. 143.

34 Williams, *Klaus Fuchs*, p. 65.

35 Clark, *The Greatest Power on Earth*, p. 6.

36 See Andrew and Mitrokhin, *Mitrokhin Archive*, p. 168.

CHAPTER 12
Hiroshima and Nagasaki

1 Andrew and Mitrokhin, *The Mitrokhin Archive*, p. 786.

2 *Glavnoye Razvedyvatelnoye Upravleniye, Entsiklopediya Voennoi Razvedki Roccii* [Soviet Military Intelligence: Encyclopaedia of Russian Military Intelligence] (Moscow, 2004), p. 183.

3 TNA Kew KV6/41/70A.

4 Williams, *Klaus Fuchs*, p. 69.

5 Andrew and Mitrokhin, *The Mitrokhin Archive*, p. 168.

6 Interview with Melita Norwood, 9 July 2001.

7 Williams, *Klaus Fuchs*, p. 75.

8 Intelligence and Security Committee, *The Mitrokhin Inquiry Report* (London: The Stationery Office, June 2000), pp. 60–1.

9 TNA Kew AB1/8.

10 TNA Kew AB16/105, 16/158.

11 Ibid. See also TNA Kew AB16/181.

12 TNA Kew AB1/325.

13 See Williams, *Klaus Fuchs*, p. 9.

14 Holloway, *Stalin and the Bomb*, p. 127.

15 Ibid.

CHAPTER 13
Proliferation

1 H. Montgomery Hyde, *The Atom Bomb Spies* (London: Hamish Hamilton, 1980), p. 20.

2 Ibid., pp. 21–2.

3 Anthony Glees, *The Secrets of the Service: British Intelligence and Communist Subversion 1939–1951* (London: Jonathan Cape, 1987), p. 310.

4 Peter Hennessy, interview with Gouzenko, *The Times*, n.d., cited Glees, *The Secrets of the Service*, p. 311.

5 Hyde, *The Atom Bomb Spies*, p. 29.

6 TNA Kew AB16/155.

7 Interview with Melita Norwood, 31 October 2000.

8 'Still another agent, codenamed "Tina", surfaced in London only in May and June 1945. "Tina" was a secret member of the British Communist Party, recruited for intelligence work by the GPU in 1935. She worked for the British Association on Non-Ferrous Metals and provided on several occasions in 1945 all of the up-to-date research for the "Enormoz" project in the metallurgical field.' Weinstein, and Vassiliev, *The Haunted Wood*, p. 194.

9 September 16, 1945, No. 1413. VENONA files can be viewed at http://www.nsa.gov/venona/releases/16_Sept_19.

10 Hyde, *The Atom Bomb Spies*, p. 36.

11 Williams, *Klaus Fuchs*, p. 65.

12 Hyde, *The Atom Bomb Spies*, p. 39.

13 Holloway, *Stalin and the Bomb*, pp. 161–3.

14 Hyde, *The Atom Bomb Spies*, p. 60.

15 Ibid., p. 63.

16 'Although the full report of the Royal Commission, which amounted to some seven hundred and thirty-three pages, was published under the date 26 June, it was not tabled in the House of Commons and so made generally public until 15 July, as a courtesy to the Soviet Union.' Hyde, *The Atom Bomb Spies*, p. 67.

17 Margaret Gowing, 'The Origins of Britain's Status as a Nuclear Power', Oxford Project for Peace Studies, OPPS Paper no. 11 (Oxford: OPPS, 1988), p. 7.

18 Williams, *Klaus Fuchs*, p. 96.

19 Jurgen Kuczynski, 'Publishing Lenin in 1919', *Labour Monthly*, November 1973.

20 TNA Kew KV2/1256. Jurgen's wife and family joined him in Berlin in February 1947.

21 TNA Kew KV2/1253/575A; KV2/1256.

22 Ibid.

23 TNA Kew KV2/1253.

24 The moderator prevents a nuclear pile from 'going mad'. Material such as graphite or heavy water is used in nuclear reactors to slow down the neutrons produced by fission so that they are not absorbed, or 'captured', by the nuclei they encounter, but split them.

25 Holloway, *Stalin and the Bomb*, p. 184.

26 Ibid., pp. 186–7.

27 TNA Kew AB16/105.

28 TNA Kew PREM8/1280.

29 TNA Kew KV6/42/170.

30 However, while observation at 12 Lawn Road was discontinued it was later reinstated at 62a Belsize Park Gardens.

31 TNA Kew KV6/43/227a.

32 TNA Kew KV6/43.

33 TNA Kew KV6/43/224B.

34 TNA Kew KV6/43.

35 TNA Kew KV2/1256.

36 Ibid.

37 Interview with Melita Norwood, 31 October 2000.

CHAPTER 14
'Sonya Salutes You'

1 Richard Aldrich, *The Hidden Hand* (London: John Murray, 2001), pp. 8–15; see also Walton, 'British Intelligence and Threats to National Security'.

2 Walton, 'British Intelligence and Threats to National Security'.

3 'Mrs. Melita Norwood and the British Non-Ferrous Metals Research Association. 12th September 1999.' Copy of a letter from the Director of BN-FMRA (1950–73) to the Home Office.

4 *Guardian*, 1 January 2002.

5 Gowing, 'The Origins of Britain's Status as a Nuclear Power', p. 9.

6 Ibid.

7 Ibid., p. 10. See also Peter Hennessy (ed.), *Cabinets and the Bomb* (Oxford University Press, 2007).

8 Foote, *A Handbook for Spies*, p. 8.

9 The only other British spy to have received this honour was John Cairncross, one of the Cambridge Five, who had been presented with the award in 1944 for his 'contribution to the epic Soviet victory at Kursk'. See Andrew and Mitrokhin, *The Mitrokhin Archive*, p. 166.

10 Ibid., pp. 532–7.

11 Gordon Lonsdale, *Spy* (London: Mayflower-Dell, 1965), p. 91.

12 Ibid., p. 108.

13 Peter Wright, *Spycatcher* (New York: Viking Penguin, 1987), p. 130.

14 Melita Norwood interview, 16 July 2001.

15 Andrew and Mitrokhin, *The Mitrokhin Archive*, p. 535.

16 Ibid., p. 536.

17 Quoted in Michael Randle and Pat Pottle, *The Blake Escape: How We Freed George Blake – And Why* (London: Harrap, 1989), p. 10.

18 H. Montgomery Hyde, *George Blake, Superspy* (London: Constable, 1987), p. 13.

19 In March 1963 rumours were circulating in Westminster about the Minister for War, John Profumo, and a call-girl, Christine Keeler, who was allegedly having an affair with the Soviet naval attaché. Having denied any involvement with Keeler to the House, threatening to issue writs for libel and slander, he confessed to the affair in June and resigned from the Cabinet, giving up also his Privy Council membership and parliamentary seat. Lord Denning released the government's official report on the affair in September, which unsurprisingly claimed that the 'Profumo Affair' had not posed a threat to national security. Anthony Blunt, the 'Fourth Man' in the Cambridge spy ring, Keeper of the Queen's Pictures and a cousin of Elizabeth Bowes-Lyon (later the Queen Mother), was offered immunity from prosecution in exchange for a full confession on 25 April 1964.

20 TNA Kew PREM13/128 I.A.E.A. 'Safeguards & the Revised United Kingdom–United States Agreement for Co-operation in the Civil Uses of Atomic Energy'.

21 Ibid.

22 Ibid. Those 'sensitive negotiations then under way' coincided with MI5's internal investigation of Sir Roger Hollis. In 1966 Hollis wrote personally to Sir Frank Soskice thanking him for his 'splendid support' in what had been a difficult year. Roger Hollis to Frank Soskice, 10 January 1966, Soskice Papers, House of Lords Record Office.

23 Melita Norwood interview, 10 March 2002.

24 Andrew and Mitrokhin, *The Mitrokhin Archive*, pp. 519–20.

25 Melita Norwood interview, 12 December 1999.

26 Viktor Rozov, 'Tovarishi moi …', *Zavtra* 40 (45), 1994.

27 Ibid.

28 ISC Report, p. 20.

29 ISC Report, p. 21 (when ISC Reports wish to conceal information a row of asterisks (****) is used).

30 Ibid.

31 Ibid., p. 22.

32 Ibid.

33 Ibid., p. 23.

34 Ibid.

35 David Rose, 'A Singular Spy', *Observer*, 9 May 2004; 'Street of Shame', *Private Eye*, 14–27 May 2004.

36 ISC Report, p. 23.

37 Ibid., p. 20.

38 *Independent on Sunday*, 12 September 1999.

39 Ibid.

40 ISC Report, p. 33.

41 Ibid., p. 13.

42 Ibid., p. 17.

Bibliography

Aldrich, Richard, *The Hidden Hand: Britain, America and Cold War Secret Intelligence* (London: John Murray, 2001).

Al'tman, V. V. (ed.), *Imperializm i borba rabochevo klassa: Pamyati Akademika F. A. Rotshteina* [Imperialism and the Struggle of the Working Class. Essays in Memory of Theodore Rothstein] (Moscow: Akademii nauk, CCCP, 1960).

Andrew, Christopher, and Oleg Gordievsky, *KGB: The Inside Story* (London: Hodder & Stoughton, 1990).

Andrew, Christopher, and Vasili Mitrokhin, *The Mitrokhin Archive: The KGB in Europe and the West* (Harmondsworth: Penguin Books, 1999).

Beckett, Francis, *Enemy Within: The Rise and Fall of the British Communist Party* (London: John Murray, 1995).

Blunt, Wilfrid, *Married to a Single Life* (Salisbury: Michael Russell (Publishing) Ltd, 1983).

Blunt, Wilfrid Scawen, *My Diaries: Part Two 1900–1914* (London: Martin Secker, 1919).

Boyle, Andrew, *The Climate of Treason* (London: Hutchinson, 1979).

Branson, Noreen, *History of the Communist Party of Great Britain, 1927–1941* (London: Lawrence & Wishart, 1985).

Bruce Lockhart, Robert, *Memoirs of a British Agent* (Harmondsworth: Penguin Books, 1950; first published 1932).

Buchan, John, *Mr Standfast* (London: Pan Books, 1964; first published 1919).

Bullock, Alan, *Hitler: A Study in Tyranny* (Harmondsworth: Pelican Books, 1962).

Challinor, Raymond, *The Origins of British Bolshevism* (London: Croom Helm, 1977).

Clark, Ronald W., *The Greatest Power on Earth: The Story of Nuclear Fission* (London: Sidgwick & Jackson, 1980).

Cohn, Laura, *The Door to a Secret Room: A Portrait of Wells Coates* (London: Lund Humphries, 1999).

Cooke, M. A., 'The Friends of Leo Tolstoy', *Millgate Monthly*, February 1909.

Costello, John, *The Mask of Treachery* (London: Collins, 1988).

Crankshaw, Edward, *The Shadow of the Winter Palace: The Drift to Revolution 1825–1917* (Harmondsworth: Penguin Books, 1976).

Damaskin, Igor, with Geoffrey Elliott, *Kitty Harris: The Spy with Seventeen Names* (London: St Ermin's Press, 2001).

Degras, Jane, *Documents on Soviet Foreign Policy*, 3 vols. (London: Oxford University Press, 1951–3).

Faligot, Roger, and Remi Kauffer, *The Chinese Secret Service* (London: Headline Book Publishing, 1987).

Fisher, Louis, *The Life of Lenin* (London: Phoenix Press, 1964).

Foote, Alexander, *Handbook for Spies* (London: Museum Press, 1949).

Glavnoye Razvedyvatelnoye Upravleniye, Entsiklopediya Voennoi Razvedki Roccii [Soviet Military Intelligence: Encyclopaedia of Russian Military Intelligence] (Moscow, 2004).

Glees, Anthony: *The Secrets of the Service: British Intelligence and Communist Subversion 1939–1951* (London: Jonathan Cape, 1987).

Gowing, Margaret, 'The Origins of Britain's Status as a Nuclear Power', Oxford Project for Peace Studies, OPPS Paper no. 11 (Oxford: OPPS, 1988).

Hennessy, Peter (ed.), *Cabinets and the Bomb* (Oxford: Oxford University Press, 2007).

Holloway, David, *Stalin and the Bomb* (New Haven, CT and London: Yale University Press, 1994).

Holman, Michael. J. de K., 'Translating Tolstoy for the Free Age Press: Vladimir Chertkov and His English Manager Arthur Fifield', *Slavonic and East European Review* 66, 2 (April 1988), 184–97.

Holmes, Colin, 'Immigrants, Refugees and Revolutionaries', in *From the Other Shore: Russian Political Emigrants in Britain, 1880–1917*, ed. John Slatter (London: Frank Cass, 1984).

Hyde, H. Montgomery, *George Blake, Superspy* (London: Constable, 1987).

Hyde, H. Montgomery, *The Atom Bomb Spies* (London: Hamish Hamilton, 1980).

Intelligence and Security Committee, *The Mitrokhin Inquiry Report* (London: The Stationery Office, June 2000.)

Kendall, Walter, *The Revolutionary Movement in Britain 1900–21* (London: Weidenfeld & Nicolson, 1969).

Kennedy, Bart, 'The Wandering Romanoff', *Evening News* (2–21 August 1900).

Kershaw, Ian, *Hitler 1936–1945, Nemesis* (Harmondsworth: Penguin Books, 2000).

Klugmann, James, *History of the Communist Party* (London: Lawrence & Wishart, 1969).

Knightley, Philip, *The Second Oldest Profession: Spies and Spying in the Twentieth Century* (London: Pimlico, 2003).

Koestler, Arthur, *The Yogi and the Commissar and Other Essays* (London: Cape, 1945).

Krivitsky, Walter, *I Was Stalin's Agent* (London: Hamish Hamilton, 1939).

Lenin, V. I. *Collected Works*, vol. 51, *Letters July 1919 – November 1920* (Moscow: Institute of Marxism-Leninism, 1965).

Le Queux, William, *Strange Tales of a Nihilist* (London, 1892; reprinted London, 1894).

Longford, Elizabeth, *A Pilgrimage of Passion: The Life of Wilfrid Scawen Blunt* (London: Weidenfeld & Nicolson, 1979).

Lonsdale, Gordon, *Spy* (London: Mayflower-Dell, 1965).

Marwick, Arthur, *The Deluge: British Society and the First World War* (Harmondsworth: Penguin Books, 1967).

Merson, Allan, *Communist Resistance in Nazi Germany* (London: Lawrence & Wishart, 1985).

Meynell, Francis, *My Lives* (London: Bodley Head, 1971).

Page, Bruce, David Leitch and Phillip Knightley, *Philby: The Spy Who Betrayed a Generation* (London: Sphere, 1977).

Jean-Michel Palmier, *Weimar in Exile: The Anti-Fascist Emigration in Europe and America* (London: Verso, 2006).

Pares, Bernard, *Russia* (Harmondsworth: Penguin Books 1940).

Pelling, Henry, *Popular Politics and Society in Late Victorian Britain* (London: Macmillan, 1968).

Pelling, Henry, *The British Communist Party* (London: A & C Black, 1958).

Philby, Kim, *My Silent War* (London: Granada, 1969).

Pincher, Chapman, *Too Secret Too Long* (London: New English Library, 1985).

Potter, Stanley Carlyle, 'Reminiscences of Tchertkoff and Tuckton's Russian Colony', *Christchurch Times* 15 March 1963.

Porter, Bernard, 'The British Government and Political Refugees, c. 1880–1914', in *From the Other Shore: Russian Political Emigrants in Britain, 1880–1917*, ed. John Slatter (Frank Cass, London 1984).

Preston, Thomas, *Before the Curtain* (London: John Murray, 1950).

Randle, Michael, and Pat Pottle, *The Blake Escape: How We Freed George Blake – and Why* (London: Harrap, 1989).

Rohwer, Jurgen, and Mikhail S. Monakov, *Stalin's Ocean-Going Fleet: Soviet Naval Strategy and Shipbuilding Programmes 1935–1953* (London: Routledge, 2001).

Rooke, Peter, *Cheshunt at War 1939–1945* (published by the author, 1989).

Rose, David, 'A Singular Spy', *Observer* (9 May 2004).

Rothstein, Andrew, *A History of the U.S.S.R.* (Harmondsworth: Penguin Books, 1950).

Rothstein, Theodore, *From Chartism to Labourism* (London: Martin Lawrence, 1929).

Sassoon, Donald, *One Hundred Years of Socialism: The West European Left in the Twentieth Century* (Fontana Press, 1997).

Slatter, John, *From the Other Shore: Russian Political Emigrants in Britain, 1880–1917* (London: Frank Cass, 1984).

Sudoplatov, Pavel, and Anatoli Sudoplatov, *Special Tasks: The Memoirs of an Unwanted Witness – A Soviet Spymaster* (London: Little, Brown, 1994).

Taylor, A. J. P., *The Struggle for Mastery in Europe 1848–1918* (Oxford: Oxford University Press, 1954).

Thomas, Hugh, *The Spanish Civil War* (London: Hamish Hamilton, 1997).

Thompson, Willie, *The Good Old Cause: The British Communist Party 1920–1991* (London: Pluto Press, 1992).

Troyat, Henri, *Tolstoy* (Harmondsworth: Penguin Books, 1970).

Weinstein, Allen, and Alexander Vassiliev, *The Haunted Wood: Soviet Espionage in America – The Stalin Era* (New York: The Modern Library, 1999).

Werner, Ruth, *Sonya's Report* (London: Chatto & Windus, 1991).

Wilde, Oscar, *De Profundis*, online at www.upword.com/wilde/
de_profundis.html.

Wilde, Oscar, *Lord Arthur Savile's Crime* (London, 1891).

Wilde, Oscar, *Vera, or the Nihilists* (London, 1880).

Williams, Robert Chadwell, *Klaus Fuchs, Atom Spy* (London: Harvard
University Press, 1987).

Woolf, Leonard, *Downhill All the Way: An Autobiography of the Years
1919–1939* (London: Harcourt Brace Jovanovich, 1975).

Wright, Peter, *Spycatcher* (New York: Viking Penguin, 1987).

Unpublished Theses

Miller, Alexander, 'British Intelligence and the Comintern in Asia:
The Noulens Case' (MPhil thesis, Faculty of History, University of
Cambridge, 2007).

Walton, Calder, 'British Intelligence and Threats to National Security,
c. 1941–1951' (PhD thesis, Faculty of History, University of Cambridge,
2006).

Index

History of British Intelligence

ISSN 1756-5685

Series Editor
Peter Martland

With the recent opening of government archives to public scrutiny, it is at last possible to study the vital role that intelligence has played in forming and executing policy in modern history. This new series aims to be the leading forum for work in the area. Proposals are welcomed, and should be sent in the first instance to the publisher at the address below.

Boydell and Brewer Ltd, PO Box 9, Woodbridge, Suffolk, IP12 3DF, UK

Previously published in this series:

British Spies and Irish Rebels: British Intelligence and Ireland, 1916-1945, Paul McMahon (2008)

CPSIA information can be obtained
at www.ICGtesting.com
Printed in the USA
LVOW04*2305120116

470367LV00006B/26/P